The New Shell Guides

Sussex

The New Shell Guides
Sussex

John Godfrey

Introduction by Max Egremont

Series Editor: John Julius Norwich
Photography by Nick Meers

Michael Joseph · London

MICHAEL JOSEPH LTD

Published by the Penguin Group
27 Wrights Lane, London W8 5TZ, England
Viking Penguin Inc., 40 West 23rd Street, New York, New York 10010, USA
Penguin Books Australia Ltd, Ringwood, Victoria, Australia
Penguin Books Canada Ltd, 2801 John Street, Markham, Ontario, Canada L3R 1B4
Penguin Books (NZ) Ltd, 182–190 Wairau Road, Auckland 10, New Zealand

Penguin Books Ltd, Registered Offices: Harmondsworth, Middlesex, England

First published in Great Britain in 1990

Typeset in Linotron 10/11pt Plantin by Cambrian Typesetters, Frimley, Surrey
Colour reproduction by Scantrans, Singapore
Printed and bound by Kyodo-Shing Loong Printing, Singapore

A CIP catalogue record for this book is available from The British Library

ISBN 0 7181 3283 1

Title page photograph: Arundel and the River Arun

Contents

Note on using the Gazetteer 5

Introduction *by Max Egremont* 7

Gazetteer 15

The Norman Heritage *by John Godfrey* 28

Sussex by the Sea *by John K. Walton* 88

The South Downs Way *by Miles Jebb* 132

Literary Sussex *by Michael Birkett* 150

Maps 186

Index 189

Note on using the Gazetteer

Entries in the Gazetteer are arranged in alphabetical order. 'The', if part of the name, follows the main element: **Witterings, The** (alphabeticised under W).

Entry headings consist of the name of the place or feature in **bold** type, followed by a map reference in parentheses: **Chichester** (1/2E). The figure 1 is the map number; 2E is the grid reference.

If a name mentioned within the text of an entry is printed in capital letters – i.e. BRIGHTON – this indicates that it has its own entry in the Gazetteer.

Bold type is used for certain places, buildings or other features of interest or importance referred to within Gazetteer entries.

Every effort has been made to ensure that information about the opening to the public of buildings, estates, gardens, reserves, museums, galleries etc., and details of walks and footpaths, were as accurate as possible at the time of going to press. Such particulars are, of course, subject to alteration and it may be prudent to check them locally, or with the appropriate organisations or authorities.

John Julius Norwich was born in 1929. After reading French and Russian at New College, Oxford, he joined the Foreign Office where he served until 1964. Since then he has published two books on the medieval Norman Kingdom in Sicily; two historical travel books, *Mount Athos* (with Reresby Sitwell) and *Sahara*; two volumes on the history of Venice; a book about Glyndebourne; an anthology of travel writing; *The Architecture of Southern England*; and *Byzantium: the Early Centuries*, the first volume of a three-volume history of that city. Since 1970 he has also compiled an annual anthology of poetry and prose, *A Christmas Cracker*. He was general editor of *Great Architecture of the World*, *The Italian World*, and *The Heritage of Britain*; he is now general editor of the *Oxford Illustrated Encyclopedia of Art*.

In addition he writes and presents historical documentaries for television and frequently broadcasts on BBC radio. He is Chairman of the Venice in Peril Fund, Co-Chairman of the World Monuments Fund and a member of the Executive Committee of the National Trust.

John Godfrey was educated in Surrey and at the University of Sussex, where he studied under the distinguished historian Lord Briggs of Lewes, and he has lived in Sussex for most of his adult life. He is an Assistant County Secretary with West Sussex County Council, with special responsibility for the coast and countryside, and a director of a small company which arranges walking and heritage tours in Sussex. He is active in conservation organisations and lectures on local history. He lives with his wife and three sons in Maltravers Street, Arundel.

Lord Egremont was born in 1948 and educated at Eton and Oxford. He has written two biographical studies: *The Cousins* and *Balfour*; and three novels: *The Ladies' Man*, *Dear Shadows*, and *Painted Lives*. He lives at Petworth in West Sussex with his wife and four children.

John Walton is a senior lecturer in History at the University of Lancaster. He has written extensively on the social history of seaside resorts. His most recent books are *Lancashire: a social history 1558–1939* and *The National Trust Guide to Late Georgian and Victorian Britain*. He is currently working on a social history of fish and chips.

Miles Jebb is the author of several books on walking, including *A Guide to the South Downs Way*. He has walked the Way and also ridden along it on horseback, from end to end.

Lord Birkett was born in 1929, the son of a famous lawyer. He was educated at the Downs, Stowe and Trinity College, Cambridge. He has been a film director and producer for most of his life – his films include *The Caretaker* and *The Marat/Sade* and more recently he was Deputy Director of the National Theatre and Director for Recreation and the Arts at the G.L.C.. Nowadays he is much engaged in the musical world.

Nick Meers was born in Gloucestershire in 1955. He graduated from Guildford School of Photography in 1978, since when his lenses have captured many aspects of life and landscape all over the world. In addition to many assignments for the National Trust, he has made the photographs for several of the New Shell Guides and for *The Spirit of the Cotswolds* by Susan Hill.

Acknowledgements

I would like to record my thanks to Chris Hare, who helped me with the research for this book; Sarah Backhouse, who typed the manuscript; David Bomford, Judith Brent, Alison and Tim McCann and Nicholas Plumley, who read the text and made a number of helpful suggestions; Jenny Dereham and Robyn Ayers of Michael Joseph Ltd.; and my wife, Sally, for her tolerance and support.

The author and publisher would also like to thank the National Trust, English Heritage and private owners for their permission to photograph and feature their properties in this book.

Introduction

MAX EGREMONT

Go to the top of Blackdown, near Haslemere on the border of Surrey and Sussex. Look south across what seems to be almost unbroken woodland in the direction of the English Channel and you see the Sussex Weald, Tennyson's view of 'green Sussex fading into blue'. Now leave West Sussex and drive to Ditchling Beacon on the South Downs, the highest point in the eastern part of the county. Climb through the outline of an iron-age fort to one of the most glorious views in England. Here is the Sussex downland, Swinburne's 'green smooth-swelling unending Downs' that form a great ridge between the Weald and the sea.

Sussex by the sea

Here too is the road that takes you across to Brighton, another side of Sussex: 'Sussex by the sea'. Go further east to Eastbourne, one of the least ravaged of Sussex towns, although developers have had their way with part of it. Walk along the promenade, past the beds of gaudy but splendid municipal planting, to the pier which juts out into the grey green waters. At the pier's end is a white ramshackle Victorian palace of pleasure, a reminder of the days when the south coast was packed with trippers from London. Hastings, Worthing, St Leonard's, Brighton, Bognor Regis, Littlehampton: these are the seaside towns of Sussex, victims not only of the easy availability of modern package tours to

Sheep grazing below Ditchling Beacon

the Mediterranean but also of their own success between the two World Wars when miles of red and white bungalows or new housing estates were built for people attracted by the health-giving powers of the sea air and supposedly mild climate.

The sea is the narrow strip which divides England from continental Europe. Sussex's position, a short sea voyage from France, has made her among the most receptive of English counties to European settlement and influence. The Romans left the brilliant pavement mosaics at Bignor and the remains of the palace of Fishbourne. The gabled tower and shingled helm roof of the Saxon Church at Sompting, unique in this country, derive from a Rhineland style probably introduced to Sussex during the 10th or 11th-century corn and wool trade. In Norman times Sussex's geographical position led to a profusion of new parish churches. Later came the blast furnaces introduced into the Sussex Weald from France at the end of the 15th century to modernise the iron industry; then the martello towers of the Napoleonic wars to guard against invasion and the fortifications built against the German threat in 1940.

This European connection gave Sussex two of the greatest monastic foundations in England: Battle Abbey and the Cluniac Priory of St Pancras at Lewes. Much survives at Battle, established by William the Conqueror after his victory in 1066 but Thomas Cromwell, Henry VIII's chief minister, razed the Cluniac Priory to the ground. The excavations show the extent of his vandalism but the loss of this most magnificent of early Sussex buildings did not prevent Horace Walpole from marvelling at 'the holy land of abbeys and gothic castles' on the borders of Sussex and Kent as he travelled around Battle, Herstmonceux, Bodiam and Bayham. Again these were perhaps inspired by buildings of similar magnificence seen by their builders while on military campaigns in France or the Low Countries. Certainly the great rebuilding at Cowdray, Parham and Glynde by the Tudor and Stuart nobility in the 16th and 17th centuries shows a wish to rival the palaces of Italy and France.

The coastal landscape was always subject to change. The silting up of rivers and estuaries has left such towns as Arundel and Steyning, once ports, stranded inland and, further east, Rye looks over a flat marshy landscape where once the sea came in. In the late 13th century Old Winchelsea disappeared after violent channel storms and flooding. In the 17th century the prosperity of Brighton declined after erosion made herring fishing difficult, only to revive when

Herstmonceux Castle

tourism arrived a hundred years later. Worthing and Bognor followed Brighton into the holiday trade, as did Hastings and St Leonard's with Decimus Burton's early 19th-century classicism, now set about with hideous modern development. Later came Eastbourne, enlarged in the 1860s to take advantage of the public's demand for sea air and made more accessible by the railway age.

The Weald

That is Sussex by the sea: a tarnished vision of health and pleasure, once the source of the European influence which has shaped so much of the country's history. Now move inland, first to a landscape of soaring escarpments and deep valleys at variance perhaps with some people's idea of tame southern England. 'The Weald is good, the Downs are best' wrote Kipling and it is hard not to agree when standing on the high ground at Treyford, Bignor or Ditchling Beacon. But you should press on down the northern side into a more secret Sussex of thick woodland and fields hedged about with yet more trees. This is the Weald, where land and houses are now much sought after by those who wish to live within commuting distance of London. How hard it is to imagine that for some four hundred years this quiet country was the centre of a thriving iron industry. Then charcoal was replaced in the smelting process by the coal of the north of England and the closing of the iron furnaces drove restless unemployed labour into the smuggling gangs of the 18th and early 19th centuries when Sussex was a far less placid place than it is now.

The Weald, originally an almost impenetrable forest, was tamed first by early medieval clearances and colonisation and then through the cutting down of trees to make charcoal for the iron masters' furnaces. Oaks were planted for ship and house building and flourished in the clay soil. This is where I live, in the West Sussex town of Petworth. Sussex is divided into two parts, each quite distinct. Petworth shows its feudal past, with the great house towering over the town, dominating it just as the castle does at Arundel. In East Sussex the feudal tradition is not so strong and towns such as Lewes owe their appearance more to the large houses of successful professional people, such as Gideon Mantell, the esteemed 18th-century physician and geologist. But in Petworth and Arundel the Percy, Seymour, Wyndham and Norfolk families were autocrats on their own domains. It is significant that in the Civil War East Sussex was largely for Parliament and West Sussex for the Crown. In the east, many of the fine Jacobean or Elizabethan houses such as Gravetye or Bateman's (later Rudyard Kipling's home) were built by ironmasters rather than the more princely patrons of the west.

The Egremonts of Petworth House

The high point of my own family was perhaps the time of the 3rd Earl of Egremont, who lived at Petworth from 1763 until 1837. He inherited a property that had passed through the female line directly from the Percys, or Earls of Northumberland, to whom it had been granted by Henry I's Queen Adeliza in the 12th century. The fields around Petworth still have the medieval lyncheting, or ridging, and the area has a strong agricultural tradition, shaped

Arundel Castle and the River Arun

NORFOLK ARMS
The Arun Art Centre

partly by Egremont who reclaimed much of the land to the north of the town. He drained the pastures, experimented with cattle and pig breeding and planted the crops needed to feed the expanding industrial towns of the north of England. Lord Lieutenant of the County, he lived mostly on his Sussex estates and had a house in Brighton where he joined the rather raffish circle of the Prince Regent and his extraordinary new Pavilion. Egremont invested in various local projects; among these were the Rother Navigation, the Wey and Arun Canal and the Chain Pier at Brighton. The canals carried timber, corn and other goods inland, away from a coastal trade menaced by Napoleon's blockade. The Chain Pier at Brighton, built after the Napoleonic wars in 1823, allowed passengers to step straight from their stage coaches into the packet boats which took them across to France and continental Europe. Egremont was also a considerable patron of the arts. He brought Turner to Sussex and commissioned those great pictures of the park and house that are a matchless celebration of light and landscape.

The Changing Face of Sussex

Egremont lived through a time of change. Agriculture flourished in 18th-century Sussex and this is reflected in the proliferation of good Georgian buildings in the towns, villages and countryside. In the fields travellers would have noticed a significant fall in the amount of fallow land. Then with the end of the Napoleonic wars in 1815, farming entered a depression and Cobbett could write of 'a shocking decay, a great dilapidation and constant pulling down' in rural England. The county, however, survived better than most other areas and Cobbett on one of his rides noted 'I have seen no misery in Sussex; nothing at all to be compared to that which I have seen in other parts; and as to these villages in the South Downs, they are beautiful to behold.'

The railways hastened change. They brought about the decline of the canals and turnpikes and made Sussex easier to reach from London. As early as 1810 the sale particulars of a house near Worth stressed the ease of transport by turnpike road to and from the capital. Appreciation of wild scenery and the sea air combined with the new trains to lure more people into the county. Sussex began to turn away from its native industries towards tourism and recreation.

Agriculture became less important. The repeal of the Corn Laws in 1846 seemed at first to have little effect on farming but in the 1870s cheap corn began to arrive from America, Russia and Poland. The First World War saw a brief revival in prices which then fell in the 1920s and 1930s. They rose again in the Second World War and remained high for most of the postwar period until the problem of food surpluses began to affect even the protected area of the Common Market. But the mechanisation and improved efficiency of farming had brought about a dramatic decline in its workforce so that men were forced off the land, often leaving the countryside altogether.

Paradoxically this gradual process coincided with some of the most famous literary appreciations of the Sussex landscape. Rudyard Kipling bought Batemans, in Burwash, in 1902 and four years later Hilaire Belloc, a Frenchman by birth, moved to Shipley to become entranced by 'the great hills

View towards Chichester from The Trundle, near Goodwood

of the south country'. Kipling's short stories and children's books, particularly *Puck of Pook's Hill* and *Rewards and Fairies*, contain lyrical evocations of the landscape of the Downs and the Weald and Belloc's *Four Men* describes a long walk across the county. A lesser known poet of Sussex is the traveller and political campaigner Wilfrid Scawen Blunt (1840–1922), the squire first of Crabbet and later of Newbuildings near Southwater, who writes of Worth Forest and the north Sussex countryside where 'the London smoke comes down upon us' and the great city seems to reach out 'with its dark arms'.

These writers celebrate a pastoral version of Sussex that was already starting to fade. Until the First World War the growth in population was concentrated on the coast or the railway routes, leaving the rural villages largely untouched or even in decline because of the precarious condition of agriculture. Then transport improved between the wars and most parts of the county came within reach of a main road or railway line. New building began to change the appearance of Sussex almost as much as the great forest clearances of the Middle Ages.

On the coast, houses and bungalows snaked out from what had once been small fishing villages or elegant resorts. In parts of West Sussex, feudalism exerted power perhaps for the last time to stop such developments on the larger estates. Elsewhere little could be done. Even the Downs were not immune to change. Farming increased production in the two World Wars and eventually its methods and machinery were advanced enough to plough up thousands of acres of high pasture.

Since 1945 these pressures have been recognised. With the Town and Country Planning Act of 1947 came the idea of planned development to curb the worst excesses. But the population of Sussex continued to grow. Crawley new town brought the first large concentration of industry to the county. Gatwick airport became the second largest in Britain. But often those who moved to Sussex were anxious to preserve its traditional character and beauty. Towns such as Rye, Chichester and Lewes have large conservation areas where development is either forbidden or strictly controlled. Parts of the Downs have been set aside for the natural regeneration of wild flowers and grasses.

As always, it is hard to get the balance right. The county must not become a lifeless museum, a network of antique shops, over-tasteful tea rooms, heritage trails or picnic areas complete with litter bins and public lavatories designed in a suitably rustic style. We must have a living Sussex where farming can be both commercial and respectful of the countryside, where enterprise is controlled yet not stifled, where the towns and villages are more than suburban dormitories. But the threat remains of Blunt's 'dark arms' of thoughtless progress and 'Nature's face stamped out of beauty by the heel of Man'. We must keep those timeless landscapes of the sea, the Weald and the Downs that have drawn people for centuries to this part of England: the views from Ditchling Beacon, the walks in Ashdown Forest or across Duncton Hill where you can still find Belloc's south country and be glad that you were Sussex born.

Gazetteer

Albourne (2/2D) *see* Hurstpierpoint

Alciston (2/4E)
A small village to the north of Alfriston, famous for its medieval tithe barn. Alciston lies below FIRLE Beacon, at 712 ft one of the highest points on the Downs, with commanding views over the surrounding countryside. A steep footpath leads from the east of the village and joins the South Downs Way near the crest of the hill. Several archaeological sites have been located in this area, although sadly many have been lost in recent years due to modern farming techniques.

Alciston village itself is situated on either side of a narrow street which peters out into a rough bridleway, at which point is the imposing tithe barn, once the property of BATTLE Abbey. That the Abbey had considerable landed interests in this part of the county is evident from the sheer size of the barn. It is 170 ft long and thus one of the largest structures of its type in the county. Another good example in Sussex is at SULLINGTON. The dilapidated, honeycombed structure next to the barn is all that now remains of the old dovecot. Pigeons rather than doves would have been found in its nesting holes, as these birds are now known to have formed an essential part of the medieval diet.

The nearby church of St Mary dates largely from the 13th and 14th centuries, although recent excavations have found evidence of a much earlier, Saxon, building. The church was built on a small hillock to protect it from flooding, which until fairly recent times represented a serious threat to low-lying land. Alciston used to be the scene of the custom of 'Easter skipping', when both children and adults would skip over a twenty yard-long rope outside the local inn.

Due north of Alciston is the small village of **Selmeston**, noted for some interesting archaeological remains from the Stone Age. In a

Medieval tithe barn, Alciston

sandpit to the south-east of the largely Victorian parish church, archaeologists in the 1930s unearthed remains of axes and tools and several pieces of pottery and cooking implements.

Realising that the native Sussex dialect was fast disappearing the Reverend W. D. Parish, a 19th-century vicar of Selmeston, recorded all that he could of this rustic vocabulary. Words he identified included 'sprucer' for liar and 'pharisees' for fairies. Today dialect words are rarely heard in Selmeston or, indeed, anywhere in Sussex. When the church was restored and rebuilt in the 1860s, the vicar ensured that the unique octagonal pillars, carved from English oak and distinguished by their capitals, were not adversely affected by the work of the restorers.

Due north of Selemston is the small downland village of **Ripe**. The church of St John the Baptist is a fine example of the Perpendicular style. The motif on the doorway is the Pelham buckle and symbolises the sway that the Pelham family had over the parish and, indeed, much of this part of East Sussex. The village also contains the delightful Old Cottage, with many strange and wonderful carvings, some of which at least must be fairly modern additions. Ripe was the home of Malcolm Lowry, author of *Under the Volcano*.

Carved wood detail on Old Cottage, Ripe

Alfriston (2/5E)

An ancient and well-preserved village north-east of Seaford, which possesses an imposing parish church known as the 'cathedral of the Downs'. Parking is the main problem in Alfriston, with double yellow lines requiring the visitor to use one of the village's two car parks. The truncated stone edifice in the centre of the village is all that now remains of the market cross, one of only two in the county to have survived at all, the other being the far grander example at CHICHESTER. The Star Inn is perhaps the best-known of Alfriston's pubs and the nearby Smugglers' Inn was once the home of one Stanton Collins, who was transported to Australia in 1831 for his illegal activities. The building has six staircases and one of the rooms has no fewer than five exits, a reminder of a smuggler's need to make a quick escape from his pursuers.

The church, dedicated to St Andrew, stands on The Tye or village green next to the Cuckmere river. It takes the shape of a symmetrical Greek cross, with a large central tower. Alfriston has every reason to be proud of its 'cathedral' for such lofty proportions in a parish church are seldom seen. According to folklore, it had been proposed to build the church to the west of the village street but supernatural forces moved the stones each night to The Tye. When four oxen were noticed lying with their backsides touching, thus forming a cross, this was taken as a sign that divine providence intended that the church should be built on its present site. It is also said – this time with more historical justification – that the early Christian martyr St Lewinna was murdered at this spot by the heathen Saxons. The saint's remains were later interred in the church and attracted pilgrims from this country and overseas. However, the folk of Alfriston did not keep a sufficiently careful eye on their famous relics, for a group of Flemish travellers were able to steal the sacred bones and take them back to Flanders, some time before the Norman Conquest.

To the south of the church, by the river bank, is the timber-framed Clergy House. This fine 14th-century building was the first building to be acquired by the National Trust and is open to the public in spring and summer. The purchase, undertaken in 1896, led to its careful restoration by Alfred Powell, whose work helped to establish the reputation of the Trust. The Congregational Church of 1801, with arch-shaped upper windows, has earned the praise of architectural historians, though by Alfriston's standards it is rather a modern building. Like LEWES, the Cuckmere valley has always had strong associations with Noncomformity and there are a number of good chapels in the area.

To the north-west of the village are the sites of ancient burial grounds that certainly predate the Christian era and demonstrate the prehistoric origins of Alfriston as a place of human settlement. North of the village, just off the A27, are Drusilla's Zoo Park and the English Wine Centre. Drusilla's is one of the best small zoos in the south and the English Wine Centre, 200 yards away, stocks more than 40 varieties of English wine. Tours by arrangement. The Youth Hostels Association has a hostel at Frog Firle to the south of the village, on the road to Seaford.

On the east bank of the Cuckmere river is **Lullington**, which can be reached on foot from Alfriston by following the footpath across the white-painted bridge over the river. Lullington boasts one of the smallest churches in the country, being only the chancel of a much larger medieval building. It is suspected that the Black Death of the 14th century so reduced the population that the parishioners who survived threw in their lot with neighbouring Alfriston. As a result, the church at Lullington was allowed to fall into decay and ruin, until what remained was rescued and restored in the 19th century. Lullington Heath is an important National Nature Reserve and an unusual example of chalk heathland where, it is claimed, the gorse flowers all the year round.

Further downriver is the village of **Litlington.** Here is to be found Sussex's only 'white horse', cut into the steep slope of High and Over Hill above the west bank of the river. The horse, covered during the Second World War to prevent its becoming a landmark for German pilots on bombing raids, is still rather grubby and in need of a good clean. It is best seen from the valley. The village church dates from the 13th century. Inside are fine old oak timbers and a large font made of Sussex marble. This is a shelly limestone, usually grey or brown, which was quarried around Petworth. The weather-boarded bell tower is typical of those Sussex churches which could not afford a steeple, but is none the less pleasing for that. Also on the

Lullington church

Downs around the village is a late Stone Age burial mound, which has the distinction of being one of the smallest in the county. Litlington is famous for its tea gardens and is an especially delightful place to visit in the early summer.

Amberley (1/4D)

A charming village in the Arun valley adjoining the famous Wild Brooks and once the summer home of the Bishops of Chichester. Much visited and much loved, Amberley remains one of the most attractive villages in the county. It grew up around the ancient church built, it is said, by St Wilfrid, who converted the pagan Saxons to Christianity. The attractions of the area were quickly recognised and in about 1100 Ralph Luffa, Bishop of Chichester, built St Michael's church and the castle, which was a summer residence of the bisbops until the 16th century. Domesday records that, at nearly 3,000 acres, Amberley was one of the bishops' largest land-holdings in the county. Other land under their control included BISHOPSTONE.

Bishop Luffa was also responsible for building CHICHESTER Cathedral and the fact that both churches were built at the same time probably accounts for the fine chancel arch in Amberley church and the carved capitals in the three Norman windows. The church was extended in the 13th century by Ralph Nevill who was not only Bishop of Chichester but also Chancellor of England. Because of his larger retinue, he required a more imposing east end of the church

for ordinations and ceremonial. It was at this time that the murals to the right of the chancel arch would have been painted. In the top left-hand corner may be seen *Christ in Majesty* with the world between His feet. Below this is a *Resurrection* scene with Christ rising from a stone coffin and sleeping soldiers beneath (see *The Norman Heritage*, p. 28).

The castle was built to defend the upper reaches of the Arun valley but soon acquired the domestic character of a summer retreat for the hard-pressed bishops. The popularity which Amberley enjoyed is reflected in the register of Bishop Robert Rede (1397–1414), which records that many of his official documents were signed here. The castle never saw action and is now an hotel and restaurant. Its one memorable moment in history was on 14 October 1651 when Charles II, in the course of his flight to France after the Battle of Worcester, spent the night at the castle under the protection of Sir John Briscoe.

The village contains many attractive brick and flint cottages with thatched roofs and has long been popular with artists, walkers and fishermen. Amberley station – which provides access to the area via the attractive Arun Valley railway line – is a mile south of the village, on the South Downs Way at HOUGHTON bridge.

North of the village are the Amberley Wild Brooks, the water meadows of the River Arun which flood in the winter and are a haven for wildlife. Happily, a scheme to drain the area some years ago was defeated and the brooks are now managed with nature conservation in mind.

Angmering (1/4E)
A brick and flint village between Arundel and Worthing which retains something of a rural atmosphere despite considerable new building. Angmering lay on the old Roman road across Sussex, which ran from Pevensey to Chichester through some of the best agricultural land in the region. Not surprisingly, the coastal plain attracted substantial Roman settlement and the two major estates in the area were centred on BIGNOR and Angmering. The villa at Angmering, parts of which were built in AD 70 and 80, was a grand house suggesting very considerable wealth and social position. The site of the villa is not accessible to the public.

When the Saxons arrived they too chose this spot as their base, under their leader Angemar. At the time of Domesday, parts of the manor were in the Rape of BRAMBER, controlled by the de Braose family from Bramber Castle. Much of the village of Angmering today dates from the 18th and 19th centuries. Of particular note are the church of St Margaret – restored by the local squire in the 1850s, reputedly as the result of a Derby win – and the county library, nicely converted from the old school building.

Another interesting building is Chant's Cottage in the High Street, which has a brick and half-timbered front. George Chant was a local shepherd who lived here and brought up ten children on a tiny income. The hardship of their lives can be imagined.

Ardingly (2/3C)
(Arding-lye), north of Haywards Heath, is a pretty Wealden village and the home of the famous South of England Show. The site was a defended position above a narrow valley formed by one of the tributaries of the River Ouse, now dammed to form a large reservoir which covers nearly 200 acres and is available for fishing. The parish church of St Peter contains good memorial brasses to members of the Culpeper and Wakehurst families who lived at **Wakehurst Place**, a mile north of the village on the B2028. The house was originally built by Sir Edward Culpeper in 1590 and is now the country home of the Royal Botanic Gardens, Kew. The 250 acres are open to the public and contain many unusual plants, shrubs and trees. Sadly, the gardens were badly damaged in the storm of October 1987, but restoration is in progress.

Ardingly College is a school of the Woodard Foundation and belongs to the same family as Lancing College (near SOMPTING) and HURSTPIERPOINT College, all founded by the indefatigable and visionary clergyman Nathaniel Woodard, to provide 'comprehensive and classless' education. Founded in 1858, the present buildings were opened in 1870. They are of red brick, in the form of two courtyards, one open to the south, the other closed.

Just outside the village is the permanent showground of the South of England Agricultural Society, where in early June each year the three-day South of England Show takes place. The Show attracts large numbers of entries from all over southern England and, apart from the events in the show rings and arenas, there are hundreds of stalls and attractions for all the family. At other times of the year events are held regularly at the showground, ranging from horse trials to antiques road shows. Details of the

The Thatched Cottage, Amberley

annual programme are available from the Secretary at the showground.

Arlington (2/5E) *see* Hailsham

Arundel (1/4E)
A small hill-top town, with a familiar skyline made up of the castle of the Dukes of Norfolk, the parish church and the Roman Catholic Cathedral. Like LEWES and STEYNING, Arundel developed where the major east-west route through Sussex crossed the river valley, at the highest point to which the river was conveniently navigable. From earliest times, the Arun gap was of strategic importance and a defended position was established at Burpham. The documented history of the town begins with the Norman Conquest. King William gave the Rapes of Chichester and Arundel, which together made up the Honour of Arundel, consisting of nearly 60,000 acres, to Roger de Montgomery, one of his most trusted lieutenants. Montgomery, who also held land in Shropshire and in Wales, built an impressive castle at Arundel, commanding the river crossing and controlling communications. From here he governed much of modern West Sussex, as well as his estates further afield.

The town which grew up in the shadow of the castle was created a borough and the port of Arundel was established, with ships bringing in manufactured goods from London, wine from France and sea coal from Newcastle, and exporting local primary products – lime, timber, corn and wool. In the 16th century the castle and estate passed to the family of the Dukes of Norfolk through the marriage of Thomas Howard, the fourth Duke, to the heiress of the last Fitzalan Earl of Arundel, and has been the seat of the Dukes of Norfolk since the 19th century.

Arundel was held for the King in the Civil War. The castle was besieged by the Parliamentary army, who mounted cannon on the church tower. Following the successful siege Colonel Morley of GLYNDE and Sir William Springate of RINGMER were appointed joint governors of the castle, but within a few weeks Springate contracted typhoid fever. His young Puritan wife, heavily pregnant, made the difficult journey from London to see him before he died and left a vivid account of events in a letter to her grandson, Springet Penn of Warminghurst. 'When we came to Arundel', she writes 'we met with a most dismal sight: the town being depopulated, all the windows broken with the great guns, and the soldiers making stables of all the shops and lower rooms.' She found her husband in his quarters but despite her ministrations he died within a few days, just 23 years old.

It was not until 1800 that the castle was fully restored; there was a further restoration, amounting almost to a rebuilding, between 1890 and 1903. As a result, little of the medieval castle remains today. Of Montgomery's buildings, which provided for a big motte and two baileys

Arundel Castle

to the north and east, only the gatehouse remains; there is also the shell keep built on top of the motte by Henry II towards the end of the 12th century. What the visitor sees today, while resembling the original plan of the castle, is thus essentially a 19th-century Gothic confection, commissioned by the 15th Duke of Norfolk and paid for out of the income derived by the family from their ownership of the steel town of Sheffield. The splendid mahogany library survives from the 18th-century restoration and the castle contains paintings by Holbein, Van Dyck, Reynolds and Gainsborough. The castle is set in over 1,000 acres of parkland to which the public have unrestricted access; dogs, however, are not permitted. A popular spot for picnics is Swanbourne Lake, reached by the tree-lined Mill Road. The Wildfowl Trust reserve in Mill Road has 1,000 ducks, geese and swans from all over the world. The castle and other venues in the town are used for the annual Arundel Festival which takes place in late August, and the international touring cricket team traditionally play their first match of the season at the castle ground, against the Duchess of Norfolk's XI.

Although the history of Arundel is inextricably bound up with that of the Norfolk family, the borough has always taken pride in its independence, and castle and town have not always seen eye to eye. Until the 1832 Reform Act, political conflict focused on the choice of the town's two Members of Parliament. The principal inns, The George and The Crown, were associated respectively with the Tories and the Whigs. The 19th century saw a prosperous town, the centre of a large and flourishing agricultural estate, with extensive trade by road, river and railway. A great deal of rebuilding took place and Arundel today is essentially a Georgian and Victorian town, the skyline completed with the construction of the Roman Catholic Cathedral in 1870, designed by John Hansom, inventor of the hansom cab. There are few very distinguished buildings, but good examples of brick and flint cottages survive in Arun Street and King Street, together with gentlemen's brick houses in Maltravers Street and some timber-framed buildings, often disguised, such as the old Crown Inn in the Square, now divided into shops.

The parish church of St Nicholas should not be missed. The building was erected in 1380, a rare example in Sussex of a decision being taken, in the late medieval period, to replace an existing Norman church. Under the same roof are the Church of England parish church and the Roman Catholic Fitzalan Chapel, private chapel of the Dukes of Norfolk with access only from the castle. The two parts of the building were divided by a solid, brick wall, now replaced by an iron and glass screen which is opened from time to time in these more ecumenical days.

A mile or two up the Arun valley from Arundel is the delightful downland village of **Burpham**. The place derives its name from the ancient *burh* or earthworks south of the church, which encloses a promontory overlooking the river, now used as a cricket field and children's playground. The parish church of St Mary the Virgin is built largely of flint rubble, with some use of local clunch, or hard chalkstone, inside. The roofs are tiled except for three courses of Horsham slabs on the north side of the nave and the west side of the north transept. (see *The Norman Heritage*, p. 28). In the churchyard is the

Maltravers Street, Arundel

Bluebell Railway near Sheffield Park

grave of the Reverend Tickner Edwardes, who was vicar of Burpham from 1927 to 1935. He kept bees and wrote several novels, one of which, *Tansy*, was made into a popular silent film.

South of Arundel are the villages of **Lyminster** and **Poling**. Both are places of considerable antiquity; Lyminster is mentioned in King Alfred the Great's will in 901. It was then called Lullyngminster: the present spelling was only standardised about 100 years ago, one of the first executive actions of the newly elected County Council which ruled in favour of this spelling rather than the alternative Leominster. The village is associated with a famous Sussex dragon legend, as the home of the monster of the Knucker Hole, a deep pool beside the church. The name derives from the Old English word *nicor*, meaning 'sea monster'. After doing a great deal of damage in the surrounding countryside, the dragon was eventually slain by a brave young farmer's boy called Jim Pulk – or by a gallant knight, in another version of the legend.

Poling was the site of the Sussex headquarters of the Knights Hospitaller. Founded in Jerusalem, the Order was dedicated to providing hospitality and care to the sick. Initially, its work was among pilgrims to the Holy Land and those involved in the Crusades, but it spread throughout Europe and was well established in this country. At Poling the Knights had a preceptory, or training establishment, and from here the affairs of the Order in Sussex were managed. Their chapel and other buildings are now incorporated in a private house known as St John's Priory. The patron saint of the Order was St John the Baptist and the present day descendants of the Knights Hospitaller are the St John Ambulance Brigade, the voluntary first-aid and ambulance organisation.

Ashdown Forest (2/4B)

Part of the great forest known to the Saxons as the Weald, Ashdown Forest was for over three centuries a royal hunting ground, having been granted to the Duke of Lancaster by his father, Edward III, in 1372. Even before the Duke and his men took to hunting deer, Ashdown Forest had been used by man. There is evidence of Celtic habitation before the Romans cut their way through to build a road to their castle at PEVENSEY. During the Middle Ages, and even more so in Tudor times, much of the forest was cut down to be burned for charcoal. Sussex was, of course, a major area for the iron industry and charcoal was essential for the smelting process. It is said that many of the cannon that helped defeat the Spanish Armada were produced in Ashdown Forest. The industry went into gradual decline during the 17th century, largely because the small bands of iron masters who lived and worked in the woods refused to adopt new methods.

The parish church of St Michael at **Withyham** was rebuilt in the 1660s after being struck by lightning. The wall painting of the *Last Judgment* is by Earl de la Warr, who was rector of the parish in the 1850s. The de la Warrs, lords of the manor of BEXHILL, owned Ashdown Forest for many years. On the southern edge of the Forest, at Heron's Ghyll, is one of the few remaining fords in Sussex, where traffic has to drive through a normally shallow tributary of the River Ouse.

On the fringe of Ashdown forest, on the busy A22 London to Eastbourne road is the village of **Forest Row**. First mentioned by this name in 1338, Forest Row was then a single row of houses on the western edge of the forest. It was an example of what are known as 'waste-edge' settlements, 'waste' meaning wild or uncultivated land. Other examples on the fringe of Ashdown Forest are **Coleman's Hatch** and **Nutley** which has an interesting post-mill. Nutley still has something of the appearance of a pioneering settlement, reflecting the way in which agriculture penetrated but did not conquer this part of the High Weald.

West Hoathly (Hoath-lye) is a hill-top village about 600 ft above sea level and on the extreme western edge of Ashdown Forest. As is to be expected in such a wooded area, there are many old timber-framed buildings, including the 15th-century Priest's House which houses a local museum of village life and is open from April to October. To the south is **Horsted Keynes.** The area remained very backward in terms of agricultural development for many hundreds of years but the introduction of new methods by the owners of the Broadhurst Estate (the Trevors of GLYNDE) in the late 18th century, combined with the later arrival of efficient systems of land drainage resulted in the development of a productive agricultural district.

Today, Horsted Keynes is best known as the northern terminus of the Bluebell Railway, the restored section of the old East Grinstead to Lewes line named after the bluebell woods through which it runs. Vintage steam trains run from SHEFFIELD PARK station to Horsted Keynes and back daily during the summer months and less frequently at other times of the year. There is ample car parking at Sheffield Park station, a museum and shops.

Ashington (1/5D) *see* Washington

Ashurst (2/1D) *see* Washington

Balcombe (2/3B)

A village in the High Weald north of Haywards Heath and close to the expanding new town of Crawley. Something very nasty indeed must have happened here at one time, for the name of the place means 'valley of dread'. But Balcombe today is an attractive village with an air of prosperity, reflecting its convenient location on the London to Brighton railway line and its closeness to the motorway system. The village centre contains many listed buildings, a number of them hung with plain clay tiles in the typical Wealden fashion. Underneath timber-framing abounds and some of the houses, such as The

Balcombe railway viaduct

Half Moon pub, have Horsham slab roofs. The parish church of St Mary was much restored and enlarged in Victorian times but retains its 15th-century tower and broached spire.

Among the distinguished country houses in the area, Stone Hall, south of Balcombe Place, stands out. This late 17th-century house, with red and blue brickwork and stone quoins, is the home of the owners of Balcombe Estate, part of whose land has been flooded to create ARDINGLY reservoir. The countryside round about is hilly and many of the houses outside the village centre have been built on vantage points with magnificent views.

Through this varied terrain, the Victorian railway engineers built the London to Brighton line; the crossing of the Ouse valley gave them the opportunity to display, in Balcombe viaduct, the full range of their technical and aesthetic skills. The result is memorable: 1,475 ft long, with 37 brick arches and a classical balustrade, Balcombe is one of the most impressive railway viaducts in the country. It can be seen from the Haywards Heath road but is best approached on foot. Note particularly the way in which each pier is arched at the bottom as well as the top and the seemingly endless vistas presented by the serried ranks of piers. Through the valley flows the River Ouse, nowadays only a modest stream, but in the 19th century sufficiently deep to enable materials for the construction of the viaduct to be shipped upriver, the navigation thus playing its part, as it so often did in the provision of the more efficient form of transport which was to take its place.

Barcombe (2/4D)

A pleasant village to the north of Lewes, a popular spot for anglers and for picnicking beside the River Ouse. Although the church of St Mary, with its distinctive shingled broach spire, was greatly restored during the last century, it retains many of its older features, including a 13th-century lancet window on the north side. There are several interesting old buildings in the village, including Shelley's Folly, which was built around 1700 and displays the emblem of the Shelley family at the back of the house. The house is not open to the public.

Barcombe Mills, to the north of the village proper, was a fashionable picnicking spot in Edwardian times where artists used to paint the old mill buildings in their lush and picturesque

surroundings. The last working mill ceased grinding corn in 1934 and was destroyed by fire five years later, so today Barcombe Mills survives in name only. There are, however, splendid views from this spot, with the great chalk outcrop of Mount Caburn visible to the south, rising up above the water meadows.

The railway through Barcombe was closed some years ago, although its presence is still felt in the surviving station buildings.

Battle (3/3D)
Situated on the A2100 to the north-west of Hastings, the town is renowned as the site of the Battle of Hastings in 1066. The Benedictine Abbey of St Martin at Battle was founded by William the Conqueror on the scene of the decisive encounter between the Saxon army and the invading Normans on 14 October 1066, the high altar being placed on the spot where Harold fell, mortally wounded by an arrow. Traditionally, the Abbey was founded as the result of a vow made by William before the battle in which he promised to build a monastery if God granted him victory. Another theory is that his action was prompted by a desire to achieve personal salvation by atoning for the loss of life in the battle. Similar motives inspired the foundation, by William de Warenne and his wife Gundrada, of the Priory of St Pancras at LEWES.

Part of the Abbey is now a private school but much of the site, cared for by English Heritage, is open to visitors. A circular tour leads from the Abbey gatehouse to the battlefield and the Abbey ruins. The Abbey occupied the high ground on the ridge where the Saxon army waited for the assault of the Normans from the lower ground of Senlac moor. The stream which still flows through the valley is reddened by the soil in the vicinity, symbolic, it is said, of the blood shed in the battle. Signposts mark a walk around the battlefield and topographical models describing the course of the battle are placed at intervals.

During the Middle Ages the Abbey acquired great power and wealth and frequently came into conflict with other landowners. After the dissolution of the monasteries in the mid-16th century, it had several owners. The gunpowder industry was established at Battle in 1676. The workshops, which were only a short distance from the Abbey, were finally closed in 1874 on safety grounds. In 1976, in celebration of the bicentenary of the United States of America, generous donations by American citizens enabled the British Government to buy the site of the battle and the remains of the Abbey.

The Norman parish church of St Mary dates also from the time of the Conquest, although it is largely 12th-century in construction. In the churchyard is the tomb of Isaac Ingall, who died in 1798 at the age, so it is claimed, of 120; he was reputed to have been a servant at the Abbey for 100 years. There are a number of fine Georgian buildings in Battle, most notably The George Hotel. Several of the cottages near the Abbey

Battle Abbey and the site of the conflict of 1066

date from about 1700 and are in a fine state of preservation. One of the oldest domestic buildings in the town is Lewins Croft, a timber-framed house in Mount Street which is believed to be over 400 years old.

Battle market, once an important commercial occasion, was last held in 1967. Its passing brought more than one tradition to an end: the custom of allowing the local pubs an hour and a half's extension of drinking hours on market day lapsed with the closure of the market. This would no doubt have pleased Guy Hayler, a founder of the temperance movement, who was born in one of the cottages near the Abbey. Another notable historical personality associated with Battle is Sir Anthony Browne, Henry VIII's Master of Horse, who acquired the Abbey and much other property on the dissolution of the monasteries, including Cowdray House at EASEBOURNE.

The Norman Heritage

JOHN GODFREY

The Normans have been described (by John Julius Norwich in his introduction to *The Norman Achievement* by Richard F. Cassady) as: 'The most energetic, vital and gifted people ever to burst upon the European continent.' Nowhere was their impact greater than in Sussex.

Outside the church of St Ouen in Rouen, capital of Upper Normandy, stands a fine statue in Caen stone of Rollo the Norseman, unmistakably Viking in his helmet, moustaches and cross-gartered leggings. Rollo it was who led Norwegian explorers and then settlers to the lower Seine valley and founded what was to become the Norman race, rulers of the virile and expansionist Duchy of Normandy with territorial interests not only in what is now France, but also in Sicily and the Crusader states of the Eastern Mediterranean.

By the middle of the 11th century, Norman power was firmly consolidated. Always adaptable when it suited their interests, the Normans had abandoned their old gods and Norse language in favour of Christianity and the richer, far more flexible French tongue. Norse survived only in the region of conservative Bayeux, capital of Lower Normandy, and it was to Bayeux that the future Duke William, the Conqueror, was sent as a boy to learn something of his Norse origins.

Chancel arch, Bosham church

Expansionist Normandy soon began to take an interest in England, for 200 years torn and divided between competing Scandinavian and German raiders and settlers. Aware of the need to appease his neighbour across the Channel, Edward the Confessor granted lands – including, in Sussex, the manor of Steyning – to religious and secular interests in Normandy and, in 1065, formally recognised Duke William of Normandy as his legitimate successor to the English throne, thereby purporting to deny the right of the English nobles meeting in council or Witan to select the new monarch.

As Edward's health failed Harold Godwinson, Earl of Wessex and a contender for the succession, sailed from Bosham to Normandy for talks with William. This episode is depicted in the Bayeux Tapestry (which is actually an embroidery) in which the church of the Holy Trinity at Bosham is not only explicity identified but may easily be recognised from the great Saxon chancel arch illustrating the relevant panel. It was as the result of this historic meeting that Harold was persuaded – or forced – to swear the famous oath to support William's claim to the throne of England on Edward's death.

The swearing of the oath is the central episode depicted in the Bayeux Tapestry; it was the subsequent breaking of this oath by Harold when he assumed the crown himself on Edward's death the following year that, in the Norman view, justified the invasion of England which took place in September 1066. In using the Tapestry as an historical source, it is important to appreciate that it was conceived and executed as an effective exercise in self-justification following the successful invasion, rather than as an objective account of what occurred.

Whatever the rights or wrongs of the matter, the fact is that William's army landed in Sussex at Pevensey on 28 September 1066. Harold was in the north of England, defeating the Norwegians and Scots at Stamford Bridge, near York. After a gruelling forced march south they were already exhausted and demoralised when they reached the hill of Senlac, 6 miles from Hastings; there, on the morning of 14 October, they faced the invading Normans who were rested, superbly equipped and ready to fight. The outcome of that day, rightly regarded as a watershed in English history, was the death of Harold, the defeat of the English army and, on Christmas Day 1066, the coronation of Duke William as King of England.

The invasion and the critical military engagement having both taken place in Sussex, William was in no doubt as to the strategic importance of the county, lying as it did at the fulcrum of his new, united kingdom. Consequently, he took special care to place the control of Sussex in the hands of men whom he knew he could trust. Making use of the old Saxon divisions of the county into Rapes, based on the river valleys, he assigned to each of his principal lieutenants and supporters a substantial Sussex estate, comprising woodland, Downs and coast.

The men who were thus established in Sussex were among the greatest in the land and were at the centre of national political life. They included Roger de Montgomery, William's cousin and close friend, who was given the Rapes of Chichester and Arundel, William de Warenne, probably his son-in-law, who was given Lewes and Robert de Mortain, William's half-brother and one of his most trusted advisers, who received Pevensey Rape. Each lord built a castle to defend his territory, to command communications routes and to impress the English with the power and efficiency of the new order.

The original castles were probably no more than hastily-constructed earth mottes, each with an enclosure defended by a timber palisade. As the invasion developed into conquest and occupation, however, the original simple structures were replaced by much more substantial stone-built fortifications on the lines of those built in Normandy to establish and defend the boundaries of the Duchy. Thus the first major Norman buildings to be constructed in Sussex were probably the great Rapal castles of Chichester, Arundel, Bramber, Lewes, Pevensey (where the Normans built within the fortifications established by the Romans) and Hastings.

At Chichester and Pevensey, the Norman builders had to make the most of level sites with few natural strategic advantages, throwing up at Chichester a substantial motte, the remains of which may be seen today in Priory Park. Elsewhere, topography was more in their favour and the sites chosen at Arundel, Bramber, Lewes and Hastings take advantage of hill-top situations, controlling river crossings and/or access by sea. The plans of the castles followed those of prototypes across the Channel, such as Arques-la-Bataille, near Dieppe; being unfamiliar with local building materials and in the absence of immediately available good quality building stone, the Norman masons imported stone from the great quarries of Caen through the coastal ports and upriver to the chosen sites.

Along with the establishment of secular power came ecclesiastical control, the rebuilding of cathedrals in major population centres and the spread of the influence of monasticism. There were already links between England and the Norman church – the Abbey of Fécamp had long owned land in Steyning, for example – but the arrival of the Normans had an enormous impact on the church in England. Within 10 years, all the dioceses in the country except Worcester were held by non-English bishops, abbeys and monasteries were established, cathedrals built or renewed and a massive church building programme put in hand. In this way, the new rulers hoped to win the hearts and minds of the conquered English.

The monastic tradition was well established in France by the time of the Conquest, centring on the powerful Abbey at Cluny in Burgundy. In Normandy the Abbeys at Fécamp, Jumièges and Caen were major centres of monastic influence. William and his lieutenants were anxious to establish similar centres in England, not only for the reasons of *realpolitik* described above, but also in an attempt to secure personal salvation. Medieval military leaders were concerned about the impact on their souls of the responsibility they bore for lives lost in battle, and commonly sought atonement by endowing religious foundations. Thus, in Sussex, William founded the Benedictine Abbey of St Martin on the site of the Battle of Hastings, the high altar placed, so tradition has it, on the spot where Harold fell, fatally wounded.

Perhaps in emulation of their royal master, perhaps as the result of genuine piety, William de Warenne and his wife Gundrada founded the Priory of St Pancras at Lewes, the first and principal foundation of the Cluniac Order in England. From Lewes, de Warenne established subsidiary communities elsewhere around the country, including the Priory at Castle Acre on his lands in Norfolk. The remains of Lewes Priory can be seen today at Southover, but they give little indication of the original scale and magnificence of the buildings: the Priory church is reckoned to have been larger than Chichester Cathedral. Much of the site was destroyed when the railway was built by the Victorians, but one positive result of their vandalism was the discovery of the de Warennes' grave slabs, which can now be seen in the church of St John the Baptist, Southover High Street.

The cathedral of the South Saxon See was moved from Selsey to Chichester in 1075 in accordance with the decree of the Council of London, which provided for cathedrals to be moved into larger centres of population from the smaller and more isolated places where they had often originally been established. A church had previously existed on the site chosen in Chichester and it is probable that the new cathedral, credited to Bishop Ralph Luffa (1091–1123), was based on this building. Completed in 1108, the Cathedral was badly damaged by fire 6 years later and had to be rebuilt; the work was finally completed towards the end of the 12th century.

This building is the basis of the present cathedral, which consists of a nave with aisles, two towers at the west end, north and south transepts and an aisled presbytery with an apse and ambulatory. Chichester Cathedral has been described as 'homely'; it certainly inspires little of the awe of Durham or Salisbury. But it is perfectly suited to its surroundings, the interior sturdily Romanesque and the famous spire a reassuring landmark for walkers on the Downs and for sailors; Chichester is the only English medieval cathedral to be clearly visible from the sea.

At Boxgrove, about 3 miles east of Chichester, is the striking parish church of St Mary and St Blaise, apart from the Cathedral itself probably the most important surviving ecclesiastical building in the county with roots in the Norman period. Boxgrove Priory was founded in the early 12th century by Robert de Haye as a cell of the Abbey of Lessay in Normandy. The building which now serves as the parish church was the central feature of the Priory and the remains of other buildings, now in the care of English Heritage, can be seen in the adjoining field.

Little survives of the original 12th-century building other than the crossing, the transepts with their arches into the nave and chancel and one or two blocked windows. The present nave, with its mixture of round and pointed arches, is Early English, built about 1220, but enough is left of the original 12th-century structure to give a clear indication of its strength and proportions. There are many similarities with Chichester Cathedral, whose development was more or less concurrent, including details of some of the original Norman decoration to the piers and capitals. Today Boxgrove, with its pleasing 15th-century painted ceiling and feeling of light and spaciousness, is one of Sussex's greatest architectural treasures.

While Boxgrove's Norman origins have been obscured by its later refinement, St Mary's at Climping has changed remarkably little from the day it was built in the early 13th century. As a result, Climping is an outstanding example of a late Norman parish church and if it were possible

13th-century undercroft, Battle Abbey

to save just one of these in Sussex, this would be the choice of many architectural historians.

The tower was built first, probably by the nuns of Almanesches to whom Roger de Montgomery gave the manor of Climping. Its walls are over 4 ft thick and it was clearly intended to play a defensive role, providing a safe rallying point for the local inhabitants in the event of an attack by raiders. The late 12th-century decoration to the tower is most unusual, displaying the unrestrained late-Romanesque pleasure in bold, three-dimensional moulding. Look particularly at the arch around the west door and the pillars at either side, and do not miss the lancet window cut into the buttress above the door and quite surrounded – even submerged – by zigzag ornamentation. The rest of the church, built a little later by John de Climping, a future Bishop of Chichester, is also very fine, quite plain and of simple plan, the interior lit by lancet windows and the whole structure an harmonious whole.

St Mary the Virgin at Burpham, across the Arun valley from Arundel, was built with confidence at the end of the 12th century when church building in Sussex was as good as any in England. A church had existed here since pre-Conquest days, when it was Burpham rather than Arundel which defended the crossing of the Arun. It is thought that the north wall of the nave and part of the walling between the arches of the south arcade survives from this time. The north transept and the arch to the south transept are early 12th-century and, later, the south wall was pierced with two arches when a south aisle was built.

The interior is light and clean, an effect enhanced by the use of clunch, a soft limestone forming one of the beds of the lower chalk and infrequently used in Sussex for buildings of this high standard. The lightness of the stone and the quality of the vaulting in the chancel give Burpham something of the atmosphere of the great abbey churches of the Seine valley, such as Boscherville, or even La Trinité at Caen, where genuine stone vaulting was first applied in Normandy. Notice in particular the rich late Norman decoration in the south transept: zigzags, chevrons, grotesque heads and scalloped capitals.

A few miles upriver from Burpham is the showcase village of Amberley and its very fine parish church of St Michael. Amberley Castle was used by the Bishops of Chichester as a summer residence and St Michael's was probably built by Bishop Luffa, who was responsible also for the building of Chichester Cathedral. In the early 13th century, when Bishop Ralph Neville became Chancellor of England, the chancel of St Michael's was enlarged to accommodate the pomp and circumstance expected of so splendid a dignitary.

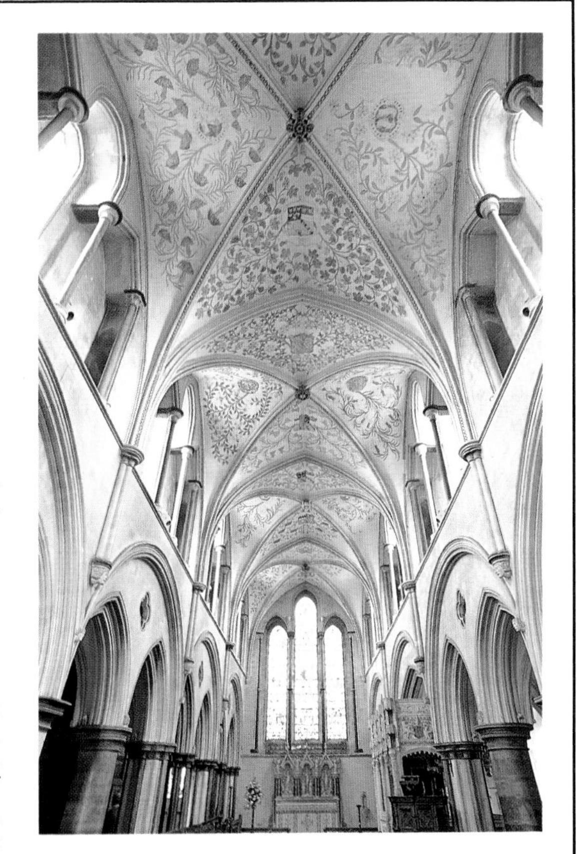

Church of St Mary and St Blaise, Boxgrove

The joy of Amberley church is the towering Norman chancel arch with its vigorous decoration; same may consider if too unrefined, but admirers of bold zigzag ornamentation need look no further. The enlargement of the chancel and the provision of larger windows to provide the rather grander setting required by the bishops result in a lighter and loftier interior than that originally built, but these later changes do not obscure the simple beauty of what remains essentially a country parish church.

Visitors to Amberley should not miss the charming little church at North Stoke, possibly dedicated, like its neighbour at South Stoke, to St Leonard, patron of prisoners. North Stoke has a Norman nave of unusual width, probably because the walls were built outside those of the original wooden Saxon church.

The final Arun valley church which deserves a mention here is St Botolph's at Hardham, just south of Pulborough. This very simple, white-painted church dates from the 11th century and is famous for having the earliest nearly complete series of wall paintings in the county. Dating from the early 12th century, they are thought to

Church of St Mary, New Shoreham

have been the work of a famous group of artists and craftsmen who were based at Lewes Priory and were also responsible for the wall paintings at Clayton. The paintings at Hardham are now much faded, a great deal of the detail of the original having been lost following their rediscovery in 1866.

If St Mary's at Climping lays claim to the title of the best Norman church in Sussex, St Andrew's at Steyning must run it very close. Indeed, the Norman nave at Steyning is undoubtedly the best in the county and has few rivals in England. The revelation comes as a surprise, but is not entirely unheralded. From the outside, Steyning looks solid and dependable, a pleasing combination of mellow stone, flint and clay tiles. But the four-square tower and the round arches of the clerestory windows should prepare the informed visitor for the interior which is to come.

It is not totally fanciful to compare Steyning's late Norman nave with that of Durham Cathedral. Although, of course, on a much smaller scale, Steyning shares with Durham a virile, northern, no nonsense approach which is unusual in the gentle south. The massive round pillars, with their decorated capitals, support lavishly carved arches, displaying all the variety of late Norman three-dimensional ornamentation. The chancel arch is higher still. Later additions to St Andrew's are less successful, but its nave is one of the prides of Sussex.

Nestling under the Downs south of Steyning is the highly unusual church of St Mary at Sompting, essentially Saxon but with Norman features. The tower, with its gabled pyramidial cap, the only example left in England of the style known as the 'Rhenish helm' or 'Rhenish helmet', is Saxon, and the arch inside is an important example of those still standing in Sussex. The church was rebuilt in the late 12th century, having been granted in 1154 to a Crusading Order of fighting monks known as the Templars.

The Templars rebuilt the nave and chancel on the original Saxon plan, with the walls in a straight line with the tower. They added the present north and south transepts, originally walled off from the main church, as chapels for the use of their members. The south transept, through which visitors enter the church today, is lower than the rest of the building, square and solid as a Crusader castle, with its own miniature chancel and sacristry. The great height of the splendid Saxon arch over the south doorway is thought to be explained by the need for Templar banners to be admitted to the church and ceremonial occasions.

Another Sussex church built for the Templars is St Mary the Virgin at Shipley, south of Horsham, probably built in about 1125. The original plan was a long simple parallelogram, with the tower intervening between the nave and the chancel, the external walls of the tower and nave lining up as at Sompting. Notice the carved stonework of the 12th-century west door, the double Norman arches of the chancel with their mouldings and corbels, and the stonework of the Norman window in the south aisle. The great treasure of Shipley – a 13th-century reliquary with scenes in Limoges enamel – was stolen in 1976 and has not been seen since.

Shoreham, an important port in Norman times as it is today, has three Norman buildings, all of considerable interest. The Marlipins in the High Street is the original customs house for the harbour, built no doubt when New Shoreham was developed in about 1100 following the silting up of the river. The settlement of Old Shoreham was abandoned, but the Church of St Nicholas survives. The church was built at the point where the River Adur was traditionally forded, an original Saxon structure being replaced by a Norman cruciform church in 1140. The building is entered through the original, much decorated Norman door arch into the south transept. The round Norman tower arches dominate the interior and there is a great variety of decoration in the carving on the inside of the arches.

The glory of Shoreham, however, is the great Norman church of New Shoreham, dedicated to St Mary de Haura (of the harbour). The building the visitor sees today is a fragment of the original and is in fact no more than the chancel, crossing and transepts, the nave having collapsed in the 18th century. The outline of the nave may be traced from the ruins in the churchyard, indicating the tremendous size of the original building.

Even in its reduced state St Mary's is spectacular, with its massive square tower and impressive arches. The tower is 81 ft tall; its first stage, with the crossing, tower arches and transepts, was probably built between 1100 and 1130. The second, top storey dates from later in the 12th century, when the present chancel or choir was built.

The most unusual feature of St Mary's is the difference between the north and south arcades of the choir. The north side has alternate solid round and octagonal columns with a strong Norman feel to them. Between them are highly decorated and slightly pointed arches with a wealth of carving. The south side, however, is unmistakably Gothic, with fluted columns stretching right up to support the vaulted roof. The two arcades are thought to have been built at the same time, so the effect produced by the use of the contrasting styles must have been deliberate.

This survey has so far been restricted to West Sussex, for no other reason than that the great Norman churches of the county are concentrated in the western division. There are, however, a handful of East Sussex churches that deserve a final mention: first, the round-towered Norman churches of the Ouse valley and second, the beautiful flint church of St Andrew at Bishopstone, near Newhaven.

St Michael's, Lewes, the nameless parish church at Southease, and St John's, Piddinghoe, all have 12th-century round towers, built of flint. Various explanations have been put forward for this unusual shape, including the suggestion that, unless stone or brick is used in combination with flint, it is difficult if not impossible to construct corners in this irregular and intractable material. A similar explanation has been advanced for the round church towers of Norfolk. Another idea is that the towers were originally intended to double as watchtowers or lighthouses, at a time when the estuary would have been much wider and deeper than it is today. The towers might have been used to guide ships into safe havens along the estuary or to Lewes itself, or to warn of the approach of those with less friendly intentions. Whatever the reason, the round towers of the Ouse valley are an oddity and the simple buildings attached to them a point of interest.

Church and the River Ouse at Piddinghoe

St Andrew's at Bishopstone, tucked away in the Downs near Newhaven, is of particular interest and should not be missed. There is much evidence of Saxon work, including a sundial inscribed 'Eadric'. The tower and the north aisle are Norman, while the interior contains some good moulding and ornamentation. Bishopstone is a peaceful spot and it was here that the naturalist and writer W. H. Hudson paused while collecting material for his little masterpiece *Nature in Downland*. It is also a good place to conclude this survey of Norman churches in Sussex.

Bishopstone derives its name from its ownership by the Bishops of Chichester, a fact that neatly illustrates the range of the influence of the Norman church. In their castles, cathedrals, monasteries and parish churches the Normans changed for ever the face of England. The effects they had on our society, law, government and economy were fundamental but intangible. Their heritage of splendid buildings remains for us to enjoy today and nowhere is this more evident than in Sussex.

Bayham Abbey (3/2B) *see* Frant

Beachy Head (3/1F) *see* Eastbourne

Bell's Yew Green (3/2B) *see* Frant

Berwick (2/5E) *see* Firle

Bexhill (3/3E)
A seaside resort between Eastbourne and Hastings which grew up in the late Victorian period and is now largely a residential and retirement town. Bexhill was developed as a resort by the Earls de la Warr in the 1880s. Previously, it had been little more than a fishing village with a reputation for smuggling. Around St Peter's church can still be found traces of the old Bexhill. The church itself stands on a Neolithic earthwork, remains of which were largely destroyed when the church was restored during the last century. Inside, parts of the original Norman church can still be found, such as the arches in the west tower. Older still is the very fine and well-preserved Anglo-Saxon coffin lid. Several weatherboarded cottages survive in Church Street, while the old Manor House is believed to date from the 14th century and to have been built for the Bishop of CHICHESTER.

The development of modern Bexhill meant a rapid growth in housing and the appearance of promenades and other standard features of English seaside resorts. The gardens at Egerton Park were commissioned by the de la Warr family, while the Pavilion on the seafront is named after them. The de la Warrs were the lords of the manor and had a hand in the founding of the State of Delaware in the USA. The Pavilion is a daring 1930s building by Erich Mendelsohn and houses a theatre, concert hall and other entertainment facilities. Bexhill was considered very advanced when mixed bathing was permitted on its beaches in 1900. Today, Bexhill features over three miles of level promenade and the gently shelving beach is ideal for swimming and subathing.

The Bexhill Costume Museum, in Old Manor Gardens, is very popular with visitors. The costumes are set in period surroundings, with almost as much attention given to contemporary artifacts as to the clothes themselves. The tableaux date from the 18th century to modern times and include a cotton dress worn by the infant Winston Churchill.

Bignor (1/3D) *see* Bury

Billingshurst (1/4C)
A Wealden village which the coming of the railway and recent housing development have transformed into a small town, astride the London to Bognor Regis road between Horsham and Pulborough. The name may derive from the association of the place with a family group of Saxon settlers known as Billa's people who chose this *hurst* or 'wooded hill' for their camp. Billingshurst has always been situated on an important communication route and the village retains something of a coaching air with a number of old inns, such as the 16th-century Olde Six Bells, which have catered for the needs of travellers for centuries.

Corner of Church Street and the High Street, Bexhill

The parish church of St Mary stands on a commanding site above the main road, surrounded by a large churchyard and a number of attractive Wealden cottages, some of them tile hung. St Mary's is of Norman origin and was restored in the 19th century. Externally, the dominant feature is the 120 ft, eight-sided spire, covered with wooden shingles. There has been a clock on the church since at least the 17th century and the present timepiece dates from 1884. Its mechanism is a half-size replica of that of Big Ben at Westminster.

Most of Billingshurst's timber-framed houses were built in the 16th and 17th centuries. More than 80 are still standing today, confirming a growing and prosperous Tudor community with, incidentally, a ready supply of local timber from the Wealden forest. By the 17th century the villagers were an independent-minded lot and, as was common throughout the Weald of Sussex, small farmers and traders embraced the new, radical beliefs of the Puritans. Nathaniel Hilton, the village parson, was a noted Puritan and a number of people from Billingshurst attended the Quaker meeting at the Blue Idol, COOLHAM. The Unitarian chapel was built in 1754 and, outside the Puritan strongholds of LEWES and the Cuckmere valley, is one of the oldest Nonconformist churches in Sussex. It was founded by William Turner and William Evershed. An examination of the gravestones in the churchyard reveals a large number of Eversheds; a few years ago Eversheds from all over the world united here to celebrate their common heritage.

Wealden radicalism also found political expression here in the work of the suffragette Beck sisters, who provided the Women's Hall and the Mothers' Garden, both still in use today.

In 1816 the Wey and Arun Canal was opened and New Bridge, on the A272 to the west of Billingshurst, became a commercial centre of considerable activity. William Cobbett records his visit in *Rural Rides*, when he breakfasted at the King's Arms while his coach changed horses on the journey from London to Bognor Regis. The coming of the railway heralded the demise of both canal and coach traffic and early industry became established around the station, some distance from the town. One of the first industries was the manufacture of wooden hoops for barrels, which lasted until metal hoops came into general use after the First World War.

Home now of many commuters who travel up to London on the Arun Valley railway line, Billingshurst has a comprehensive school, a popular recreation centre and a new public library. There is talk of a bypass but for the time being traffic continues to rumble through the centre of the town as it has since Roman times.

Bishopstone (2/4E)

Situated on the coast between Newhaven and Seaford, Bishopstone is noted for its fine Saxon parish church. The old village of Bishopstone, to the north of the residential development around the railway station, still retains its rural character, enhanced by the large number of beech trees here. In the early 8th century the parish was granted to the Bishops of Chichester and it remained under their control until the 17th century. The importance of this connection is demonstrated not only in the name of the village but also in the Saxon church. Until the 11th century it was still common for parish churches to be built of wood, so to find a stone structure dating from about 750 is clear evidence of the ecclesiastical importance of Bishopstone. With a fine 12th-century tower, St Andrew's is also renowned for its light interior. The sundial above the south doorway bears the name 'Eadric', who was perhaps either a Saxon benefactor or one of the original craftsmen.

The area to the south-west of the village, still marked on maps as 'Tide Mills', was once a small hamlet which developed around in 18th-century tide mill. Unfortunately both the mill and the cottages nearby were used for artillery practice during the Second World War and today 'Tide Mills' survives in name only, although the ruins of farm buildings and cottages can be found. It is possible to park here and walk down to the beach to swim.

There are memorials in St Andrew's church at Bishopstone to the Catt family who for many years owned and worked the mill. The Sussex naturalist and writer W. H. Hudson recorded in *Nature in Downland* a visit he made to Bishopstone church on a summer afternoon. His seat was beside the open door,

> so that while following the service I could let my eyes rest on the landscape. That was a beautiful picture I had to look at, with the doorway for a frame . . . And by-and-by, into that green enclosure came a white calf, and remained there for some time, standing motionless in the centre of the picture. The brilliant sunlight made it luminous and it was like a calf hewn out of a block of purest white chalk.

Recently, several Sussex flint barns in the area

have been converted into houses, despite objections from some local people who wished to see them retained as farm buildings to preserve the rural identity of the village.

Bodiam (3/3C)
A small village on the eastern River Rother, famous for its perfect late medieval castle and very close to the Kent border between Hurst Green and Northian. According to Domesday, Osbert de Bodeham lived here in the 11th century. Later the estate passed to the de Wardeux family and then, through marriage, to the Dalyngrydges of East Grinstead. Until 1385 Bodiam remained a small hamlet of little importance, but the threat of French invasion soon brought it to prominence. In 1377, RYE had been sacked by a French raiding party and it was feared that the French might make a concerted attempt to sail a flotilla up the eastern Rother, which forms the border between Sussex and Kent. It was with this in mind that Sir Edward Dalyngrydge, recently returned from the wars in France, applied to the King for permission to build a castle at Bodiam. His request was granted and Sir Edward was able to build what was regarded as a vital inland defence, guarding the upper reaches of the Rother valley and the Kent Ditch. The invasion never materialised, however, and Bodiam marks the end of the great castle building period of the Middle Ages. It never saw an arrow or a shot fired in anger, although it was partly razed by General Waller's Parliamentary army during the Civil War. Thereafter, it gradually fell into decay until in 1829 it was proposed to dismantle it entirely; fortunately this scheme was forestalled by 'Mad' Jack Fuller of BRIGHTLING, who saved the castle. Restoration work was begun at the end of the last century by the then owner, George Cubitt; he sold the castle to Lord Curzon of Kedlestone, sometime Viceroy of India, who completed the work. On his death in 1926 Curzon left Bodiam to the National Trust, who still own the castle and the surrounding land. It is open to the public in spring and summer.

Hidden among tall trees, the parish church of St Giles is charming, if a little eccentric. The roof, somewhat curiously, steepens half-way up, possibly a legacy of the major restoration work carried out during Victorian times. Inside there is a colourful stained glass window, dedicated to the Cubitt family. The upholstered pews are a feature unique to Bodiam. One of the church bells, which were all remodelled in 1961, is also of interest: it is dedicated to the late Emperor Haile Selassie of Ethiopia. The then rector, the Reverend A. E. Cotton, had been a military adviser to the Emperor during the Second World War, and the Emperor demonstrated his gratitude by giving a generous donation towards the cost of the new bells.

Bognor Regis (1/3F)
A seaside resort and residential town between Selsey Bill and Littlehampton, with associations with George V. The original settlements from which Bognor developed were a hamlet on the coast and the village of Bersted, a mile from the sea. Nothing very much happened here before 1785 when Sir Richard Hotham, a successful London hatter, bought 1,600 acres of land and attempted to develop a fashionable resort to rival BRIGHTON and Weymouth. Hotham built between Bersted and the sea, but not on the sea front itself, and his work can best be seen today in The Dome, Upper Bognor Road. The Dome was built as Hothampton Crescent in about 1787 and is now occupied by the West Sussex Institute of Higher Education, following careful restoration by the County Council. Early Bognor was probably the model for Jane Austen's *Sanditon*.

Alas, the dream of a fashionable 'Hothampton' succeeding at Bognor was not realised and the town developed during the 19th century as a very ordinary seaside resort, with few buildings of any distinction. George V was sent to nearby Aldwick to convalesce after an illness in 1929 and awarded the town its royal suffix of 'Regis'. Today, Bognor has all the usual amenities of a minor seaside resort and the Bognor Regis Centre on the front includes the Alexandra Theatre. Annual events include a clowns' convention and an international birdman rally, when intrepid volunteers attempt to take flight from the pier.

Just east of Bognor, beyond South Coast World, is the village of **Felpham.** William Blake, the poet and writer of 'Jerusalem', described Felpham as 'a sweet place for study'. He lived here for four years and his house can be seen in Blake's Road, near the church of St Mary, which has a solid tower and a Sussex marble font.

Bolney (2/2C)
On the A23 north of Brighton, close to the junction with the A272 from Cowfold to Cuck-

The Dome, Upper Bognor

Bodiam Castle (National Trust)

field. 'Eye' is an old word for 'island' and as Bolney lies beside a tributary of the River Adur, it may at one time have been an actual island in the marshy valley. The village today has a single main street leading to the parish church of St Mary Magdalene, which has a Norman nave and chancel and a splendid lych gate outside. The tower, built in the 1530s, carries a peal of eight balls – hence the name of the village pub. The Bolney Stage on the A23 dates from the 16th century and was originally a coaching inn. The most impressive house in the village is Wykehurst, a Victorian mansion built by E. M. Barry with a terrace which has good views south to the Downs.

A couple of miles south of Bolney on the way to Brighton is **Hickstead**, the home of the All England Show Jumping Course. Fixtures are held from April to September; details can be obtained from the Secretary.

Bosham (1/2E) (Bozzum)
The best view of Bosham, perhaps the most painted and photographed village in Sussex, is from across the creek with the spire of Holy Trinity church taking centre stage. Bosham is one of the most accessible of the sailing villages around CHICHESTER Harbour and has a bustling, salty air which – almost – conceals its sleek prosperity. Visitors should remember that this is one of the places where King Canute is supposed to have demonstrated his inability to control the tides: cars are parked on the harbourside road at low tide at their owners' peril! All too often drivers have found, after visiting Bosham's friendly inn and shops, that their cars are under water, the tide having come in while they were away.

This pleasant spot has witnessed some important events in English history. The Romans landed in Chichester Harbour and Bosham is

Church and millstream at Bosham

thought to have been an important settlement in the Roman period.

The manor of Bosham later came into the hands of Earl Godwin of Wessex, father of King Harold, and it was from here that Harold sailed in 1064 when he visited Duke William of Normandy. The Bayeux Tapestry shows the church of the Holy Trinity where Harold paused to pray before setting sail. His crossing of the Channel led to his famous oath in support of William's claim to the throne, to the Norman invasion, the Battle of Hastings and the end of the Saxon kingdom. Bosham became the property of the new King, William the Conqueror, and at the time of Domesday was one of only two manors in Sussex held directly by the King (see *The Norman Heritage*, p. 28).

Bosham church is thought to stand on the site of a Roman basilica occupied in the 7th century by a Celtic monk who founded a small community here before the conversion of Sussex to Christianity under St Wilfrid, whose base was at SELSEY. The chancel arch is one of the finest Saxon arches in England and can be clearly recognised in the depiction of the building in the Bayeux Tapestry. The church was remodelled in the 13th century, when the chancel was lengthened and new lancet windows added. A tour of Bosham should conclude with a stroll on Quay Meadow, the exact spot from which Harold sailed for France. It is now owned by the National Trust.

Botolphs (2/1E) *see* Bramber

Boxgrove (1/3E)
There is an outstanding church in this relatively plain village north-east of Chichester, where the coastal plain meets the dip slope of the Downs. One of the most important medieval buildings in Sussex, Boxgrove Priory should not be missed. The building which remains, and which now serves as the parish church, was the central feature of a Benedictine priory founded in the early 12th century by Robert de Haye as a cell of the Abbey of Lessay in Normandy. Of some 70 monasteries in Sussex during the Middle Ages, the domestic buildings have survived in only about a dozen – the best example being Michelham Priory, near HAILSHAM, now owned by the Sussex Archaeological Society. Some former monastic churches – including that of Boxgrove – have been preserved as parish churches; a few others have been converted to secular use.

De La Warr chantry chapel, Boxgrove Priory

Saint Mary's House, Bramber

The 12th and 13th centuries were periods of great building activity in southern England and many churches were rebuilt and extended. There are striking similarities in style between churches such as Old and New SHOREHAM and Boxgrove, and the Abbey of Lessay. Originally founded for three monks only, the Priory steadily grew into a large and prosperous community, which endured successfully until the Dissolution of the Monasteries in 1537. What now remains is the parish church dedicated to St Mary and St Blaise, and some ruins in the care of English Heritage. The church dates mainly from about 1220; the style follows closely the development of CHICHESTER Cathedral, as there was much contact between the neighbouring foundations. The chancel is one of the most important Early English buildings in the county and the 15th-century painted ceiling is also notable (see *The Norman Heritage*, p. 28).

The village of Boxgrove does not reflect the distinction of the Priory, but there are some good cottages in the lane leading to the church and, in the main street, the 17th-century Nightingale Cottages and the 18th-century Derby Almshouses, built by the Countess of Derby who lived at HALNAKER House, are worth a visit.

Bramber (2/1D)
Historic village dominated by the romantic ruins of Bramber Castle, in the Adur valley, north of SHOREHAM. The Rape of Bramber was given by William the Conqueror to his trusted lieutenant, William de Braose (see *The Norman Heritage*, p. 28). At the time of the Conquest, the river was navigable to Bramber bridge, as most of the estuary was under water. De Braose chose this position to build his castle on top of the massive natural chalk outcrop which dominates the valley. The water came right up to the castle walls and the Norman soldiers built quays to receive goods and passengers. De Braose also built a chapel for the use of the garrison, which in due course became the parish church of St Nicholas, patron saint of sailors.

Bramber became an important military and administrative centre for this part of Sussex and church and castle saw many important visitors during the Middle Ages, including King John in 1216 on his way from Canterbury to Winchester. Between 1285 and 1302, Edward I was here on no less than five occasions. The church was expanded to cater for the growing population and for visiting fishermen and sailors, while the monks who had originally occupied the building were moved to other accommodation across the river at Beeding. In the 15th century the lands of the de Braose family were transferred to Magdalen College Oxford, who presented rectors to the benefice of Bramber until 1952.

The waters eventually retreated from Bramber, leaving the village high and dry above the meadows of the river valley. While remaining a borough and returning two Members of Parliament, Bramber declined and, in the Civil War, the castle was all but destroyed by the Parliamentary army. Today only a tall fragment survives of what once must have been the mighty keep, but the site is well worth a visit. A walk round it gives a good impression of its natural strategic position and the grounds, which are maintained by the National Trust in a semi-wild and informal state, are ideal for picnicking.

Having also looked into the church, the visitor should walk down the High Street towards the bridge, past an interesting museum devoted to the smoking of tobacco. The other important building in the village is St Mary's, a fine 15th-century house built originally as a monastic inn for pilgrims going to Canterbury and run by the monks who were the Wardens of the Bridge. It was refashioned in about 1470 for William of Waynflete, Bishop of Winchester and founder of Magdalen College, Oxford. In the 19th century the house was owned by Alfred Musgrave, when it was the inspiration for the Sherlock Holmes story *The Musgrave Ritual*.

Two other famous names associated with Bramber are Charles II, who came through here on his way to France after the Battle of Worcester and was very nearly discovered by Parliamentary guards at the bridge, and the anti-slavery campaigner William Wilberforce, who was Member of Parliament for Bramber, although he rarely came here. Within an area of a few square miles, the three 'rotten' boroughs of Bramber, Steyning and New SHOREHAM, all with tiny populations, returned together six MPs until the Reform Act of 1832.

Across the river is the village of **Upper Beeding**, consisting of a single village street, a parish church some distance from the village and a great deal of undistinguished modern development. Upper and Lower Beeding are some miles apart, 'upper' signifying the fact that this was the principal settlement of the tribe and 'lower' the location of a subordinate settlement, probably an outlier used for pasturing animals and without a resident population. William de Braose founded the Benedictine priory of Sele here in 1075 on a site to the north of the present church. This was dreadfully restored in the 19th century and the site of the priory is now occupied by a

Leper's window, Botolphs church, Bramber

house. Upper Beeding played an important role in the development of the system of turnpike roads in the early 19th century and the toll cottage from the village, probably the last to close in Sussex, is now in the Weald and Downland Museum at SINGLETON.

A famous resident of Upper Beeding was the shepherd Michael Blann, who began his career on the Downs above here when he was nine years old. During the course of a long life Blann developed a considerable reputation as a singer, gathering new material as he travelled the Downs and visited the sheep fairs at Lewes and Findon. His song book has been published by WORTHING Museum, which also has a number of interesting exhibits on the life of South Downs shepherds in the 19th century.

Downriver from Upper Beeding, on the west bank of the Adur, is the hamlet of **Botolphs**, which takes its name from the tiny church dedicated to St Botolph, patron saint of travellers. The dedication is particularly appropriate today as the church lies just off the South Downs Way on a spot that marks the position of an old river crossing. Indeed, the original dedication of the church was to St Peter de Vetere Ponte (of the old bridge). There may well have been a river crossing here in Roman times; certainly a flourishing community had developed by the Middle Ages, beside the wide river estuary and with its own wharves. As the sea receded Botolphs, like Bramber, lost its importance and prosperity until by Tudor times few inhabitants remained.

A leper colony – the Hospital of St Mary Magdalen – was situated between Bramber and Botolphs. The inmates were discouraged from visiting the more populous and fashionable Bramber and two low windows were provided in the chancel of Botolphs's church to enable them, kneeling on the grass in the churchyard, to see the altar and to participate vicariously in the celebration of the Mass.

Brede (3/4D)

A small village on the A28 north of Hastings which gives its name to the nearby river. Brede is full of legends and myths. Here once lived the famous (or infamous) Brede Giant, Sir Goddard Oxenbridge. Sir Goddard was real enough and stood over 7 ft tall. His tomb, which is disappointingly normal is size, may be seen in the parish church. In the centuries since his death, the story spread throughout Sussex that he had been a blood-thirsty ogre who regularly roasted

'Mad Jack' Fuller's folly, Dallington near Brightling

young children for his supper. His foul deeds were finally ended when the children of Sussex made a giant wooden saw and, after stupifying him with strong ale, cut him in two, with the West Sussex children on one end of the saw and the East Sussex children on the other. How this story arose is not known, but it was extremely popular throughout the county during the last century.

The Oxenbridge family lived at Brede Place, built in medieval times and said to be haunted by several ghosts. So widely circulated were stories of supernatural activity in the vicinity that the Society for Psychical Research undertook a study of the area. Brede Place was gutted by fire in 1979.

The parish church of St George dates from the 14th century. Inside are some interesting artifacts, including an alms box of 1687 and a carved chest from the same period that belonged to Dean Swift.

During the winter of 1830, rural riots among impoverished labourers led by a mythical 'Captain Swing' spread throughout southern England. Threatening letters, often followed by acts of arson, characterised the uprising. The disturbances began in Brede on 4 November, when Thomas Abell, the overseer of the local workhouse who was judged to be brutal and overbearing, was tied to a dung-cart and unceremoniously dumped over the parish boundary.

Brightling (3/2C)

North-west of Battle, Brightling is famous as the home of 'Mad Jack' Fuller. John Fuller (1757–1834) was a wealthy eccentric who earned his nickname from his passion for constructing bizarre follies, including a pyramid shaped mausoleum built in 1810. The Fullers earned a fortune during the 17th century as iron founders. John inherited the estate at the age of 20 and thus had 57 years in which to indulge his fancies as politician, patron of the arts, maverick builder and paternalistic squire. As the local Member of Parliament, Fuller was suspended from the House of Commons on several occasions for his outlandish behaviour, once describing the Speaker as: 'That insignificant little fellow in a wig'. At 22 stone, Fuller was no 'little fellow' himself and was known affectionately as 'The Hippopotamus'. More significantly, he commissioned several paintings from Turner, saved BODIAM Castle from demolition, built a lighthouse at Beachy Head and provided work for unemployed men on his famous follies.

In the grounds of Brightling Park, home of the Fullers, are to be found The Rotunda, where Fuller is said to have played all-night card games and The Tower, from which he is said to have observed the restoration work at Bodiam Castle. Also in the grounds is an astrological observatory, designed by Sir Robert Smirke. It is said that part of the manor house was demolished to facilitate its construction. On a hill between Brightling and Dallington is The Sugar Loaf, so called because it resembled the shape in which sugar crystal was delivered to grocers. It was built as a replica of the spire of Dallington church, Mad Jack having wagered one night that the church could be seen from Brightling on a clear day. Perhaps his most famous folly is Brightling Needle, or The Obelisk, built on Brightling Beacon to celebrate Nelson's victory at the Battle of Trafalgar.

Inside the parish church of St Thomas Becket there are memorials to the Fuller family and a fine Gothic-style barrel organ which Mad Jack presented to the church in 1820. The church of St Giles at nearby **Dallington** is of interest because of its stone spire, a rarity in Sussex, and the timber-framed house which adjoins it.

Brighton (2/3E)

The largest town in Sussex, centre of culture and fashion, Brighton contains some of the best examples of 19th-century architecture in the country. Unlike other important towns in Sussex, Brighton began life not as a market town or a political or military centre but as a fishing port, and a pretty poor one at that. The fishermen and their families lived in mean cottages beneath the cliff, on land long since covered by the sea. Those who did not depend on the sea for their livelihood had their homes on the higher ground, in the labyrinth of medieval streets which now form the famous Brighton Lanes. Although the buildings in the area contained within the modern West, North and East Streets now date mainly from the early 19th century or later, the street pattern was established many centuries ago and the pedestrian alleys of the Lanes provide the modern visitor with an authentic impression of the feel and atmosphere of the original settlement of Brighthelmstone, as it was then known.

Fishing remained important in the local economy and indeed continues to this day. In 1820 a visitor recorded that: 'The fishery employs nearly 100 boats, carrying some three, some four and others five men each. The mackerel season commences in April, the herring season in October, and are together said sometimes to have produced £10,000 per annum'. By this date, however, the role of Brighton as a resort town was already well-established and work had begun on the construction of the Regency squares and terraces for which the town is famous.

The initial stimulus for the meteoric rise of Brighton to the pinnacle of fashion was the arrival of Dr Richard Russell of Lewes, who, in 1753, published his *Dissertation concerning the Use of Sea Water in Diseases of the Glands* which advocated the value of both drinking and bathing in sea water as a restorative. Russell was the founder of modern Brighton and, indeed, of the English seaside resort. He discovered the chalybeate spring in what is now St Anne's Well Gardens HOVE, which he enclosed in a basin and used for treating his patients. Within a short time the number of people coming to Brighthelmstone to take his cure justified his building a large house on the site of what is now the Royal Albion Hotel so that he could personally supervise his patients' progress. Since very few

Dukes Lane, Brighton

WINDOW
Brighton
Festival
30

Brighton Royal Pavilion at sunset

visitors were able to swim, sea bathing was supervised by 'bathers' for gentlemen and 'dippers' for ladies. Both sexes – who, of course, bathed separately – entered machines built on high wooden wheels and drawn by a horse. While the visitor prepared for the plunge by undressing and donning a loose, diaphonous robe, the machine was drawn into the sea. He or she was then grasped by the attendant and vigorously plunged several times into the water. It became popular for gentlemen visitors to gather close to the ladies' bathing place and to observe through telescopes and spy-glasses members of the fair sex entering the water.

The 'bathers' and 'dippers' acquired considerable reputations, including 'Smoaker' Miles and Martha Gunn, who was known as the 'Queen of the Bath'. She became a dipper when bathing started in 1750 and continued to supervise the beach until her death, aged 89, in 1815. In spite of the rigours of the regime recommended by Dr Russell, patients and visitors were soon flocking to Brighthelmstone: early fashionable visitors included the Countess of Huntingdon and Henry and Hester Thrale, friends of Dr Johnson. Johnson himself was less enthusiastic: an expedition to the Downs provoked his comment that the place was 'so truly desolate that if one had a mind to hang oneself for desperation on being obliged to live there, it would be difficult to find a tree on which to fasten the rope'.

It was the patronage of the Prince of Wales, later George IV, which secured Brighton's place as the most fashionable resort in the country. The Prince first came to the town in 1783, shortly after his 21st birthday, and was given a tremendous reception. From 1785 the visits became an annual event. He stayed at Grove House (later known as Marlborough House) on The Steine, the open space around which the early development of fashionable Brighton took place. Shortly afterwards the Prince leased a plot of land on The Steine and commissioned Henry Holland, who was working for him on Carlton House in London, to build what became known as The Marine Pavilion. The first Pavilion was a simple classical building with a semicircular portico in the centre. In 1810, the Prince decided to enlarge the building and a year or two later William Porden was commissioned to put up a large Stables (now The Dome concert hall) and a Riding House (now the Corn Exchange).

These new buildings were Indian in style and their success prompted the Prince Regent, as he became in 1811, to instruct John Nash to rebuild the Pavilion in a similar style. The result is the Royal Pavilion we know today, one of the most dazzling and exotic buildings in the country. Dating from between 1815 and 1822, the interior of the Pavilion was decorated in the Chinese style and most of the original wall hangings are still in place today. In recent years, Victorian decorations have been replaced by faithful re-creations of the original brilliant designs. Of particular interest are the Music Room, the Banqueting Room and the Great Kitchen. The Pavilion, now in the care of Brighton Borough Council, is currently undergoing further restoration which may conceal parts of the exterior and cause the temporary closure of certain rooms.

The patronage of the Prince Regent, combined with the inability of fashionable society to travel on the Continent during the wars with France, both ensured Brighton's success as a resort and led to the dramatic development of the town. Initial development was concentrated round The Steine but building soon spread up on to the east cliff where Royal Crescent, the first series of houses to be built facing the sea, was completed in 1807. The houses are faced with mathematical tiles, hanging tiles made to imitate brick, which are a feature of seaside architecture. In Sussex they occur here in Brighton and also, in large numbers, in LEWES. To the west of the town centre, Bedford Square was completed in 1818, followed by Regency Square, Russell Square and Cannon Place.

The 1820s saw the development of Regency Brighton as we know it today. It was largely the creation of three architects who lived in the town: Amon Wilds, his son Amon Henry Wilds and Charles Busby. The masterpiece of the Wilds and Busby partnership is Kemp Town, built to the east of the town centre for Thomas Read Kemp, one of the joint Lords of the Manor. The estate, which consists of two terraces facing the sea (Arundel and Chichester Terraces) and a crescent with two wings (Lewes Crescent) opening into a large square (Sussex Square), was begun in 1823. All the façades were finished by 1827; the construction of the houses behind them was left to the taste of individual purchasers. Kemp himself moved into No 22 Sussex Square, where a wall plaque records his residence.

As well as its public buildings, estate developments and individual houses of the Regency period, Brighton is rich in Victorian architecture, particularly church architecture. The ancient parish church of St Nicholas, on a hill outside the old town, was comprehensively restored by R. C. Carpenter in 1853. It had been replaced as parish church by the new church of St Peter, a fine Gothic Revival edifice to the north of The Steine and The Level, designed by Sir Charles Barry in 1824–8 when he was still under thirty. Brighton's other notable churches include the soaring St Bartholomew in Ann Street, whose nave is higher than that of Westminster Abbey, and the Unitarian Church in New Road, designed in Greek Doric style by Amon Henry Wilds in 1820. St Bartholomew was one of several churches built by the remarkable Father Arthur Wagner (1825–1902) who was the son of H. M. Wagner, vicar of Brighton from 1824 to 1870.

Brighton Rock

The Brighton Society and Brighton Borough Council produce an excellent walking guide to the centre of the town which is available free from the Tourist Information Centre at Marlborough House, Old Steine.

Today, Brighton has much to offer visitors of all ages. Of particular interest are the inter-

Madeira Drive, Brighton

nationally known Brighton Festival held in May each year, concerts at The Dome and excellent drama at The Theatre Royal, founded in 1806. There is also a racecourse for Flat racing, the modern Prince Regent Swimming Centre, the Aquarium and Dolphinarium, a museum and art gallery, a marina with berths for 2,000 boats, the Palace Pier and children's entertainments. Brighton acts as host to many events, conferences and exhibitions, including a Motor Show in June and the London to Brighton Veteran Car Run in November. Accommodation is available to suit all pockets, including a youth hostel at Patcham and camping at the Sheepcote camping and touring caravan site, and there is a very wide choice of places to eat and drink.

East of Brighton, beyond the marina and Roedean School, is the village of **Rottingdean.** It was once an agricultural community on the coast, where the custom was for the labourers at harvest time to accompany the last wagon from the fields to the village pub on the seashore where beer was supplied by their employer. Rottingdean is the home of the Copper family, who have kept alive the Sussex tradition of unaccompanied folk singing. The pastoral calm and seaside location of the village attracted artists and writers in the 19th century, including Rudyard Kipling and Sir Edward Burne-Jones. For Kipling, however, the village became too busy and he retreated to BURWASH, where he lived for 34 years until his death.

Another village within the Brighton urban area is **Stanmer** to the north of the main town. Stanmer House and Park were the home of the Pelhams, Earls of Chichester, and the place retains an estate village atmosphere despite the fact that the University of Sussex has grown up in the park and the house was for many years used by the University. The house and park are now owned by Brighton Borough Council and it was their desire to see a university established in the town which led them to make the site available. The University, the first to be built in this country since the Second World War, opened in 1962 and has established a considerable reputation in social studies and in scientific fields.

Broadbridge Heath (1/5B) *see* Horsham

Burgess Hill (2/3D)

A modern town between Brighton and Haywards Heath, with a long-standing tradition of brick and tile making. The name of the place is derived from the family of Burgeys who owned a large farm in the area, but the story of modern Burgess Hill really begins in 1828 when all the commons and wastes of the manor of Keymer were enclosed by Act of Parliament. The costs of obtaining the legislation were met by the sale of 200 acres of St John's and Valebridge Commons for speculative development. So began the construction of villas and cottages, a process which was hastened by the arrival of the London to Brighton railway in 1841. Towards the end of the 19th century there was a rapid growth in house building and, within a short time, Burgess Hill had become a thriving country town. Further growth took place after the Second World War and the town today has a population of over 24,000, with a bustling commercial centre and considerable local employment.

In earlier times the area was of some agricultural importance – on Fairplace Hill an annual sheep fair was held from the 14th century until 1912 when it was finally discontinued. Although the traditional agricultural way of life was drastically affected by the enclosure of the commons in the early 19th century, another important local industry, brick and tile making, continues to this day. Taking advantage of the availability of good quality Wealden clay, the thriving works in Nye Road produces the well-known Keymer hand-made sand-faced clay tiles and fittings. Open days are held at the works from time to time, when visitors may watch the traditional processes in operation. Brick making has long been a feature of the area, which is situated on a rich seam of gault (a series of beds of clay and marl), as reflected in the names of one of the few older houses in the town, Marle Place, and of the adjoining parish of CLAYTON.

Burpham (1/4E) *see* Arundel

Burwash (3/2C)

Situated on the A265, west of Etchingham, the village is famous as the home of Rudyard Kipling whose house, Batemans, stands between the wooded hills and the River Dudwell. Today Burwash is prim and proper, with characteristic weatherboarded houses and a neat little church. It was not always so. Writing in 1870, the Sussex historian M. A. Lower recalled the time when Burwash was notorious 'for the lawlessness of the lower portion of its population. Smuggling, sheep-stealing and burglary were rampant and it was scarcely safe for a wayfarer to pass after nightfall over Burwashdown'. Rudyard Kipling came to live at Burwash in 1902 and stayed until his death in 1936. It was the recollections of old men in the village that inspired him to write many of his poems, including 'The Smugglers' Song'. However, it is probably his poem 'Sussex' that most accurately captured his sense of pride in his adopted county:

> No tender-hearted garden crowns,
> No bosomed weeds adorn
> Our blunt, bow-headed, whale-backed Downs
> But gnarled and writhern thorn –
> Bare slopes where chasing shadows skim,
> And through the gaps revealed
> Belt upon belt, the wooded, dim
> Blue goodness of the Weald.

Batemans is owned by the National Trust and is open to the public. The mill at the house grinds flour from time to time when the house is open.

Kipling's former home recalls Burwash's other great legacy, the iron trade. Batemans was built in 1634 for a local ironmaster and the village has other reminders of its industrial past. In the churchyard of St Bartholomew's is the grave of one of the first really successful iron workers in Sussex, marked by an iron 'headstone' dating from the 1300s. The church is late Norman and contains several memorials to those who prospered when 'iron was king'. In the High Street are a number of splendid timber-framed cottages, the most notable of which, Rampydene, was built in 1699 as the home of a well-to-do wood merchant. Burwash is still very wooded although, being situated on a high ridge, the area suffered badly in the 1987 storm.

Bury (1/4D)

A pretty village across the River Arun from Amberley and just off the busy A29 London to Bognor Regis road. Bury lies below the Downs and gives its name to the steep hill up which drivers on the A29 labour, to be rewarded at the top by a splendid panorama of the Arun valley, dominated by the chalk pits at HOUGHTON Bridge. Bury is a quiet place of mainly sandstone houses, a manor house (now a prep school), the parish church of St John the Evangelist and the Edwardian mock Tudor Bury House, where the writer John Galsworthy lived and died. The church was probably built at the end of the 12th century on the instructions of the Abbey of Fécamp, Normandy, to whom the manor had been given by William the Conqueror. It is best known for its shingled spire, reminiscent of the Wealden churches of HORSHAM and BILLINGSHURST, although it is built of the downland materials of flint, stone and chalk.

In days gone by, a ferry across the Arun connected Bury with Amberley and provided a low level route for travellers as an alternative to the track which followed the ridge of the Downs. From time to time arrangements are made to re-open the ferry for the benefit of parties of walkers, and a very popular amenity it is too.

West of Bury lies a series of memorable villages, all sheltering under the Downs, which at Bignor Hill reach a height of over 800 ft. This well-protected, south-facing site beside Stane Street which runs from Chichester to London was chosen by the Romans as one of their largest and most successful agricultural estates in southern England. The estate was controlled from the villa at **Bignor**, conveniently situated a day's journey from the markets at Chichester. The villa contains some of the finest Roman mosaic pavements outside Italy, which came to light when a farmer's plough first turned up some fragments of tile in 1811. The mosaics include representations of Venus, Ganymede and Medusa and scenes with gladiators.

The Old Shop, Bignor

Excavation of the site is continuing, as is the development of the excellent exhibition displays.

Bignor's parish church of the Holy Cross, like its neighbour at Sutton, formed part of the endowments of the great Priory of St Pancras at LEWES. Drastically restored by G. E. Street in the 1870s, the church is notable for its early Norman font, a crude tub-shaped bowl on a modern base. The other building of interest in the village is The Old Shop, a 15th-century timber-framed and thatched cottage of the Wealden type, with infillings of brick, flint, stone and plaster.

Between Bury and Bignor is the hamlet of **West Burton** which contains the solid, late 16th-century Coke's House. Beyond Bignor is **Sutton**, a pretty village containing good examples of the use of nearly all Sussex building materials. Further north, on the A29 towards Pulborough are the villages of **Watersfield** and **Coldwaltham**, whose names alone confirm their location beside the Amberley Wild Brooks, prone to winter flooding and low mists. Stane Street runs through Coldwaltham just north of the church and its metalled track is sometimes only half hidden beneath the surface of the ground. A visitation in 1724 revealed that 26 families lived in the village and the population has hardly grown since then: the charmingly situated primary school, beside the parish church, is today the smallest in West Sussex.

Buxted (2/4C)

On the A272, north-east of UCKFIELD and dominated by Buxted Park. Buxted House was once a fine Georgian mansion with an impressive avenue of pine trees dating from the same period. Unfortunately, the house was badly damaged by fire in 1940 and the avenue was affected by the 1987 storm. The 13th-century church of St Margaret, also within the grounds, has been much restored. Several features, including the shingled broach spire, were added in the 18th century. The Jacobean pulpit is noteworthy, not only for its age but also because William Wordsworth's brother was once the vicar here and preached over a thousand sermons from it. The wall that runs along a ditch close to the church was designed to stop livestock straying without interrupting the open view from the house and is known as a ha-ha. The old village of Buxted was once situated within the Park but in 1836, desiring greater privacy, the owner of the house, Lord Liverpool, forced the villagers out. Their cottages were demolished and new ones built on the site of the present village.

Hogge House dates from the late 16th century and was the home of Ralph Hogge, known as the father of the Wealden cannon-founding industry. It is said that cannon from Hogge's foundry were used to help defeat the Spanish Armada in 1588.

Catsfield (3/3D)

A pleasant village situated off the A269 between Bexhill and Battle, with a prominent Methodist church, whose lofty spire dominates the village, making the parish church of St Laurence appear very humble by comparison. With the arrival of Huguenot refugees from France in the 17th century this part of Sussex gained a reputation for its strong links with Nonconformity and the Methodist church, built as recently as 1912, demonstrates the continuation of this tradition. The parish church dates from the 13th century but suffered considerably at the hands of Victorian restorers. In the churchyard is the grave of Sir Thomas Brassey, an associate of George Stephenson the locomotive designer, who later became responsible for railway construction throughout the British empire.

Chailey (2/3D)

North of Lewes on the A275, Chailey is said to be at the geographical centre of Sussex. It is one of the largest parishes in the county, with a boundary totalling 24 miles. The village is centred around the parish church of St Peter, which overlooks the charming village green. The Old Rectory, to the west of the church, stands beside a moat which, according to local tradition, was dug personally by the incumbent parson during the early 18th century. Ades, a Georgian mansion to the east of the church, and The Hooke, dating from the late 17th century, are two other buildings of architectural note in the village.

A few miles away is **North Common**, now a nature reserve. The common, with its old smock windmill, was once a popular meeting place for gypsies. Near by is the well-known Chailey Heritage, which was founded in 1903 by two London social workers as a home for seven

Pump on the village green, Newick

physically handicapped East End children. It now caters for 200 handicapped children from all parts of Britain and overseas. The school has a remarkable chapel designed by Sir Ninian Comper, dedicated in 1913 and complete with its original furnishings. At one time, Chailey Heritage had an annexe at Tide Mills, near BISHOPSTONE, where the children were able to enjoy the therapeutic benefits of sea air and swimming.

South Common overlies the gault formation of the Wealden beds, whose clays made it famous for high quality pottery. Today the potteries have closed, but there is still a thriving brickworks.

East of North Chailey, on the A272, is the village of **Newick**, where cottages and houses are grouped attractively around a large triangular green which sports a fine pump, erected in 1897, the year of Queen Victoria's silver jubilee. Just off the green, School Cottage is of interest. Formerly Lady Vernon's School, the building was put up in 1771 to house a school for 12 poor girls. The parish church of St Mary has a sandstone tower and is of Norman origin. The Bull Inn on the green is said to be haunted by a strange, ball-like object which rolls across the floor of the bar, apparently from nowhere to nowhere. The actor Dirk Bogarde spent his childhood in this part of Sussex and described his early life in *A Postillion Struck by Lightning*, the first volume of his autobiography. It was at Newick that he had his first major role, in an amateur production of R. C. Sherriff's *Journey's End* in 1934.

Other notable buildings include Newick Farmhouse, Founthill House and The Old Rectory, which has some very fine wrought-iron railings. The two famous cricketing brothers of the interwar years, James and John Langridge, were coached at Newick by Thomas Baden-Powell, cousin of the founder of the Scout movement.

Chanctonbury Ring (1/5D) *see* Washington

Charleston Farmhouse (2/4E) *see* Firle

Charlton (1/3D) *see* Goodwood

Chichester (1/2E)

Cathedral city and county town of West Sussex, Chichester lies in the south-west corner of the county, between the Downs and Chichester Harbour Area of Outstanding Natural Beauty.

The town was founded by the Romans, evidence of whose impact on the area is all around. The town plan of Chichester, with its four intersecting streets and town wall, graphically illustrates the city's Roman origins. The Romans came to Chichester Harbour in the 1st century AD, and the settlement they established at the head of the **Fishbourne** Channel is one of the most important Roman sites in Britain. As the conquest of southern Britain was completed, the decision was taken to build a great house or

palace on the site, probably to accommodate the puppet British king Cogidubnus who ruled a large territory occupied by the Regni tribe.

Fishbourne Roman Palace was on a lavish scale and probably the largest non-military Roman building in Britain. Completed by the end of the 1st century, it consisted of a great central courtyard and three subsidiary courtyards and, like the neighbouring city of Noviomagus (Chichester), was intended to show the native population just what could be achieved by the

Chichester Cathedral

Roman Empire. The palace was destroyed by fire in about 300 and used as a source of building materials for Noviomagus. The ruins remained undisturbed and undiscovered until 1960, when quantities of Roman material were turned up by a plough. The excavation of the site was led by Professor Barry Cunliffe, then of Southampton University and the palace, with its splendid mosaics, museum and well-equipped education building, is now owned and managed by the Sussex Archaeological Society. A popular feature of the programme of activities at the palace are the regular visits by authentically dressed members of the Ermine Street Guard, whose displays of Roman army drill and equipment are both enjoyable and instructive.

The Cathedral of the Holy Trinity in West Street is the principal building in Chichester. The only English medieval cathedral to be visible from the sea, it was built by the Normans and dedicated in 1108. In 1114 it was badly damaged by fire and, when rebuilt, became a popular place of pilgrimage, containing as it did the shrine of St Richard, Bishop of Chichester, who was canonised in 1262.

The spire of the Cathedral, now thankfully free of the scaffolding which covered it for many years, can be seen for miles around in the flat landscape. Closer inspection reveals an unusual feature in the separate bell tower, built because it was feared the central tower was not strong enough to take the Cathedral bells. These fears were proved to be justified when, in 1861, the spire crashed down into the nave, causing considerable damage.

Market Cross, Chichester

Ostriches on the gates of Pallant House Gallery

Inside, the Cathedral has a quiet, reflective atmosphere which complements that of the city as a whole. The 12th-century panels in the south aisle showing *Christ coming to the house of Mary of Bethany* and *The Raising of Lazarus*, should not be missed. The nave is separated from the choir by the 15th-century Arundel Screen, which was taken down in the 19th century but re-erected in 1961. Other changes made during the 1960s include the installation of a modern pulpit in 1966 and the commissioning of a series of tapestries by John Piper representing the *Trinity*, the *Evangelists*, and the *Four Elements*. Among other modern works of art in the Cathedral are Graham Sutherland's *Noli Me Tangere* and a stained glass window by Marc Chagall.

Beside the Cathedral is the Prebendal School, the oldest school in Sussex, where the Cathedral choristers are educated. To the south, the Bishop's Palace Garden is open to the public, with access from the cloisters and St Richard's Walk, or from South Street via Canon Lane.

West Street, the Clock Tower and the Cathedral, Chichester

Other medieval buildings in Chichester include the 13th-century St Mary's Hospital (which can be visited by the public at certain times), an example of an early hospital with its own chapel and still used today to house deserving elderly people of the city, the Guildhall in Priory Park, the market cross in the centre of town and a large number of churches and later chapels, many of them now redundant and used for a wide variety of new purposes, including a social centre, a bookshop and even a Chinese restaurant.

Like other Sussex towns, Chichester suffered during the Civil War and was in some decay by the late 17th century, but the 18th century saw a considerable revival in the city's fortunes and it is to this period that many of Chichester's most distinguished domestic buildings belong. Westgate House (or Wren House) in West Street was completed in 1696, Pallant House in 1712 and the city walls were repaired in the 1720s. Throughout the city houses were rebuilt or refronted and the results can be seen today in and around St Martin's Square and The Pallants.

Pallant House is of particular interest: it is open to the public and houses a significant collection of contemporary art, given to the city by the late Dean Hussey, patron of artists such as John Piper and Graham Sutherland. It is probably the finest 18th-century house in Chichester, built by the wine merchant Henry 'Lisbon' Peckham as his home and business premises, complete with an observation tower from which he could observe his ships returning to Chichester Harbour laden with fine wines and other goods from Spain and Portugal.

The period 1790 to 1815 saw Chichester enjoying considerable prosperity as the centre of a booming agriculture area, with corn and livestock markets held in the city twice weekly. The scale of the operation is suggested by the size and opulence of the old corn exchange building in East Street, built in 1832–3. Markets are still held on Wednesdays and Saturdays at the cattle market close to Eastgate Square and attract many visitors.

Today, Chichester is an important administrative centre and a popular residential area, particularly for those working in the high technology industries of south Hampshire. Many people are attracted by the location of the town, with its easy access to both the countryside and the sea. Modern amenities include the fine

Festival Theatre in Oaklands Park. Every July the city devotes itself to a two-week programme of festivities, with events ranging from symphony concerts in the Cathedral to fireworks at Goodwood Racecourse. Also in the summer, the Cathedrals of Chichester, Winchester and Salisbury are hosts in turn to the Southern Cathedrals Festival.

Close to the town is Chichester Harbour, the complex of tidal channels and creeks of great interest to walkers and naturalists and the playground of some 10,000 weekend sailors. Harbourside villages such as BOSHAM attract many visitors, and from the millpond at Fishbourne, south of the main road, there is a splendid walk to Itchenor and East Head, following the shoreline. Details of this and other walks around the Harbour, boat trips and other information are available from the Harbour Office at Itchenor. The best beaches for swimming and sunbathing are at West WITTERING; places to visit in the area include Goodwood House and the Weald and Dowland Museum at SINGLETON. Other museums in the city are the District Museum in Little London, the Museum of Mechanical Music at Church Road, Portfield and the Royal Military Police Museum at Roussillon Barracks on the A286 Midhurst road a mile north of the town centre.

Chiddingly (2/5D)
A secluded village to the north-west of Hailsham, whose parish church is famous for its stone spire. There are very few stone church spires in Sussex, and that at Chiddingly is by far the most impressive. Rising to a height of 128 ft, it stands out for miles in the landscape of the Sussex Weald. Inside the church are several memorials to the Jefferay family, who lived at nearby Chiddingly Place. The Tudor mansion is now a ruin, although the magnificent timber-framed barn from the same period has been carefully restored.

Stonehill House, one and a half miles north-east of the church, is an early Tudor house which has been saved from decay. The building makes an impressive sight with its heavy oak timbers and close studding. The bay window was added a century later, during the reign of Elizabeth I. One of Sussex's most celebrated literary figures was born in the parish: M. A. Lower was the author of *A Compendious History of Sussex*, published in 1870, a founder of the Sussex Archaeological Society and a determined upholder of Victorian moral values.

Christ's Hospital (1/5C) *see* Horsham

Church Norton (1/2E) *see* Selsey

Cissbury Ring (1/5E) *see* Findon

Clapham (1/5E)
A small village on the Downs, north-west of Worthing. Clapham's main claim to fame is its association with the Shelley family of Michelgrove. The Shelleys were one of the leading

Whig families in the county during the 18th century. Locally, the centre of the Whig interest was The Crown Inn in the High Street of the ancient and rotten borough of ARUNDEL. Today, the building is no longer an inn but the connection with the family is recalled in the name of one of the shops which now occupy the building, Shelley's.

Michelgrove House was built on the ridge to the east of Arundel in the early Tudor period and was occupied by the Shelleys for 350 years.

The pond at Patching

In 1800 Sir John Shelley sold it to the Duke of Norfolk who subsequently demolished it. The clock tower from the stable block now forms an attractive feature in STEYNING High Street.

St Mary's church in the village dates mostly from the 13th century and contains a number of monuments to the Shelley family, the most poignant of which is that erected by Sir John Shelley to his wife Wilhelmina, who died in 1772

IN MEMORY OF
FRANCIS EVERED LUNT
BISHOP OF STEPNEY
GREATLY LOVED

Church of St Mary, Climping

aged 23. He composed her epitaph himself: 'She was a pattern for the world to follow. Such a being both in form and mind perhaps never existed before.'

Close by is the village of **Patching** which has a celebrated pond, the 13th-century church of St John and one of the smallest primary schools in West Sussex.

Clayton (2/2D) *see* Pyecombe

Climping (1/4E)
An unspoiled village close to the sea between Littlehampton and Bognor Regis with a splendid Norman church. The coastline here was once much further out to sea than it is today and the lost parish of Cudlow and the manor of Atherington are now beneath the waves. The village consists of a single street of mainly brick and flint cottages leading to the sea, a pub, an hotel and, to the north of the A259, the parish church of St Mary. Climping is a favourite spot for visitors as it provides access to one of the few remaining stretches of undeveloped coastline in West Sussex. From the large car park at the end of The Street, visitors can enjoy several miles of sand dunes and beaches, free of urban clutter and modern 'amenities'. As a result, Climping becomes quite crowded in the summer holiday months.

Like many attractive places in the county, Climping was held before the Norman Conquest by Earl Godwin, father of King Harold. Roger de Montgomery, Duke William's close companion who became Lord of Arundel and Chichester, gave Climping to the nuns of Almanesches. Most of the church of St Mary dates from the 13th century and is attributed to the vicar, John de Climping, who subsequently became Bishop of Chichester; all architectural historians are united in praising the result as one of the best medieval village churches in the country (see *The Norman Heritage*, p. 28).

Close by, Roger de Montgomery enabled the Benedictine monks of the Norman abbey of Seez to establish a chapel and the house occupied by their bailiff was the foundation of the present Bailiffscourt Hotel. Bailiffscourt was built for Lord Moyne by the architect Amyas Phillips in a highly plausible and accomplished medieval style. On the death of Lord Normanby in the early 1970s the estate was divided, but the National Trust has secured covenants which should preserve for ever this unspoiled and attractive stretch of coastline. The County Council produces a useful walking guide to Climping beach, copies of which are available locally or from County Hall, Chichester.

Coldwaltham (1/4D) *see* Bury

Coleman's Hatch (2/4B) *see* Ashdown Forest

Coolham (1/5C) *see* Coneyhurst

Coneyhurst (1/5C)
A hamlet south-east of Billingshurst, with strong associations with the Society of Friends, or Quakers, and the founder of Pennsylvania.

Friends in this part of Sussex, despite persecution, decided in 1691 to settle on a suitable place for regular meeting. A farmhouse at Coneyhurst was purchased and the timbers of the first floor removed from the two large store rooms at the south end, in order to make a room of suitable height for the meeting house; the floor was left at one side to form a gallery reached by a narrow flight of stairs. In the roof are two small bedrooms, the larger of which is known as 'the Prophet's Chamber' as it was used for the accommodation of visiting Friends.

This lovely building, its ancient timbered walls roofed with Horsham stone, has had a chequered history of use and neglect. Originally used as a meeting house in the 17th century, it was closed for this purpose from 1793 to 1869, when it was colour-washed in blue. It was quite possible that it gained the name of the 'blue idle meeting house' – the word 'idle' then being widely used for any unoccupied building or silent factory – hence the name by which the meeting house is known today.

The Blue Idol meeting house is open to visitors at all reasonable hours and the rest of the building is run as a guest house; the bedrooms are named after notable Friends with associations with Coolham and Warminghurst. The graveyard beside the meeting house contains the graves of Friends who died for their faith in Horsham gaol. The village school at nearby **Coolham**, known as the William Penn School, is unusual in that it operates as a controlled school in association with the Society of Friends.

In the late 17th century there were many Friends in the district. William Penn lived for 15 years at **Warminghurst**, only four miles away due south, and worshipped regularly at this meeting house. Often he would ride over on horseback with his wife Gulielma, while their children rode in the family coach drawn by a team of oxen. It was chiefly West Sussex yeomen who helped to found Pennsylvania: the constitution of the new state was drafted, with the help of Algernon Sydney, at Warminghurst. Gulielma did not accompany her husband on his first voyage but stayed at Warminghurst until Penn's return in 1686.

The parish church of the Holy Sepulchre at Warminghurst is one of the architectural treasures of Sussex: a light, clean interior with all the original 17th and 18th-century fittings, including a three-decker pulpit and box pews. The church is now in the care of the Redundant Churches Fund and is usually locked. The key is kept at the adjoining Warminghurst Farm.

Coombes (2/1E) *see* Sompting

Cowdray (1/3C) *see* Midhurst

Cowfold (2/2C)

Situated at the busy junction of the A272 and the A281 Horsham to Henfield road, Cowfold is a village worth exploring. The temptation is to drive straight through, but in fact there is a surprising amount to see.

The parish church of St Peter can easily be visited from the small car park on the village green, just east of the crossroads. The churchyard is remarkable and unexpected, the cottages round it facing inwards rather than out to the busy A272. Although none of the houses is exceptional, as a group they have considerable character and provide a charming setting for the sturdy Wealden church with its solid, reliable tower.

The most famous feature of the church is the remarkable monumental brass to Thomas Nelond, Prior of St Pancras's Priory in LEWES, who died in 1433. The Priory, founded in 1077, was the principal house in England of the Cluniac order, and Prior Nelond is shown, life size, in the dress of a Cluniac monk. He stands with hands folded and an expression particularly solemn and dignified. But the most memorable feature of the brass is the beautifully engraved canopy above the Prior's head, consisting of an arch and representations of the Virgin and Child, St Pancras and St Thomas à Becket. The brass is underneath the carpet in the nave and is not normally accessible.

There are a number of attractive houses and cottages in the village and the Victorian village hall and library in the centre is particularly good. Outside the village there are two fine modern country houses – The Clock House (1913–4) and Ivory's (1921) – and a mile away to the south is the Monastery of St Hugh's Charterhouse, more commonly referred to as Cowfold Monastery. It was founded here in 1873, when the Carthusians were forced to leave France. The spire is a landmark for miles around, providing a similar visual focus in the western

Church of the Holy Sepulchre, Warminghurst

Weald to the spire of CHICHESTER Cathedral on the coastal plain.

Crawley (2/2B)
The most successful of the first generation post Second World War new towns, with a buoyant local economy driven by the expanding Gatwick Airport and a booming industrial estate. The town, which straddles the A23 London to Brighton road, now has 85,000 inhabitants and is the largest inland town in the county. Its origins lie in the three settlements of Crawley, Ifield and Three Bridges, but there is evidence of prehistoric occupation of the area in the iron workings at Broadfield and Bewbush. The original village of Crawley developed from a clearing in the Wealden forest made by the early pioneers and iron workers. Later, its position alongside the coach road to London gave it added importance. Early buildings still to be

Houses along the edge of the churchyard at Cowfold

seen in the High Street include The Tree, based on an original hall house of about 1500 and The George Hotel which has provided overnight accommodation for travellers since the 17th century. The unusual 'gallows' carries the inn sign across the High Street and The George looks much the same today as when Thomas Rowlandson drew it in the 18th century. Another building of interest in the town centre is the Victorian bandstand in Queen's Square, which was moved from the old Gatwick race-course.

To the west of Crawley town centre is the village of **Ifield**, which includes The Plough Inn, a Friends' meeting house dated 1676, Ifield Mill and the Barn Theatre. **Three Bridges** is to the east of the town and grew up around the railway station on the London to Brighton line, which here is joined by the Arun Valley line to Littlehampton and Bognor Regis. There was also a branch line from Three Bridges to East Grinstead – now closed but available to walkers and known as the WORTH Way. Three Bridges is typical of the residential and commercial areas which developed around railway stations in the late Victorian period.

The postwar new towns were conceived as a response to the continuing outward sprawl of London and were a key element in the early planning of the south-east region, together with the creation of the metropolitan green belt. Crawley was one of eight new self-supporting towns established in a ring round the capital, each providing not only housing but also local employment, which Crawley has been outstandingly successful in attracting. Twenty thousand people work in the 180 factories on the Manor Royal industrial estate alone. The master plan for the development of the new town was produced by Anthony Minoprio who envisaged a series of residential neighbourhoods, based on the village concept and incorporating existing communities, all grouped around the town centre. Neighbourhood centres were provided with sufficient shops for day to day needs, a school, a church and a pub. Community centres followed as funds became available. Broadfield and Bewbush, south of the town centre, are the most recently built neighbourhoods and work is now under way on Maidenbower, extending the built-up area east to the new town boundary of the M23. The Borough Council takes great pride in the expansion of the town, as is evident from their motto of 'We grow and we rejoice', but it is likely that Maidenbower will mark the completion of the development of Crawley. The town has two leisure centres, an excellent new arts centre known as The Hawth and over 1,000 acres of public open space.

To the north of the town is **Gatwick Airport**, the second busiest international airport in the world, which grew from a pre-1939 airfield on the site of the old Gatwick racecourse. The airport now handles over 20 million passengers a year; its development was completed in 1988 when the new North Terminal (which is six times the size of the Albert Hall) was opened by Her Majesty The Queen. Plans for a second runway have been abandoned and in 1979 the former British Airports Authority signed a binding agreement with the County Council not to build one for at least 40 years: indeed, the North Terminal stands today in the only position in which a second runway could have been built. More than 15,000 people are employed at the airport and this figure will rise rapidly as the capacity created by the new terminal is taken up. Gatwick Airport plc prides itself on being 'the airport in the country' and thousands of new trees have been planted in the carefully landscaped grounds, providing a splendid introduction to the United Kingdom for visitors from overseas.

On the south-east fringe of Crawley and soon to be engulfed in the expanding new town is **Worth**, best known for its Saxon church. Worth means 'an enclosure in the forest' and the place gave its name to Worth Forest, a remnant of the great Wealden forest which effectively separated the settlements of the Sussex coast from the interior of the island. Up in the High Weald pioneers established clearings where they kept animals and gathered timber. It was here that the Sussex iron industry had one of its main centres, the other being the countryside around

The Blue Idol meeting House, Coneyhurst

Church of St Nicholas, Worth

BATTLE. The industry created considerable wealth and the late Elizabethan Rowfant House, east of the village, was probably built for the local ironmaster, Robert Whitfield.

The early occupation of the area is reflected in the 11th-century parish church of St Nicholas which provided a focus for a scattered community in this remote, wooded country. Despite extensive Victorian alterations the church has more Saxon work than any other in Sussex, notably the apsidal chancel, heavy arches and external decoration with pilaster strips. The population grew as communications improved. The railway came first to Three Bridges; later there was a connecting branch line to EAST GRINSTEAD. The line was closed in the 1960s, bought by the County Council and made available for walkers and riders. At the suggestion of a local primary school the route was given the name 'Worth Way', since for nearly all its length it runs through the large rural parish of Worth. A leaflet about it is available from County Hall, Chichester.

Substantial Victorian buildings in the area include Crabbett Park, designed in 1873 by Wilfrid Scawen Blunt of rose brick with stone dressings and Paddockhurst, an imitation Tudor mansion with additions by Sir Aston Webb, architect of CHRIST'S HOSPITAL. Paddockhurst is now Worth Abbey, a Benedictine monastery which also includes a school.

Crowborough (2/5B)

One of the principal centres of the High Weald, Crowborough has expanded in recent years, with extensive new housing and shopping developments. Crowborough is the highest town in Sussex, about 800 ft above sea level. It therefore boasts commanding views over the surrounding countryside, especially from the Beacon, an open space in the centre of the town.

Until the last century it was a wild and barren place, inhabited only by smugglers and iron smelters. The Sussex iron industry was once based around Crowborough, and with its decline in the 18th century the future for the small community must have seemed bleak. But urban development expanded in Victorian times and several famous writers made their homes here, including the naturalist Richard Jefferies and Sir Arthur Conan Doyle, the creator of Sherlock Holmes. This expansion was generated by the arrival of the railway in 1868, which highlighted Crowborough's proximity to London and its convenience for city businessmen who wished to escape from the smog and grime of the capital.

Crowborough has modern facilities, including a shopping centre and a sports complex, all catering for a new generation of commuters who wish to make their homes in a rural environment.

Cuckfield (2/3C)

A distinguished village on the old coach road from London to Brighton. William de Warenne, Norman Lord of LEWES, had a hunting lodge here, deep in the Wealden forest, and he and his wife Gundrada founded a church on the site of the present parish church of Holy Trinity. This 13th-century building, with a shingled broach spire and Horsham slab roof, commands an impressive view south to the Downs. Close to the church is the 17th-century school with mullioned and transomed windows. The King's Head, in the High Street, was a popular staging post in the 18th and early 19th centuries and the street, with its brick pavements, retains a coaching air today. The Talbot was the seat of local justice, where the Cuckfield magistrates sat for the last time in 1888. It is also the scene of

the annual election of the Mayor of the Independent State of Cuckfield, an office whose significance is more bibulous than political.

Notable houses in the village include Ockenden Manor and Cuckfield Park. Ockenden Manor, now an hotel and restaurant, was bought by William Burrell in 1608. He was one of the leading iron-masters of the county and his descendant, the barrister and diarist Timothy Burrell, lived here from 1683 to 1714. Cuckfield Park was built in 1580 by another Sussex iron-master, Henry Bowyer, and for hundreds of years was the seat of the Sergison family, from whom the pub beside Muster Green, HAYWARDS HEATH, takes its name. The house is approached via an Elizabethan brick gatehouse and what was, until the storm of October 1987, a fine avenue of lime trees. Unfortunately it is not open to the public. The Sergisons refused to let the London to Brighton railway cross their land in 1841, with the result that the line was built to the east, leading to the rapid development of what became Haywards Heath.

Cuckfield was a market town from the 13th

The High Street, Cuckfield

century and the history of the place is illustrated in the small museum which has been established by the Cuckfield Museum Trust in the old reading room of Queen's Hall in the High Street.

North-west of the village, at **Handcross**, is the garden of Nymans, owned by the National Trust and open to the public from April to the end of October. One of the great Wealden gardens, Nymans features rare and beautiful shrubs, plants and trees from all over the world. It is best visited in spring when the azaleas and rhododendrons are in bloon.

Dallington (3/2D) *see* Brightling

Devil's Dyke (2/2D)

This famous viewpoint on the Downs above Brighton overlooks a string of pretty, spring-line villages with the Weald of Sussex beyond. At nearly 700 ft above sea level, Devil's Dyke has been a favourite objective for expeditions

Fulking Hill, Perching Hill, Edburton Hill and Truleigh Hill from Devil's Dyke

from Brighton since the town began to attract fashionable visitors in the 18th century. Indeed, one of the reasons for the success of Brighton compared with resorts like WORTHING or BOGNOR is the proximity of the Downs and the ability to combine pastoral delights with the excitements of the social round of the town. To help visitors reach the Dyke a railway was constructed from the town centre. In the 1880s, when the railway was complemented by a cable car suspended across the Dyke and a cable lift up the steep north escarpment of the Downs, the area became a bustling attraction.

Today it is difficult to recapture the scene at the Dyke as it was in late Victorian and Edwardian times, all trace of the railway and cable cars having long since disappeared. The Dyke, however, remains popular and now has a pub, restaurant and large car park. A modern

activity which attracts both participants and spectators is hang gliding: the gliders are a fine sight as they launch off from the hill, circling graciously with their gay colours hundreds of feet above the farmland below. From the hilltop there are fine views north across what Kipling so accurately called 'the wooded, dim, blue goodness of the Weald' to the North Downs, west to Chanctonbury Ring and east to Newtimber and Wolstonbury Hills. The car park is a good access point to the **South Downs Way**, the long-distance footpath and bridleway which runs along the crest of the escarpment.

The Dyke itself is the steep-sided natural ravine to the south of the car park, said to have been created by the Devil in a thwarted attempt to flood the Christian communities of the Weald. The Dyke and the hill top are owned by Brighton Borough Council, who bought hundreds of acres of downland in the 1920s to protect them from development. The land is now managed with conservation in mind and sheep grazing has been re-introduced. Two hundred and ninety acres of the adjoining land to the west – the Fulking escarpment – has recently been bought by the National Trust and is managed in association with their 235 acres of woodland and downland at Newtimber. The Trust is negotiating to buy further land in the area and it is to be hoped that, before too long, much of the downland here will be managed for conservation and public access. There is already an excellent modern youth hostel at Tottington Barn near Truleigh Hill, just beyond the radio masts which can be seen from Dyke Hill, looking west.

Below the hill runs an attractive road from Pyecombe to Upper Beeding which follows the spring-line; water gushes out of the chalk and across the road below the Shepherd and Dog pub at **Fulking.**

Edburton has a simple 13th-century church dedicated to St Andrew, and a well-known smoked salmon establishment. On the hill to the south are the remains of an earthwork, possibly an early motte and bailey castle, which marked the boundary between the Rapes of BRAMBER and LEWES and thus the historic boundary between the counties of West and East Sussex (see *The Norman Heritage*, p. 28). The early Georgian flint and red brick Perching Manor Farm and its adjoining barn are noteworthy. These villages well illustrate the traditional sheep/corn agricultural system of the Downs: sheep were grazed on the steep hillsides during the day and brought down at night to manure the already exceptionally fertile arable land below.

Of particular interest in this connection is Saddlescombe, a farm resting, as its name suggests, on a ridge of land below Newtimber Hill. In 1228 the Manor of Saddlescombe was acquired by the Knights Templar, who operated a preceptory or training centre here in addition to their estate at SHIPLEY. The Order was dissolved in 1312 and its lands in Sussex passed to the Knights Hospitaller, whose headquarters were at Poling, near ARUNDEL. Saddlescombe passed eventually into private hands and the farm is the subject of a 19th-century memoir entitled *A South Downs Farm in the Sixties* which describes life here more than 100 years ago, when oxen were used to plough the fields and the farm was the home of a large community of agricultural workers. The family who lived here were Quakers and travelled into Brighton on Sundays to attend the Friends' meeting house. The donkey-wheel which was used to draw water from the well can still be seen in its weatherboarded engine house and the 16th-century timber-framed farmhouse is little changed. Saddlescombe gives the modern visitor a very good impression of what life in the Sussex Downs was like in the past – hard and primitive maybe, but also secure and predictable.

Dickers, The (2/5D)

Two small hamlets in the same Downland parish west of Hailsham. The parish church of Holy Trinity at Upper Dicker was rebuilt in the Norman style in 1843. The first vicar of the new church appears to have preferred the challenge of converting the heathen overseas to caring for his own parish and went as a missionary to Sierra Leone. He achieved a great deal and was made a bishop, but died shortly afterwards at the early age of 35. Horatio Bottomley, opportunistic politician, trickster and profiteer, had a home here in the early years of the century. He was eventually sent to prison, an experience from which he never recovered. The house where he lived, The Dicker, is now a school.

Opposite The Dicker, a minor road leads to **Michelham Priory**, situated on a peninsular beside the Cuckmere River. The Norman Lords of Pevensey built a hunting lodge here and, in 1229, Gilbert de Aquila created a priory of Augustinian monks at Michelham which flourished until the dissolution of the monasteries under Henry VIII in the 16th century. It became a Tudor farmhouse and was owned by the Sackville family from 1603 to 1897. Thomas Child, who developed the famous Michelham breed of cattle, lived here during the early years of the 19th century. The Priory is set in 6 acres of gardens surrounded by a moat which is crossed by an imposing 14th-century gateway. The property is owned by the Sussex Archaeological Society and is open to the public. There is a physic garden, a working water mill that grinds flour for sale, a forge, a wheelwright's shop and many other interesting exhibits.

Ditchling (2/3D)

A well-known village under the Downs north of Brighton and a popular spot with artists and craftsmen. The village is organised around a crossroads, above which stands the parish church of St Margaret. The manor was owned by King Alfred, who is thought to have had a palace here at the centre of a large royal estate. The church dates from the 13th century, although the exterior has been altered by restoration. Opposite the church is the timber-framed Anne of Cleves house which has late 16th-century details but little to do with Henry VIII's rejected Flemish bride. Another notable house is Cotterlings, also timber-framed but faced with black and red mathematical tiles, similar to those to be found in Brighton and Lewes.

Ditchling has always attracted artists and, during the 1920s, was the home of the sculptor and designer Eric Gill, whose work in Sussex included the war memorial at South HARTING. Another famous resident was the artist Sir Frank Brangwyn, who lived in the village for many years until his death in 1956. In Sussex, his work can be seen in the chapel at CHRIST'S HOSPITAL, where his paintings decorate the walls. There is a good local museum, housed in the old school buildings which date from 1836.

A couple of miles south of the village is Ditchling Beacon, at 813 ft the third highest point on the Sussex Downs. This fine viewpoint was given to the National Trust in memory of a young airman killed in the Second World War. The Beacon, site of one of the warning fires prepared at the time of the Armada, is the starting point for a number of waymarked walks described in a leaflet available from County Hall, Lewes.

To the south-east of Ditchling lies **Westmeston**. The parish church of St Martin has a shingled bell turret and wall paintings by the same Lewes school of artists responsible for CLAYTON and HARDHAM. Westmeston Place dates back to the 15th century and, although extended around 1882, contains some original mullioned windows. Another notable house in the parish is Middleton Manor, now run by the County Council as a training centre in country crafts and horticulture for mentally handicapped young people. The Manor house was built in about 1830 of Horsham sandstone faced with red mathematical tiles, and was used by the Army as a holding centre before the ill-fated Dieppe Raid

14th-century gatehouse, Michelham Priory

of 1942, in which many thousands of Canadian and other troops lost their lives.

The next village east is **Plumpton**. Plumpton Place has early 17th-century origins but is largely the work of Sir Edwin Lutyens, who rebuilt the house in the 1920s for Edward Hudson, owner of *Country Life* magazine, for whom he had earlier restored Lindisfarne Castle in Northumberland. Near by are the East Sussex College of Agriculture and Plumpton Racecourse, close to the railway station where trains make extra stops on race days. Plumpton Racecourse is for national hunt racing only and a new stand opened for the 1988–9 season; the course is also used for pony club camps. The Victorian signal box is a listed building and railway enthusiasts have fought hard to stop its being replaced by a more modern structure. At The Half Moon pub there is a large wall painting depicting 100 regular customers, specially commissioned in 1977 to mark Her Majesty The Queen's Silver Jubilee.

Eartham (1/3E)

A brick and flint village north-east of Chichester consisting of a large house, church, pub and a few cottages. Eartham House was owned by an obscure 18th-century poet, William Hayley: in the church there is a memorial to his son Thomas, who died in 1800 when he was only 20. His father, a friend of the writer William Blake, moved away to Felpham and Eartham House was sold to the politician William Huskisson, who was killed on the opening day of the Liverpool and Manchester Railway when he misjudged the speed of the train. The house was remodelled in the William and Mary style by Sir Edwin Lutyens in 1905 and is now a prep school. The nearby church of St Margaret was comprehensively restored in 1869 but retains a fine Norman chancel arch.

There are good walks in the area and a useful public car park is provided by the Forestry Commission in Eartham Wood. From here it is possible to walk up the old Roman road, Stane Street, to Bignor Hill and beyond.

Easebourne (1/2C) *see* Midhurst

Eastbourne (3/2F)

A large coastal town, with the Downs to the west and the Pevensey Levels to the east. Largely built during the latter half of the 19th century, Eastbourne is renowned as a distinguished and tasteful resort. The bourne or stream after which the town is named still rises from a spring in the Downs and flows underground, beneath Bourne Street, to the sea. The old town, which is situated to the east of the modern resort and about a mile inland, still retains something of its former identity. During redevelopment work in the 1960s remains of a Roman boat were found, indicating that a community of some sort had existed at Eastbourne for many centuries before the Norman Conquest. The church of St Mary is a large building of flint and stone, with a distinctive green sandstone tower. It dates from about 1200 and is particularly impressive inside. Immediately north of the church is the Old Parsonage, constructed of knapped flints and cobbles. The building is well-preserved and contains a large fireplace, designed to heat the great hall. The Lambe Inn in the High Street is thought to date from the 13th century as does the timber-framed house near by.

The modern town owes its existence to the principal local landowners in the mid 19th century: the Duke of Devonshire and Carew Davis Gilbert, whose grandfather was President of the Royal Society. The arrival of the railway opened up Eastbourne as a potential destination for visitors, and later for businessmen and the retired. The stately hotels on the seafront and the grand avenues with their prim Victorian villas are ample testimony to the patrons' desire to create a seaside town which would be 'The Empress of Watering Places'. The Duke in particular has left his mark on the town with such noble monuments as the spacious Devonshire Park gardens and the gracious theatre in its grounds. Also of architectural note are the pier, built in the 1880s by Eugenius Birch and the extravagant town hall, constructed of brick and Portland stone with a view to grandeur and little regard to cost.

The development of Eastbourne as a resort was carefully controlled and, today, a special feature of the town is the esplanade which, with its three-tier promenade, extends for three miles, backed by landscaped gardens and handsome hotels and private houses. There is safe bathing from the gently sloping shingle beach, which is sandy at low tide. Eastbourne has excellent shops and is host to a number of major sporting events, including a ladies' international tennis tournament at Devonshire Park in June each year.

The Redoubt, as the Martello tower in Royal Parade is known, was built in 1803 as part of Britain's defences against a French invasion

On the seafront at Eastbourne

during the Napoleonic Wars. Today it houses the Sussex Combined Services Museum. The Royal Sussex Regiment, whose history features in the Museum, was founded in 1701 and saw both glory and disaster, from the skirmishes of Empire to the bloody slaughter of the First World War. It was the Royal Sussex Regiment which was sent to relieve General Gordon at Khartoum, only to arrive to find the General and his men already slaughtered by the Madhi. At the Battle of Abu Klea the Dervishes were finally defeated, but the colonel and many men of the Regiment died in the fighting. According to a popular song of the time: 'They did not flinch nor fear, they stood their ground like Englishmen, and died at Abu Klea'.

On the edge of the town is Compton Place, from where the Duke of Devonshire supervised the development of the resort. The house seems to date originally from the 17th century, but was the subject of extensive remodelling. It now houses a finishing school and is not open to the public.

The Butterfly Centre in Royal Parade has over 50 different species and the Congress Theatre in Carlisle Road, built between 1958 and 1963, provides an interesting programme throughout the year. Eastbourne can boast the oldest motor-bus service in the country; a favourite trip in the summer is by open-topped bus to **Beachy Head**, the name of which is derived from the French *beau chef*, or beautiful headland. Clearly our Norman ancestors were as taken with the view as are modern visitors. Beachy Head is the most easterly and the most spectacular of the chalk cliffs that mark the line of the Downs between Brighton and Eastbourne. It is also prolific in wildlife and is a protected area. Ever since Victorian times, tourists have delighted in the views and enjoyed picnics on warm summer days overlooking the English Channel. The headland has, however, always had a sinister reputation and was known to Venetian sailors as 'The Devil's Cape', because of the number of ships wrecked there. The cliffs, too, are dangerous and subject to constant erosion, so the warning notices should be taken seriously. In 1806 a one-eyed fisherman named 'Jumper' Hutches discovered a Bronze Age hoard, including items of gold, in the cliff face and more recently further archaeological finds have been made.

Overleaf: Beachy Head

In *Nature Near London* Richard Jefferies writes of the breeze on Beachy Head: 'The glory of these glorious Downs is the breeze. The air in the valleys immediately beneath them is pure and pleasant; but the least climb, even a hundred feet, puts you on a plane with the atmosphere itself, uninterrupted by so much as the tree-tops. It is air without admixture. If it comes from the south, the waves refine it; if inland, the wheat and flowers and grass distill it'.

East Dean, *East Sussex* (2/5F)
Situated on the coast road to the west of Eastbourne, where the chalk cliffs meet the sea to the south and FRISTON Forest bounds the parish to the north. The cliffs at Birling Gap are today owned by the National Trust and make a pleasant picnic spot on a summer's day. Yet these cliffs have not always had such agreeable associations. In the 18th century, many a storm-tossed mariner met a watery grave here. The vicar of East Dean at the time, the Reverend Jonathan Darby, was so appalled by the loss of life that he set about constructing a warning beacon on the cliffs. Labourers were hired to excavate a tunnel through the chalk, emerging at a cave which overlooked the sea. On stormy nights the vicar would take himself to the cave and light a fire as a warning to passing ships. His efforts saved the lives of many seamen who would otherwise have perished on the rocks below. Today, the automatic electric beacon at Beachy Head carries on the work begun by Jonathan Darby.

East Dean village is today the size of a small town, as a great deal of development has been allowed to the north of the A259. At one stage there was a proposal to build a housing estate in Crowlink Valley, but the scheme met with much local protest and a fund was set up to buy the land and save it from the speculators. Among those who gave generous contributions was Rudyard Kipling, who lived for a while at nearby Rottingdean. The campaign was a success and Crowlink now comes under the protection of the National Trust.

The church of St Simon and St Jude is of little architectural interest, having been greatly restored in the 1880s. The pewter chalice and plate, displayed in a glass case, were discovered in a priest's coffin and are of some antiquity. One of the church bells has an inscription on it which proudly boasts: 'Surely no bell beneath the sky, can send forth better sound than I'. The red and grey brick Georgian house known as The Dipperays was built for the smuggler James Dippery, who lived to enjoy his ill-gotten gains by turning King's evidence and betraying his comrades. The Tiger Inn is one of the oldest buildings in the village, dating back to Elizabeth times.

East Dean, *West Sussex* (1/3D)
A snug Downland village, mainly of brick and flint, at the head of the Lavant valley, east of Singleton. With Singleton and CHARLTON, East Dean was part of the estates of the Fitzalans, Earls of ARUNDEL. South of the village lay a deer park originally set aside for hunting in the time of Henry II. The association of the area with hunting was maintained into the 18th century, when the Charlton Hunt was one of the most famous in England. The village is grouped pleasantly around the pond and the Star and Garter pub, a good flint building with slivers of flint, or galletts, inserted in the mortar for strength and decoration. Most of the village houses are of flint with brick dressings round the windows and doors, but a few are timber-framed. The village suffered a disastrous fire in 1852; happily, many of the older houses survived.

The village school closed in 1958 when the number of pupils dropped to eight and the school building was converted into a village hall. The old school bears the arms of the 3rd Duke of Richmond and the date 1782. The parish church of All Saints, at the top of the village street, dates from about 1150; its proportions were retained in the restoration of 1870.

East Grinstead (2/3B)
A Wealden market town on the edge of Ashdown Forest and close to the county boundary with Surrey and Kent. East Grinstead developed in the Middle Ages as an important market centre in the High Weald, serving the surrounding rural area and fulfilling a similar economic role to the Wealden towns of MIDHURST and HORSHAM. Situated on a sandstone ridge which produced good building stone and surrounded by woodland, East Grinstead retains a large number of 16th and early 17th-century buildings. Timber-framed houses in the High Street include Clarendon House and Stone House which, together with a number of other late 16th-century buildings, form one of the most attractive groups in the county. The use of local building stone is represented by the parish church of St Swithin and Sackville College almshouses. The

church was built by James Wyatt in 1789 to replace a medieval building which collapsed when the tower fell down. Sackville College, a quadrangle of low stone buildings with Horsham slab roofs and brick chimneys, was founded in 1609 by the second Earl of Dorset and continues to provide homes for 18 local elderly people. The public rooms of the College, including the banqueting hall with a splendid hammerbeam roof, are open to visitors.

West of the town, on the Surrey border, is the 17th-century Gullege Farm, combining stone and timber-framing.

As well as providing a commercial focus for local agricultural and industry, East Grinstead was for many years an assize town. As it was relatively close to London, the judges could reach the town in the winter when the deplorable Wealden roads prevented their getting to Lewes, and East Grinstead shared with Horsham the distinction of acting as a judicial centre for the county. The Judges' Lodgings in the High Street are a reminder of these days.

Following the decline of the iron industry and the emergence of Lewes as the administrative and social capital of the eastern division of Sussex, East Grinstead's importance diminished, to be revived by the coming of the railway in 1855. The railway made it possible for the well-to-do to build country houses in the area, within reasonably easy access of the capital. During the late 19th century many substantial houses and villas sprang up between East Grinstead and Horsham, taking advantage of the undulating landscape and the fine views afforded from hills and outcrops of sandstone. These houses were often associated with memorable gardens, examples in the vicinity of East Grinstead including Gravetye, Borde Hill and WAKEHURST Place.

The best Victorian country house in the area is Standen, a mile and a half south of the town. Built by Philip Webb in 1894, the house makes extensive use of traditional materials and techniques, including local stone and brick, tile-hanging and weatherboarding, and features William Morris wallpapers and textiles. Commanding views across the valley of the River Medway to ASHDOWN FOREST, Standen was built for a wealthy London solicitor James Beale and his wife, who used it as a country retreat and, subsequently, as a retirement home. The house and gardens are now owned by the National Trust and are open to the public. The house contains a flat which is let by the Trust for weekends and holidays.

The valley of the Medway, which forms the boundary between East and West Sussex, was dammed here in 1950 to create Weir Wood reservoir, a 280 acre expanse of water, part of which is now a nature reserve. Fishing is available and there are two car parks, one specially designed for the disabled.

It was the railway, too, which led to the rapid expansion of East Grinstead in Victorian times, when the commercial centre shifted from the High Street to London Road, which runs towards the station. House building continued into the present century, reflecting the growth of Gatwick Airport and improved access to central London when the railway line was electrified. Local amenities include the King's Centre, which offers swimming and indoor and outdoor sports, the WORTH Way, a six-mile walk to THREE BRIDGES, Crawley, along the track of the old railway line closed in 1967, and the Queen Victoria Hospital, famous for its pioneering work on plastic surgery. There is a local museum at East Court.

East Guldeford (3/5C) *see* Rye

East Lavant (1/2E) *see* Lavant

East Preston (1/4E) *see* Littlehampton

East Wittering (1/F) *see* Witterings, The

Edburton (2/2d) *see* Devil's Dyke

Elsted (1/2D) *see* Harting

Exceat (2/4E) *see* Seaford

Fairlight (3/4D)

A picturesque village to the east of Hastings, where wooded valleys and gorse-covered heath tumble down to sandstone cliffs. At nearly 600 ft above sea level, Fairlight enjoys commanding views over the Weald and across the Channel to France. In 1870, the Sussex historian M. A. Lower wrote: 'It is said that from this charming height there are visible no less than ten towns, two harbours, three bays, 66 churches, five castles, 70 Martello towers, one lighthouse, two monumental towers and 40 windmills'. The number of windmills and Martello towers may have drastically decreased since Lower's day, but the view is still impressive, and it is a popular spot for visitors during the summer months.

Most of the parish is within the protected confines of the Hastings Country Park, while Mallydams Wood is an animal sanctuary belonging to the Royal Society for the Prevention of Cruelty to Animals. The Country Park covers nearly 600 acres and stretches along the coast for four miles, providing spectacular views, nature trails, picnic sites and an information centre.

The Victorian church is dedicated to St Andrew. In the churchyard is the grave of T. A. Walmisley, a friend of the great composer Mendelssohn and an early admirer of Bach. His own musical genius became evident at an early age and he was appointed Professor of Music at Cambridge University at the age of 22. Another son of Fairlight is commemorated by a stone memorial close to the car park in the Country Park. Archie Belaney, known as Grey Owl, went to live and work among the Red Indians of Canada when still a youth. He became a skilled trapper and married an Indian woman. In the 1930s he returned to England, where he toured the country, giving lectures on his experiences to captivated crowds. He also wrote several books, in which he advocated a greater harmony between man and his natural environment.

Faygate (2/2B) *see* St Leonard's Forest

Felpham (1/3F) *see* Bognor Regis

Ferring (1/4E) *see* Worthing

Findon (1/5E)
Just north of Worthing on the A24 to Horsham, beneath Cissbury Ring and famous for its annual sheep fair. Despite being under siege from development thrusting out from Worthing along the euphemistically named 'Findon Valley', Findon retains a village atmosphere. At the centre is The Square, around which there are a number of brick and flint houses. Findon Manor, now an hotel but originally The Rectory, is a good flint house under a Horsham slab roof and The Gun Inn is of some historical interest. The parish church of St John the Baptist is on the west side of the main road. It is made of flint, even including the chimney at the north-east corner and has an ancient font like a cattle trough, made of Sussex marble. The church was restored by Sir George Gilbert Scott in 1876. Near by is Findon Place, built in the early 18th century and enlarged after 1786. The charming village cricket ground is off the road across the Downs known as Long Furlong.

Findon is home to one of the two great Sussex sheep fairs, the other being at Lewes. The Findon fair was first held on Nepcote Green in the 13th century and traditionally took place on 14 September. In 1959 the date was changed to the second Saturday in September. Up to 20,000 sheep are bought and sold at Findon fair and, in addition, there are many attractions for the whole family to enjoy. In the old days the sheep were driven to the fair on the hoof from remote corners of the Downs, the shepherds rising very early to get their sheep there by the time business got under way. The shepherds, wearing their traditional smocks, would meet old friends and have a good time. Later, with the coming of the railways, sheep came to Findon fair from all over southern England, driven along the roads from the nearest railhead at Steyning. As well as sheep, Findon has always had a strong association with horses. There were at one time three forges in the village and racehorses have been trained on the Downs here for many years.

Looming above Findon, 600 ft high, is the Iron Age hill fort of **Cissbury Ring**, which can be approached from either Nepcote or Findon Valley. Either way, a stiff climb is involved from the car park to the Ring and the ascent is not suitable for the faint-hearted. The climb serves to emphasise the natural defensive possibilities of the site, recognised by our Iron Age ancestors. In about 250 BC, they constructed here one of the largest forts in a series which crown a line of hills from Kent to Dorset. Second only to the mighty Maiden Castle in Dorset, Cissbury's fortifications enclose 65 acres of the hilltop, from which views extend to CHICHESTER Cathedral, SELSEY Bill and the Isle of Wight. Closer at hand can be seen CHANCTONBURY RING to the north and Highdown Hill to the west. It is estimated that some 60,000 tons of chalk were dug out of the ditch to build the ramparts, which themselves cover a further 18 acres.

An examination of the site reveals collections of depressions and mounds of earth which are the remains of the much earlier activity of flint mining that went on here in the New Stone Age, between about 4300 and 3500 BC. The mines consisted of shafts up to 40 ft deep, with galleries radiating off in which the miners toiled with primitive tools fashioned from red deer antlers to extract nodules of flint from the chalk. Flint mined in this way was much more useful for making tools and other implements than

Piper's 'Tree of Life' window, West Firle church

flints which had been lying around on the surface and exposed to the weather. Cissbury seems to have been one of the main centres for flint mining in southern England; there is a similar site at Grimes Graves, near Brandon in Suffolk, where it is possible to descend one of the old shafts which has been excavated.

Cissbury seems to have been abandoned as a fortification some time before the Roman invasion in AD 43 but was re-occupied towards the end of the Roman period, possibly as a defence against Saxon raiders. In this, of course it failed and the modern name of the place reflects a supposed association with Cissa, the Saxon lord of Chichester. Cissbury Ring is owned and managed by the National Trust and is open to the public at all times, free of charge. The growth of scrub is controlled by sheep grazing so areas of the site may be fenced off from time to time. Visitors should respect this ancient site and avoid behaviour which might damage its archaeological interest, the full extent of which remains unknown to this day.

Firle (2/4E)

Just to the east of Lewes, Firle is an unspoiled Downland village, for centuries the home of the notable Roman Catholic Gage family. Firle (or more properly, **West Firle**, although there is no East or any other) is a peaceful, feudal village which grew up around Firle Place and the parish church of St Peter. The 16th-century Sir John Gage and his wife Philippa are the subjects of the beautiful alabaster effigies in the church and there are a number of very good brasses which may be rubbed for a small fee. At his feet Sir John has a ram, taken from the family coat of arms. The ram also gives its name to the village pub. Sir John, who was a Catholic, was Vice-Chamberlain to Henry VIII and a man of considerable importance. He built Firle Place and the house has remained in the family ever since. The Gages remained Catholics until well into the 18th century. Little remains of the original house as major alterations were made in the 18th century.

There are many good village houses, some of them faced with the mathematical tiles which are such a feature of Lewes, and Firle is an excellent centre for walks on the Downs. One of the most popular walks is to Firle Beacon (712 ft), east along the ridge to the top of Bo-Peep bostal, returning to the village along the old coach road under the Downs.

A mile or so east of Firle and reached by a long access road from the A27, is **Charleston Farmhouse**, home for many years of the artists Duncan Grant and Vanessa and Clive Bell. They so decorated the house that nearly every surface in the house was painted or embellished by them and their own wallpapers, fabrics and fittings transformed what was a commonplace Sussex farmhouse into a considerable work of art. They also laid out the gardens. Here were received a constant stream of visitors, including Maynard Keynes (who lived at nearby Tilton Farm), Lytton Strachey and the young Benjamin Britten. With substantial financial assistance from a generous American benefactor, Charleston has now been restored and opened to the public in spring and summer. Such an artistic household needed someone sensible to provide direction and stability and this was the role of the housekeeper, Grace Higgens, whose portrait by Vanessa Bell is on the first floor landing. Look out also for Vanessa's self-portrait in the Garden Room.

The gardens at Charleston are a delight. Small and informal, they nevertheless have something of the atmosphere of the grander gardens at the home of Claude Monet, at Giverny near Rouen. Time spent in the quiet of the garden at Charleston will refresh and inspire the modern visitor, just as it did the leaders of the artistic and literary world of the 1930s.

In the bedroom in which Maynard Keynes wrote *The Economic Consequences of the Peace* is a portrait of Chatty Salaman, a friend of the family, who was the model for the angels painted by Vanessa Bell and Duncan Grant and their son Quentin in the nearby **Berwick** parish church. The interior of the church is covered with wall paintings, commissioned by Bishop Bell of Chichester and executed during the Second World War. Opinions on the artistic merit of the paintings differ, but the church should certainly not be missed.

Fishbourne (1/2E) *see* Chichester

Fittleworth (1/4D) *see* Pulborough

Fletching (2/4C)

A pretty village west of Uckfield in an area with many real and supposed historical associations. Riot, revel and rebellion have marked the history of tiny Fletching. During the last century, the tumultuous behaviour of the Bonfire Boys was viewed with wary apprehension by the

The Studio, Charleston Farmhouse

authorities. Today, the more riotous aspects of 5 November have given way to a colourful pageant that still attracts widespread local support on Bonfire Night. There was also once a popular May Day tradition in Fletching: young people would create fantastic maypoles out of the felled branches of oak trees from Sheffield Park and the most impressive would be chosen as the village maypole by Lord Sheffield.

In 1264 Simon de Montfort's men camped on Fletching Common before the Battle of LEWES. Legend has it that the fallen knights were later buried in Fletching churchyard, still encased in their battle armour. Two centuries later, the routed remnants of Jack Cade's rebellion sought refuge here. One of Cade's associates, Peter Denot, is commemorated by a small brass in the church. Denot was a glove maker by trade, which is evident from the illustration on the brass. The church of St Mary and St Andrew is Norman in origin. The mausoleum in the north transept, dedicated to the Sheffield family, was added in the 18th century. Also buried in the church is Edward Gibbon, author of the renowned *Decline and Fall of the Roman Empire*.

To the north of the village is **Sheffield Park,** which is the starting point for the famous Bluebell Railway, and the site of Sheffield Park Garden, owned by the National Trust. The 100 acres of gardens, including five lakes, were laid out in the 18th century by Capability Brown. The house, which is privately owned and not open to the public, was built in about 1779 by James Wyatt for John Baker Holroyd, first Earl of Sheffield.

The skull of 'Piltdown Man' was discovered at the adjoining hamlet of Piltdown in 1912 and was for many years believed to represent the 'missing link' between man and the apes. In the 1950s the remains were proved to be nothing more than a crude forgery. The perpetrators of the hoax have never been identified, but rumours abound. These range from accusations that Sir Arthur Conan Doyle was invovled in a prank to cock a snook at the scientific establishment, to claims that the whole episode was the creation of a fundamentalist Christian preacher who wished to discredit the theory of evolution. The most likely explanation is that the discoverer of the skull, a Lewes solicitor and geologist called Charles Dawson, was himself the author of this rather clumsy deception.

Fontwell (1/3E) *see* Slindon

Church of St Mary, Friston

Ford (1/4E) *see* Littlehampton

Forest Row (2/4B) *see* Ashdown Forest

Frant (3/1B)

On the border between Sussex and Kent, due south of Tunbridge Wells, Frant was once a centre of the iron-making industry. The iron industry once dominated the High Weald of Sussex, although it was extinct by the time the parish church of St Alban was built at Frant in 1819–22. Nevertheless, some of the glazing bars and the central pillars supporting the roof of the nave are made of cast iron. The church features a fine gallery, supported on thin iron shafts and an alabaster pulpit and reading desk. In the churchyard is an imposing memorial to Lord Stratford de Redcliffe who, as Sir Stratford Canning, made his reputation as a diplomat in the 19th century. While serving as ambassador to Turkey he arranged for ancient Assyrian sculptures, discovered by the archaeologist Layand, to be shipped to London and the British Museum. Shernfold Park house, rebuilt during the last century, was once the home of Colonel John By who founded Bytown in Canada, later renamed Ottawa.

Close to Frant is the charming hamlet of **Bell's Yew Green**, clustering round the friendly Brecknock Arms. Also nearby is **Bayham Abbey**, regarded by many as the most impressive monastic ruin in Sussex. On the county boundary, five miles south-east of Tunbridge Wells, Bayham was a considerable monastery, established in the early 13th century. Much remains to be seen and the ruins, now in the care of English Heritage, may be visited between Easter and the end of September.

Friston (2/5F)

A small village on the coast between Seaford and Eastbourne, dominated by Friston Forest. The forest originally comprised deciduous trees; the more recently planted conifers are a profitable addition of modern times. During the 15th century the remnants of Jack Cade's peasant army sought refuge in the woods. Today the footpaths through the Forest, past the prehistoric Long Barrow and tumuli north of Snap Hill and up to the Lullington Heath National Nature Reserve, offer visitors excellent scenic walks.

Friston village itself now merges with EAST DEAN and has lost some of its individuality as a result. The church of St Mary has a small, roundheaded window above its southern doorway which is believed to be early Norman in origin, or even Saxon. One of Friston's most distinguished residents was the composer Frank Bridge, who died here in 1941 and is buried in the churchyard. Friston Place was built in about 1650, although the timber-framing of a much earlier building is still visible. The old barn, with mullioned windows, is of a similar date.

There are good walks from Friston, either north around the Forest or south through the Crowlink valley and over the rolling cliffs of the Seven Sisters to EXCEAT.

Fulking (2/2D) *see* Devil's Dyke

Gatwick Airport (2/2A) *see* Crawley

Glynde (2/4E)

East of Lewes, with its own railway station, and famous for opera at nearby Glyndebourne. Mount Caburn, the great chalk outcrop, watches over Glynde. As its name implies, it has steeper slopes than most Sussex hills and almost looks as if it were man made. Although this is not the case, Caburn is associated with ancient habitation. Stone Age man made his home here and the site was fortified in the Iron Age, giving the village its name, which comes from *gline*, meaning 'a fenced enclosure'. During Roman times corn was exported from Glynde to the Continent and to other parts of Britain; a Roman road ran north to London.

The cottages in the village are of a style typical of mid-Sussex and few places possess such a large number of well-preserved examples. The church, however, is quite different and very unusual. It was built in 1763 in the Palladian style. The wall coverings and rich fittings of the interior are perhaps more reminiscent of a Baroque chapel or even a synagogue than an English parish church. Buried in the churchyard is John Ellman, who perfected the famous Southdown breed of sheep. The Southdown was famous for its ample proportions, high quality wool and well-kept appearance. It formed the basis of the breeding stock of Australia and New Zealand but in modern times has given way to the shaggy cross-bred, as the meat of the Southdown is rather too fatty for modern tastes. Furthermore the cross-bred is more economical, producing on average two lambs a year to the Southdown's one.

Glynde Place, next to the church, was built

for William Morley in the 1560s. During the Civil War, the Morleys were leaders of the Parliamentary cause in Sussex and Colonel Morley was joint governor of Arundel Castle following the successful seige under General Waller. In the 18th century Glynde Place became the residence of the Trevor family, one of whose members was Bishop of Durham. He it was who built the church. The association with the family is commemorated in the name of the village pub, The Trevor Arms. The house is now the home of Lord Hampden and may be visited on certain days during the summer.

At nearby Glyndebourne, the opera house was opened by John and Audrey Christie in 1934 and today enjoys an international reputation for the quality of the productions and the beauty of the surroundings in which they are presented. The summer season at Glyndebourne has become a British institution, opera goers travelling by train from London to enjoy the special atmosphere of this opera house in the country, with the traditional long intervals during which picnics are enjoyed in the grounds. Tickets for the main summer season are expensive and hard to come by, and many people prefer to visit in the autumn to enjoy performances by the touring company.

Goodwood (1/2E)

The famous 18th-century home of the Duke of Richmond and Gordon, set in a magnificent estate of 12,000 acres on the Downs north-east of Chichester. The name probably derives from the ownership of land in this area before the Norman Conquest by Godwin, Earl of Wessex and father of the future King Harold of England. But this part of the Downs had been a centre of human habitation for centuries before the Saxons arrived; Neolithic man established one of the four major Sussex hilltop settlements on The Trundle Hill. The camp on The Trundle was later surrounded by the massive ramparts of an Iron Age hill fort and the site takes its name from its shape which is like a wheel.

The precise function of these settlements or enclosures is unclear. Possibly in earliest times they were used infrequently, in time of war or other danger, but at the time of the Roman invasion The Trundle was probably operating as a market centre, providing services for a wide area. With the development of the city of Chichester the settlement on the Downs declined in importance, but it was still used as an occasional place of public assembly as late as the 17th century, when a demonstration of farmers and labourers took place here during the Civil War.

Goodwood House began life as a modest brick house built in 1720. In the late 18th century the house was substantially remodelled for the third Duke by the architect James Wyatt. Wyatt was instructed to build entirely in flint because it was the material most easily available locally. Opinions on the result vary. Some point to the craftsmanship displayed in knapping and shaping the flints, others find the overall effect, unrelieved by dressings of brick or stone, monotonous and unappealing in so large a building. It remains true that when Goodwood

was first built it set a considerable trend and a number of large houses were built of flint in the area in the next 20-30 years.

The technique of flint working can perhaps best be seen in the lodge gates on the northern boundary of the park which bear the date 1794. Also of note are the slightly earlier stables, by Sir William Chambers, where the knapped and squared flints are contrasted with limestone dressings.

The estate originally included a substantial deer park, although much of the land is now farmed. Goodwood Racecourse was laid out in 1801 by the third Duke and the first grandstand built in 1830. The coming of the railway to

Palladian church at Glynde

SINGLETON on the Chichester to Midhurst line confirmed the popularity of the course with all sections of society and 'Glorious Goodwood' in July has remained a feature of the English summer season ever since. A new grandstand was built in 1980 and there are now six Flat meetings a year with racing on 15 days. With panoramic views from the racecourse and The Trundle, a 60-acre country park, children's playground, motor circuit, airfield and golf course, Goodwood has something for everyone.

North of Goodwood, in the valley of the River Lavant, is the small and churchless hamlet of

Sussex Downs viewed from The Trundle near Goodwood

Charlton, famous for its hunt. Charlton is a common English place name, meaning 'the farmstead of the churls or free peasants'. The settlement grew up in the lush meadows of the Lavant, a winterbourne stream which flows only when the water in the underground aquifer below the chalk reaches a certain level.

The possession of Earl Godwin before the Norman Conquest, the settlements in the Lavant valley passed to the Fitzalans, Earls of Arundel, and then in 1730 to the Duke of Richmond. Under the Dukes of Richmond, Charlton became the home of the most famous hunt in England. In 1730 Fox Hall was built as a hunting lodge for Goodwood by the 2nd Duke and, by the 1740s, more than 150 hunters were stabled in or near Charlton. The finest hour of the Charlton Hunt was the run of 26 January 1738 when, after a chase lasting ten hours, the quarry was killed in Arundel Park. Today, Charlton's associations with hunting are marked by the memorial in SINGLETON church to the huntsman, Thomas Johnson, and by the name of the village pub: The Fox Goes Free.

It was in The Fox that the first Women's Institute meeting in England took place on 9 November 1915. Fox Hall has been restored by The Landmark Trust and can be rented for weekends and holidays.

South-west of Goodwood, on the road from Chichester to Petworth, is **Halnaker**, a village with a famous windmill on the skyline. The strange name of the village may signify half a strip of cultivated land – in the 17th century it was known as 'Half Naked'. In the garden of Little Halnaker, just north of the village, are the ruins of Halnaker House, an important medieval house originally built by the de Haye family, founders of BOXGROVE Priory. Like COWDRAY, Halnaker House was substantially remodelled in the 16th century and, again like Cowdray, it became ruined around 1800. Halnaker became redundant when Goodwood House was built and all that now remains are a few walls. The present Halnaker House was designed by Sir Edwin Lutyens and built in 1938.

On Halnaker Hill above the village stands the brick tower mill known as Halnaker Windmill. Built about 1750, the mill is in a simple, vernacular style which contrasts with the elegance and relative sophistication of some later windmills, products of the Industrial Revolution. The present mill ceased grinding in 1900 and the structure has been restored by the County Council as a landmark feature. Hilaire Belloc chose *Ha'nacker Mill* (for thus it is pronounced) as the title of one of his Sussex poems and the mill, standing up on the hill with its white sails gleaming, remains a much-loved landmark.

Nearer Chichester is the small settlement of **Westhampnett**. Both Westhampnett and Halnaker were on Stane Street, the Roman road from Chichester to London. From the East Gate of Chichester, the road ran over Halnaker Hill to Pulborough, where it crossed the River Arun. It then ran on a long alignment to Leith Hill, near Dorking, and north through Streatham to London, entering the city by Billingsgate. The modern A29 road between Pulborough and Billingshurst follows the line of the Roman road and a surviving section can be walked from Eartham to Bignor Hill. The parish church at Westhampnett was founded in the 8th century and the present building contains fragments of material taken from the ruins of Roman Chichester.

Old Schoolhouse, Westhampnett

Between Westhampnett and Halnaker is **Strettington**, whose name also derives from its location on the Roman road.

Goring by Sea (1/5E) *see* Worthing

Graffham (1/3D)

A straggling village south-east of Midhurst, between the sandy heaths of the western Rother valley and the scarp face of the Downs, with some pretty cottages and an over-restored parish church. There is a group of Bronz Age barrows on Graffham Down, indicating the presence of early man in the area. The barrows can easily be visited from the South Downs Way and are well worth the short detour. More recently, Graffham Down was in the news when it was featured in Marion Shoard's book *The Theft of the Countryside* (1980) as an example of traditional Downland turf being ploughed up to grow more crops. When the Saxons colonised the Weald, the village grew up in a wood or grove below the Downs (*graf ham* meaning: 'grove settlement'). In the 16th century a glass furnace was operating in the area, no doubt making use of the deposits of sand on Graffham and Lavington Commons.

South Harting seen from Harting Hill on the South Downs

Early in the 19th century, John Sergeant became Rector of Graffham and **Woolavington**. He and his wife had four beautiful daughters – Emily, Mary, Caroline and Sophia – all of whom married clergymen. Emily married Samuel Wilberforce ('Soapy Sam') of Lavington Park, the son of the anti-slavery campaigner. Samuel became Bishop of Oxford and then of Winchester before succeeding his father as lord of the manor. Lavington Park is now a school (Seaford College) and the building which was once the parish church of Woolavington is the school chapel. Graffham is the home of the Lavington Stud and there are good walks and rides on the Downs and over Lavington Common to the north, owned by the National Trust.

Great Dixter (3/4C) *see* Northiam

Hailsham (3/1E)

A small town north of Eastbourne on the A2021, bounded on the west by woodland and on the east by low-lying water meadows. Apart from the 15th-century church and 18th-century manor house, the town has little to commend it. However, some of the shops are of considerable age: some years ago, murals were found beneath the plaster work of an ironmonger's shop in the High Street. The paintings appeared to be Tudor, if not older, and carried a hand-written verse by the artist:

> The Peace of God, a quiet life,
> A content mind, a good report,
> A friend in store, what need a man with any more?

Until this century, Hailsham was famous throughout Sussex as the 'string town', due to its twine-making industry. From the finest string to the toughest rope, all kinds were produced at Hailsham, including the special cord commissioned by the Home Office for the exclusive use of the official hangman.

North of Hailsham is the village of **Hellingly**. The parish church of St Peter and St Paul stands on an old Saxon earthwork and it seems reasonable to assume that a far older building than the present late Norman church once stood on this site. Horselunges Manor, built in the early 16th century and restored in the 1920s by W. H. Godfrey of Lewes, is one of the best timber-framed buildings in the county. **Lower Horsebridge**, a hamlet in Hellingly parish, is associated with a grim historical tale from the 16th century. It was common practice for the young squire, Lord Dacre, to go hunting with the local village men. One night, after a heavy drinking session, Dacre and a group of friends went on a drunken rampage through the woods, hunting any animal that came in sight. When challenged by the gamekeeper a fight ensued and the keeper was killed. Three of Dacre's men were hanged for the murder and Dacre himself was tried by his fellow peers. He too was found guilty and hanged, a form of execution usually reserved for the lower classes. It is not recorded whether the rope used was made at Hailsham.

South-west of Hailsham, on the far side of the woods which lie on that side of the town, is **Arlington.** The parish church of St Pancras is believed once to have been linked with the Priory at Lewes, which had the same dedication. What is of interest is the variety of architectural styles, from Saxon onwards. Evidence of Roman tiles has been discovered and it seems likely that a church of some description stood on this spot before the Saxon chieftain Eorla, after whom the village may be named, established a farmstead here. Abbot's Wood, which is owned by the Forestry Commission, offers some pleasant walks including properly signposted nature trails.

Handcross (2/2C) *see* Cuckfield

Hardham (1/4D) *see* Pulborough

Halnaker (1/3E) *see* Goodwood

Hartings, The (1/1D)

South Harting is a classic Downland village close to the Hampshire border, with a broad High Street and many good houses. The three settlements of East, West and South Harting are distinguished quite early in their history, indicating that the early pioneers spread out over a large area. By the time of Domesday, Harting was one of the largest manors in the county, owned by Roger de Montgomery, lord of Arundel and Chichester. The setting of South Harting is perhaps best appreciated from the car park and picnic site on Harting Hill, which provides access to the South Downs Way from the Chichester to Petersfield road. From here, the composition is dominated by the elegant parish church of St Mary and St Gabriel with its distinctive green spire. Inside, the church contains some interesting memorials, including one to Sir Henry Fetherstonhaugh and other residents of UPPARK, the fine 17th-century house above the village on the road to Emsworth. In the churchyard are stocks, a whipping post and a

Roadside signpost in Treyford

war memorial by Eric Gill.

Distinguished residents of South Harting include the naturalist Gilbert White and the novelist Anthony Trollope, who lived here for the last two years of his life, during which time he wrote four novels.

Surrounded by first class walking and riding country, Harting is an ideal base from which to explore the South Downs; fresh opportunities are provided by the proposed extension of the South Downs Ways westwards to Winchester and by the purchase of Harting Down by the National Trust.

A mile or two east of Harting is the flint-walled village of **Elsted.** The village may take its name from Aella, first King of the South Saxons, who invaded Sussex with his sons in the 5th century. Fierce fighters though they were, it took the Saxons several years to drive the Britons out of the territory which was to become Sussex. Aella died in 516 and was succeeded by his son, Cissa, founder of modern Chichester. Today Elsted is a tranquil place, distinguished by its flint walls and attractive houses.

Near by is the downland village of **Treyford** and on Monkton Down above are six round barrows in a line known as The Devil's Jumps; such ancient burial places were often associated in folklore with magical and even sinister activities. The barrows, which are looked after by The Society of Sussex Downsmen, are accessible by means of a stiff climb from The Royal Oak pub at Hooksway, off the road from Chichester to Harting.

Sussex by the Sea

JOHN K. WALTON

Half a century ago the poet and controversialist Hilaire Belloc despaired of the Sussex coast. It had, he thought, become an alien encampment, cut off from the rest of the county, its history and traditions. There was no longer any point in trying to understand Sussex by following its shoreline:

> To-day it would be wasting time, for you would not find Sussex there any more, but only a dreary and heart-breaking procession of villas and boarding-houses, and esplanades and tin bungalows, interrupted by intervals of tufted grass growing rank upon deserted sandhills. It is but a string of London outposts all the way from Selsea to Rye save where the chalk cliffs by Beachy and the sand cliffs of Fairlight interrupt the line for a few miles.

Belloc was a Sussex patriot. His attachment was rooted in an idealised vision of an ancient Sussex landscape and countryside. He had no time for the 'exotic' new towns with their imported inhabitants, accents and building materials. But he saw no way of stopping their continuing spread.

Belloc was blind to many of the good things about this long and varied coastline and unduly pessimistic about its future. Fifty years on, the Downs still undulate to the sea between Seaford and Eastbourne, unsullied by the speculative builder who inspired such dread between the two World Wars. You can still tramp through the waving salty grasses of Chichester Harbour's deeply indented shore for mile after mile, with only the sea-birds and summer butterflies for company, except where the amateur yachtsmen have colonised the harbours and havens. Belloc admitted in 1936 that Bosham 'is still the ancient harbour and village which its history demands that it should be'; and it has kept its green, its mill, its Anglo-Saxon church tower, its tales of King Canute and its vernacular houses. Today's village is not Belloc's Bosham: it is too well manicured, insufficiently workaday and taken over by outsiders. But at least he would recognise it.

The forty miles of urban seaside offer contrasting delights of their own. There are medieval fishing quarters and old harbours, while seaside terraces and crescents chart a path from Georgian politeness through Regency frivolity and heavy Victorian respectability to turn-of-the-century exuberance. Even the surviving 'tin bungalows' of the early 20th century can display their own bohemian charm. Most of what we see has emerged in the last two and a half centuries, since the cult of sea bathing began to transform a remote and impoverished coast whose mid-18th-century inhabitants had scraped an unsatisfactory living from farming, fishing and smuggling.

These momentous changes began towards the middle of the eighteenth century, in an obscure little town called Brighthelmstone; but they soon erupted at other points along the coast and new resorts were still appearing throughout Victoria's reign and even in the inter-war years. Brighton itself soon left all rivals far behind. During the first half of the 19th century it was the only resort to grow in step with the great industrial towns, so that by 1851 it was nearly three times the size of its nearest rival. By now Hove, next door, was making its own contribution to a 'Greater Brighton' whose growth continued uninterrupted into the new century. But the second rank of Sussex resorts competed strongly against all comers elsewhere as first Hastings, then in turn Worthing, Eastbourne, Bexhill and in the 1920s Worthing again took up the running. In 1881 Sussex had England's two most populous resorts and three more in the top thirty; by 1911 it had six in the top two dozen. And this was before the building spree of the 1920s and 30s, when a tide of bungalows engulfed deserted shores and sleepy villages and threatened the Downs themselves. There was something special about the Sussex coast; and especially Brighton.

The first sea bathing visitors to Brighton found lodgings in the narrow streets of the old fishing port, and in the 1740s and 50s the locals began to rescue their town from poverty and decay by adapting and improving the buildings there. From these small beginnings, unpretentious terraces spread piecemeal through the open fields which surrounded the town, following the narrow strips of land which had belonged to individual farmers.

Similar things were happening elsewere. Brighton gained an extra boost from the writings of Dr Russell, the founder of its fashionable reputation for sea bathing. But the crucial advantage came from the sustained patronage of the Prince of Wales, later George IV, from 1783 onwards. His fashionable and raffish alternative

Royal Pavilion, Brighton

court created a snowballing demand for really opulent accommodation, which bore fruit in the early 19th century in the palatial seafront terraces to the east and west of the old town. The King's fantastic Indian and Gothic Marine Pavilion has proved an endearing and enduring attraction although its onion domes, scalloped arches, dragons and serpents went out of fashion for many years after his death. When Queen Victoria abandoned it in 1847 it was bought and saved by the Town Commissioners only after a fierce debate and the closest of votes.

Later developments sustained Brighton's distinctive blend of frivolity and affluence. At the turn of the century the Metropole Hotel became the weekend haunt of the ostentatiously rich, as sporting peers and pioneer motorists entertained stars of music-hall and musical comedy. The 'fast', dissolute lifestyle of the Prince of Wales and his friends became an enduring theme in Brighton's social life.

Fashionable Brighton mingled, gossiped and intrigued in the coffee houses, assembly rooms and circulating libraries of the late 18th and early 19th centuries. From 1823 onwards additional meeting places were provided by the piers. The Chain Pier of that year, gracefully constructed on the lines of a suspension bridge, survived until 1896; it was joined in 1866 by the West Pier, a larger and more conventional concern which became famous for its sideshows. It lives on in decaying splendour, as desperate efforts are made to restore its rotting ironwork and crumbling superstructure. But Brighton's third pier, the Palace Pier of 1899, still flourishes in all its raffish glory. Where the West Pier had performing fleas, the Palace acquired a daring collection of 'What-the-butler-saw' machines. With its gilding, filigree and onion domes it is often praised as the most elaborate and exciting of Britain's surviving seaside piers.

The West and Palace Piers were also magnets for trippers in the summer, for the arrival of the railway in 1841 turned central Brighton into a working class playground during the excursion season. The beach became invaded with minstrels, performing animals, ventriloquists and assorted musical turns, as well as vendors of everything from gingerbread to oysters. There was also a succession of more ambitious novelties. 1872 saw the opening of the Aquarium, with its mysterious subterranean tanks of elusive and strangely-shaped sea creatures. A few years later, in 1883, the neat little carriages of Magnus Volk's pioneering electric railway began to trundle along the sea-front. It survived an early embarrassment, when the combined weight of a ceremonial party of gargantuan aldermen proved too much for the

Palace Pier, Brighton

springs and brought the proceedings to a grinding halt; and it is with us still. Sadly the extension to Rottingdean which used carriages on stilts to keep the tide at arm's length for the journey along the foreshore, was short-lived: it was a wonderful piece of seaside eccentricity, known affectionately as 'Daddy-long-legs'.

At the root of Brighton's enduring success is the capacity to be many things to many people, combining the raffish, the respectable and the refined. Much the same applies to Hastings, Brighton's earliest Sussex rival. Like Brighton, it was an ailing fishing port; and it began to acquire the trappings of a resort in the 1770s. Just as Brighton's more sedate visitors and residents were able, from the 1830s, to take refuge in the carefully-policed respectability of Hove, so the planned villas and formal terraces of Decimus Burton's St Leonard's gave a similar choice to the snootier of Hastings's patrons. The American novelist Henry James, visiting Hastings in 1879, found it 'very grey and sober and English'. He concluded:

> If I were a quiet old lady of modest income and nice habits . . . I should certainly go to Hastings. There, amid the shops and the little libraries, the bath-chairs and the German bands, the Parade and the long Pier, with a mild climate, a moderate scale of prices and the consciousness of a high civilisation, I should enjoy a seclusion which would have nothing primitive or crude.

This was actually profoundly misleading. James went to Hastings in the winter and missed out on the Cockney *bonhomie* of the summer excursion season, when thousands of Londoners took advantage of cheap temperance outing tickets to get drunk at the seaside. He also neglected the delights of the old town and fishing quarter. At the east end of the seafront, where the drawn-up fishing boats meet the funfair, are the distinctive Net Stores, tarred and weatherboarded, in sharp geometrical shapes clustering in compositions to form a photographer's dream. Around them is an enjoyable sprawl of fishermen's sheds and tackle and through all this runs a miniature railway, extending from the fairground. You can buy fish here and in 1988 the Old Town Fish Palace was bang up to date with new holiday trends, offering 'Fresh Fish and Turkish Kebabs' to the day-trippers.

To the west lie more eccentricities. Pelham Crescent, dating from 1824–8, is one: an upward-curving composition nestling below a cliff, with a church in the middle and an arcade of shops below. The pier is a delight, staggering out on its spindly legs and seeming about to collapse under the weight of its buildings. The White Rock Theatre and Palace Chambers are also endearing, with their strange curves and unexpected embellishments. And the Cask and Kettle pub offers lively vignettes of Hastings's medieval and military history in a vivid sequence of tile murals from the turn of the century, reinforcing the feeling that the town's sense of its past is alive, spontaneous and fun.

Emergent resorts were also unfurling tentative new shoots to the west of Brighton in the late 18th century. Most confident were Worthing and the future Bognor Regis. Worthing became a refuge for those who found the Prince Regent's Brighton too expensive and too dissolute. It soon outgrew the limited accommodation provided by its first two innkeepers, Messrs. Hogsflesh and Bacon, and from its earliest days it had a reputation for friendly, companionable informality, with beach cricket and pony races. Even now, when Worthing is full of the denizens of sixty years of Southern Electric commuter semis and a similar span of retirement bungalows, the pier and surrounding seafront can buzz with gossip and shared reminiscences.

Worthing has kept some delightful corners, despite several postwar planning disasters. My favourites are Park Crescent, which nestles behind an absurd triumphal arch supported by coarsely-carved bearded figures and looks out on a wilderness of sycamores and horse-chestnuts; and the seafront juxtaposition of Pier and Lido. The former is an early example of 1862, with various subsequent domed and streamlined embellishments; the latter has a neat little classical pavilion, yellow and white walkways and tea dances. And there are several leafy cottagy corners, in flint or brick or stucco, which repay the effort of discovery.

Bognor is a much more private place. It was originally promoted in the late 1780s as Hothampton, the speculation of a London hatter and overseas merchant who became M.P. for Southwark and tried to establish an exclusive and aristocratic resort on his seaside estate. The remains of the original resort survive, a few minutes from the town centre. Hothampton Crescent is an extravaganza in red, grey and yellow brick, displaying its promoter's borrowed coat of arms and created in the unavailing hope of royal patronage. But the surroundings began to go down market with the arrival of Billy Butlin's funfair in the early 1930s and – after bitter controversy – his holiday camp in 1958. The camp survives, recently refurbished with an amusements centre resembling a cross between a D.I.Y. superstore and a chemical works. Facing it stands the last Edwardian bastion of the Bognor

Net drying huts on the beach at Hastings

43 Riverside Road, Shoreham Beach

B.&B. landlady and a blue ogee-capped shelter with wrought-iron waterleaf capitals which now contains 'The Magic Roundabout'.

Bognor soon becomes less plebeian as you head west past the pier; and the detached designer houses of Aldwick, with their private sea frontages, are inhospitable to the outsider. The Bognor of 1799 was described as 'desolate', because its superior visitors were too proud and aloof to mix with each other; and at this end of town very little seems to have changed. Only the exuberant façade of the Royal Norfolk Hotel, with its stucco, pediments and croquet lawn, lends any enchantment and the town as a whole still suffers from a prevailing preference for private spaces rather than public places.

The third new Georgian resort of West Sussex was Littlehampton. This old-established port began its new career in 1775, when a London coffee-house proprietor built the Beach Coffee House and Assembly Rooms on the common. Its successor, an endearing sprawl of gables, dormers, red tiles and pinkwashed timbering is still at the core of the resort's seafront; and the breezy common finds room for open grassland as well as park, kiosks and funfair. On the landward side a hundred yards of terraced housing provides a potted history of south coast resort architecture: Georgian brick, Victorian stucco and wash, assorted bays, balconies and dormers, adding up to a riot of rhythms, colours and textures. But despite the rather half-hearted patronage of the Dukes of Norfolk at nearby Arundel, Littlehampton never managed to match its neighbours as a resort.

Eastbourne, on the other hand, shows what could be done by a determined ducal patron. From the middle of the 19th century the Dukes of Devonshire and their agents presided over the conversion of a fishing village into 'the Empress of Watering-Places'; the seventh and eighth Dukes are commemorated by idiosyncratic statues in the seafront gardens. Above all, Eastbourne is a town of public gardens and expansive open spaces, of palatial hotels and substantial villas, of the comfortable Victorian and Edwardian middle classes in their leafy splendour. The Corporation inherited this ethos from the Dukes and has perpetuated it. A relic of earlier times is the engaging Martello Tower, the Wish Tower, looking like a child's sand-castle transplanted from the beach. It houses the Coastal Defence Museum, and this link between Napoleon's and Hitler's wars is a reminder of the historic front-line status of this coast. So are the successive fortifications of Pevensey Castle, from the Romans through William the Conqueror (whose invasion force landed hereabouts) to a concrete emplacement of 1940. Pevensey lies a few miles east of Eastbourne, among marshes and an outcrop of bungalows.

Beyond Pevensey is Bexhill, another late developer among the Sussex resorts. The exuberant stretch of promenade which runs eastward from the De La Warr Pavilion has kept its original turn-of-the-century character, rather South Kensington on Sea, featuring red brick with stone facings, Dutch gables, Moorish onion domes and Venetian arches. The Marina, on the seaward side of the esplanade, is an especially attractive complex of bungalows, chalets and arcades, with oriental motifs on chimneys and doorways. The De La Warr Pavilion itself is even more exotic. Its sweeping streamlined curves, as they follow the shoreline and draw in the sunshine, make a complete contrast with the faceless flats to the left and the Victorian and Edwardian fantasia to the right. This alone is worth the journey.

Bexhill, like most Sussex resorts, has kept the cottagy core of its original village, huddled defensively around the church. Survivals like this are rightly cherished. But there are other kinds of coastal settlement, equally spontaneous in their origins, which also deserve to be highlighted. These are the 'bungalow towns' which grew up at various points on the Sussex coast between the 1880s and the 1930s. They responded to a need for cheap, informal weekend cottages and holiday homes, free from the restrictions imposed by hoteliers, landladies and local authorities. Many of the early 'bungalows' were based on old railway carriages and tramcar bodies and they grew by accretion, using a range of cheap building materials. War was waged upon them by local authorities and defenders of unspoiled countryside and many were destroyed during the Second World War, or subsequently sanitised and tidied up. But some survivals convey the original makeshift, bohemian flavour. At Pagham, west of Bognor, there are two fascinating streets between the mud and waterfowl of Pagham Harbour and the shingle of the shore. Many of the dwellings have the rows of tiny oblong windows associated with mid-Victorian third class railway carriages and some display the legend 'Smoking' on the glass. In striking contrast, some owners have recently added Spanish hacienda-style arcades, with names like 'Sol y Mar' and 'Alhambra'.

There are similar survivals at New Shoreham, where ancient railway carriages were originally hauled across the Adur estuary to Shoreham Beach at low tide. One house in Old Fort Road celebrates its origins with a display of varnished wooden panelling bearing the legend 'L.B.S.C.R.' (London, Brighton and South Coast Railway), although it has also acquired a gable and a small tower. There are others; but best of all is the array of sea-going houseboats moored along the estuary: assorted barges and minesweepers, exotically decorated, with New Shoreham's Norman church as a backdrop. Nearby Riverside Road contains a dwelling with a conventional gate, drive, garage and rockery; but the 'house' is a two-masted sailing vessel, neatly moored with its prow to the shore.

After these oddities the larger bungalow settlement at Peacehaven, between Brighton and Newhaven, is an anti-climax. Its promoter promised health and independence to returning First World War veterans and its critics savaged the untidy inroads it made into clifftop downlands; but planners have tidied it into something more innocuous and less interesting than its raw beginnings threatened. The hate campaign against Peacehaven expressed a growing protective attachment to downland scenery between the wars, fuelled by the writings of Kipling, Belloc and others. The Sussex downs became sacred, an emblem of ancient Englishness and a wartime symbol of 'what we are fighting for'. Developers here came to seem greedily unpatriotic. This frame of mind saved Cissbury Hill, near Worthing, purchased by public subscription to save it from speculative building. It also protected the cliffs and downland between Seaford and Eastbourne, including Beachy Head. This airy switchback walk can still instil peace, solitude and a sense of communing with ancient mysteries. It also links the Victorian decay of Seaford's seafront with the garden city prosperity of Eastbourne, reminding us that there are many 'Sussexes by the Sea', with something, somewhere, for everyone to enjoy. Most happily of all, it offers proof that Hilaire Belloc was wrong about the fate of the Sussex coast, in more ways than one; and we are all the richer for that.

29 Old Fort Road, Shoreham Beach

Previous page: Hastings viewed from the Castle

Hastings (3/4E)
Founded by the Saxons and made famous by the Normans, Hastings combines faded Victorian elegance with the old-world charm of the eastern quarter, where the traditional fishing industry still retains a high profile. Sussex and Kent were two of the original seven kingdoms of Saxon England. Yet for several centuries, straddling the borders of the two counties, was an autonomous region centred around Hastings. Founded by a separate group of Saxons known as the Haestingas, the Hastings enclave lived in peaceful co-existence with its neighbours, in stark contrast to the bloody conflicts that broke out in other parts of the country.

The Norman Conquest of 1066 changed the political landscape for ever. Gone were the old tribal divisions and in their place was installed the nationwide feudal system of medieval England (see *The Norman Heritage*, p. 28). The ruined castle which still dominates Hastings was the first stone structure built by the Normans after their invasion and for many years its French occupants kept a watchful eye on a resentful population from the safety of their formidable battlements. The visitor who is forced to pause for breath while climbing the steep lane that leads to the castle will doubtless appreciate the invulnerability of such a stronghold to a local uprising.

The tradition of separateness from and antagonism towards the French continued for many centuries. During the Hundred Years War, French raiding parties and foreign pirates regularly attacked and plundered Hastings. After one terrible raid, the town was left a smouldering ruin and the homeless and embittered townsfolk had to rebuild it. During the Tudor period the sea proved an even greater enemy. Several times ferocious gales caused severe flooding and yet again much of Hastings was destroyed: in fact, the old Elizabethan harbour now lies beneath the modern shopping development in the town centre. Once again in the 17th century war came to Hastings: French and Dutch vessels were engaged in skirmishes with fishermen off the shore, with casualities on both sides. After a raid in 1691 a cannon ball was lodged in the tower of St Clement's church, where it remains to this day.

It was in the 18th century that the Hastings fishermen earned their notorious nickname of 'Chop-backs'. A group of them had boarded a Dutch merchant ship and, in return for its safe passage, they demanded a payment in the form of some of the ship's cargo. Initially the captain of the ship agreed, but later he went back on his word and fired on the fishermen, several of whom were wounded while trying to flee. In revenge, the entire Hastings fishing fleet set sail and recaptured the Dutch vessel. The captain was tied between two posts and cut open with an axe down the length of his spine, a traditional punishment for treachery. Until the end of the last century, 5 November was celebrated in Hastings in riotous style, townspeople dressed up in elaborate costumes, including Viking-style headgear, and burning tar barrels were rolled through the streets. The Fishermen's Museum is situated in Rock-a-Nore Road, where the tall fishermen's huts, used for drying nets, still dominate the skyline.

The Old Town is reached via George Street and is centred round the High Street. George Street itself is now largely Victorian or modern, but numbers 10, 15 and 16 are older, the first being the site of the old market. In the High Street several timber-framed Jacobean buildings remain, including Judges cake shop, founded in the middle of the last century by the Hastings family of that name. Opposite The Nelson pub, still a favourite haunt of the local fishermen, is The Old Hastings Club which has been in existence for nearly 200 years. The seafront at Hastings dates from the 1820s, when the town was developed as a seaside resort; most of the architecture is the work of Joseph Kay, James Burton and his son, Decimus. The most important architectural composition on the sea front is Pelham Crescent, developed by the 1st Earl of Chichester in the 1820s and recently comprehensively restored with the assistance of English Heritage.

Visitors should make a point of seeing The Hastings Embroidery, a modern Bayeux Tapestry created to mark the 900th anniversary of the Norman Conquest. The embroidery, which is 240 ft long, depicts scenes from English history and is on display at the Town Hall in Queens Road. Also open to the public are the famous St Clement's Caves, near the castle. Although these are very old in origin, they were greatly extended during the last century by a local eccentric. There is a strong local tradition – sadly unsubstantiated – that the caves were used for smuggling.

Hastings has a delightful Victorian pier, built in 1872, a good beach for bathing and exploring rock pools and an interesting museum of local history in the old Town Hall in the High Street.

Just over a mile west of Hastings is **St Leonard's**, which takes its name from St Leonard, patron saint of prisoners. The area was laid out in the 1830s by James Burton, in imitation of Brighton. The centrepiece of the development is all stuccoed brick and focuses on what is now the Royal Victoria Hotel. The town plan implemented by Burton features long, symmetrical colonnades flanking the central axis, while much of the architectural design is on Classical lines. The Masonic Hall is the central feature of the new town; the south elevation is based very closely on a Greek Doric temple. The pyramid in the graveyard in West Hill Road is the Burton family memorial and there is a monument to James Burton in St Leonard's Gardens. The new town also features buildings based on, among others, Gothic and Scottish baronial styles. A scholarly guide to this most interesting area entitled *A Walk Round Burtons' St Leonards* has been produced by the County Council and is available locally or from the County Hall, Lewes.

Haywards Heath (2/3C)

An undistinguished dormitory town on the London to Brighton railway line. The area was open, wild heathland, the haunt of highwaymen until the refusal of LINDFIELD and CUCKFIELD to accommodate the railway forced the promoters to build the London to Brighton line across the heath in 1841. The common land was subsequently enclosed and the whole area built over. A reminder of the agricultural importance of the place is the cattle market, established in 1867 and still one of the largest in the South of England, helped no doubt by the town's favourable position at the centre of the county and with good road and rail communications. The growth of Haywards Heath in Victorian and Edwardian times was given further impetus by the electrification of the railway in 1933, providing a rapid and frequent commuter service to the capital.

Architecturally, the only part of the town that is of any interest is Muster Green, on the A272 to the west of the town centre. The name originates from the 17th century, when householders throughout the county were obliged to send men to an annual muster of militia. Now a tree-lined open space, Muster Green is surrounded by a number of good 19th-century houses and is a designated conservation area. Just off the Green is The Sergison Arms, which dates from the 16th century and takes its name from the local landowners who lived at Cuckfield Park. The pub may originally have been founded to serve the needs of visiting militia men. Another notable building is the 19th-century Holy Cross Convent, now converted into apartments.

Royal Victoria Hotel, St Leonard's

There are two important gardens in the area, Borde Hill on the B2036 and Heaselands on the A273 a mile south of the town, both of which are open to the public at certain times under the National Gardens Scheme.

Heathfield (2/5C)

Between Buxted and Burwash, developed originally as a market centre for the East Sussex Weald and expanded with the coming of the railway from Tunbridge Wells to Eastbourne.

The church of All Saints, in old Heathfield, has a 13th-century tower and a shingled spire. North-west of the church lies Heathfield Park, now a largely Victorian house but originally built in the 17th century. It was remodelled in 1766 for General Elliott, later made Lord Heathfield as the result of his defence of Gibraltar.

Detail of The Cat House, Henfield

A couple of miles west of Heathfield is Cross-in-Hand, where there is a windmill which was originally at Uckfield.

Hellingly (3/1D) *see* Hailsham

Henfield (2/2D)
A busy village on the A281 south of Cowfold, on the east side of the Adur valley. It consists of a bustling village street with many pleasant houses and gives every impression of being a lively and enterprising place. Situated about half-way between Brighton and Horsham, Henfield was an important staging post on the coach road to London: both The George Hotel and The White Hart are fine old coaching inns. The water meadows of the River Adur are near by, there is an extensive common to the south-east of the village and The Downs Link path follows the course of the old railway line south to Steyning and north to Christ's Hospital and Guildford.

There has been a community here since the 8th century, when a small church was built by a Saxon lord. In medieval times, the wooden church was replaced by one of Caen stone, brought across the Channel from Normandy and shipped up river to Henfield. After extensions in the 14th and 15th centuries the church remained substantially unaltered until a major Victorian restoration changed its character. A local resident at this time was Nathaniel Woodard, the great improver who founded the well-known group of public schools which, in Sussex, include LANCING, ARDINGLY and HURSTPIERPOINT Colleges and St Michael's, near PETWORTH. Woodard, who had previously served as curate at New SHOREHAM, lived in Henfield from 1862 to 1891, and a plaque on the wall near the front door in Church Street records his residence.

One of Woodard's more colourful neighbours was the local joiner, Bob Ward. Ward lived on Pinchnose Green, off Church Street, the site of the old village tannery. One day Woodard's cat caught and killed the joiner's pet canary. Insensed, the eccentric Ward embarked on a campaign against his neighbour which included installing a string of metal cats with bells and seashells around his cottage and jangling it loudly whenever Woodard walked by. Years later, the metal cats were recovered and attached to the walls of the cottage, giving the place its present name of The Cat House. There is a good collection of old agricultural implements, including some of joiner Ward's tools, in the Parish Museum in the village hall.

A mile south of the village on the A2037 is **Woods Mill**, the headquarters of The Sussex Wildlife Trust. The Trust, one of the most respected county naturalists' trusts in the country, is responsible for a number of important nature reserves throughout Sussex and has a distinguished record of scientific and practical work. Here at Woods Mill it owns an 18th-century water mill set in 15 acres of woodland, meadows and marsh. In the mill there is an accurate model of an oak tree, 25 ft tall, showing the life cycle of the most common tree in Sussex and the insect, animal and bird life which it supports. A popular activity in the grounds is pond dipping in the lake. Nets can be borrowed and help given in identifying 'catches'.

Herstmonceux (3/2D)
Famous for its castle and observatory, Herstmonceux is situated on the A271 east of Hailsham. Originally built in 1440, Herstmonceux Castle was one of the first brick buildings to be erected in England and also one of the largest. For many years it was the home of the Fiennes family. It later passed to the Hare family, whose members ranged from the eccentric to the downright mad. An 18th-century Hare was believed to have been in cahoots with smugglers and, to deter inquisitive visitors, concocted the legend of 'The Herstmonceux Drummer', a ghostly apparition some 9 ft tall, who would walk through the mists on a winter's night beating a doleful tattoo on his drum. During the 19th century the castle was the home of the writer and traveller Augustus Hare, whose long and anecdotal memoirs graphically illustrate the peculiar traits of the writer and his family. The building was beautifully restored by the Lewes architect W. H. Godfrey, in the 1930s.

Shortly after the Second World War the Royal Observatory moved from Greenwich to Herstmonceux, as the smog and bright lights of London were hampering their work there. The opening of the £1m Isaac Newton Telescope by Her Majesty The Queen in 1967 marked the heyday of the Observatory in Sussex: technological changes have forced it to move yet again, this time to Cambridge.

Hickstead (2/2C) *see* Bolney

Horsham (2/1B)

Second town of West Sussex and 'capital' of the Western Weald, much developed in recent years but retaining something of its market town flavour. The name of the town ('horse meadow') tells us a great deal about the origins of Horsham. The principal Saxon settlements in Sussex were on the coast, but as the settlers penetrated the Weald to the north they cleared the forest and established extra pasture to which they drove their animals in the spring and summer. Breeding stocks were developed in these remote areas, particularly horses, and many of the coastal manors maintained links with 'outliers', as they were called, in the Weald.

Horsham developed at the point where one of the drove roads from the coast crossed the river Arun and it had the added advantage that, in winter, horses could be moved to the sandy heaths of St Leonard's Forest, east of the town, avoiding the mud of the river valley. Horses and other stock were brought to market here and as pioneers began to cultivate the Wealden forest, they came to town to buy necessities and to sell their surplus produce. Under Norman rule, William de Braose established his principal headquarters at Bramber, but he maintained three subsidiary fortifications, including Knepp Castle, within 7 miles of Horsham, enabling the occupants to get to market for supplies and return within a day.

Horsham's position as a market town was consolidated during the medieval period. A twice weekly market was established, an annual fair licensed and, in the middle of the 12th century, William de Braose's son Philip provided a new, substantial church to meet the needs of the growing community. The first document recording Horsham as a borough is dated 1235 and notes that the townspeople could pay rent to the landlord in place of manual labour. In Horsham, the payment of rent to the lord and participation in the administration of the borough were associated with certain plots of land – the burgage plots – around the market place and the church.

Towards the end of the 13th century the burgesses of Horsham were summoned to send two representatives to Parliament and in 1306 the assizes came to the town for the first time. From then until 1830, Horsham acted, in turn with Lewes and Chichester, as the county assize town.

Assize weeks at Horsham were very popular and regularly attracted many visitors, in addition to the lawyers, litigants and witnesses who crowded into the town. Following the assizes, public executions sometimes took place at Horsham Common and on Broadbridge Heath. Other executions, sometimes in public, were held at the county gaol, which was considered a model for its day. Lewes Prison succeeded as county gaol in 1843. The last execution in England by pressing to death – of a man charged with murder and robbery who refused to plead – took place in front of the gaol in Queen Street in 1844. In addition to common criminals, the county gaol accommodated many members of the Society of Friends who were persecuted in the 17th century.

The houses of Horsham were principally timber-framed buildings with roofs of sandstone slabs. The beds of hard but fissile sandstone in the Wealden clay provided slabs for floors, pavements and field walls as well as for roofs, all known by the generic name of Horsham stone. The slabs are very heavy and demand massive support – rafters measuring 6 in by 5 in were not unknown. With such roofs a sagging ridge is the rule rather than the exception. A good example is number 30 The Causeway, without doubt the best street in the town, with a large number of Wealden buildings. The Horsham Museum occupies Causeway House, a large, timbered house at the town end of The Causeway. Rooms are devoted to local trades and industries, archaeology, geology and costume, and at the rear is a fine Sussex barn, moved from a local farm and used for special exhibitions and displays.

Other old buildings in the town, mainly concentrated in The Carfax and The Causeway, are the Town Hall (built by the Duke of Norfolk in 1812 and rebuilt except for the façade in 1888), the Manor House (now the national headquarters of the Royal Society for the Prevention of Cruelty to Animals), the King's Head Hotel reputed to date from 1410 with 18th-

School band playing at Christ's Hospital, Horsham

century additions and, towards the station, Park House (1720), carefully restored by the district council and used as their offices and meeting rooms. Horsham, with Exeter and Oxford, is one of the few English towns to have a Carfax (i.e. a crossroads) and here the central space has grown into a horseshoe-shaped street which features a good Victorian bandstand.

The Wealden mud kept Horsham relatively inaccessible for centuries, as the roads in the area were notoriously impassable. The coming of the railway meant great changes for the town, which found itself an important junction, with lines to London, Guildford, Shoreham and Chichester. The line from Guildford to Shoreham is now closed, providing an excellent long-distance walk known as The Downs Link (leaflet from County Hall, Chichester).

Good access to London and the Sussex countryside and coast has enabled Horsham to develop as a popular residential and commercial centre. Further development is planned, but the town's amenities already include good shops, three first class sports centres and the Horsham Arts Centre in Park Street which houses a theatre, cinema, studio and restaurant.

A couple of miles west of the town centre is **Broadbridge Heath**, where the poet Shelley was born on 4 August 1792 at Field Place. As a child, Shelley sailed his boat on **Warnham** millpond, now a nature reserve managed by the district council. Warnham Court was the home of the Lucas family and a Lucas was a member of the County Council from 1889, when the council was established, until 1985, very nearly 100 years. Warnham brickworks supplies bricks throughout the region.

A mile or two south-west of Horsham is **Christ's Hospital**, the famous Bluecoat School, which moved here from the City of London in 1902. The Religious, Royal and Ancient Foundation of Christ's Hospital is today pleasantly situated in the peaceful and leafy surroundings of rural Sussex, but it originated in very different circumstances. The move to Horsham in 1902 represented a break with a long tradition of existence in the City of London, where the institution had flourished for 350 years following its foundation by Edward VI. The buildings at Horsham were designed by Sir Aston Webb and incorporated some of the features of the London school. Opinions on the merits of Webb's design vary, but few would deny the impressiveness of the total effect of brick and Bath stone, and the fine sense of scale in what is one of the largest quadrangles in the country.

Today Christ's Hospital is a boarding school of some 825 boys and girls and has a strong academic, musical and artistic tradition. It remains a charitable organisation, devoting its assets and efforts to the education of those who would be unlikely to be offered independent education in any other school. On most days the school band plays the pupils into lunch in the dining hall, which houses one of the Hospital's greatest treasures – Antonio Verrio's painting depicting the granting of the Royal Charter to the Royal Mathematical School. By prior arrangement, boys and girls – known as 'Verrio guides' – are available to show visitors around the school and members of the public are welcome to attend events in the modern Arts Centre, which includes a theatre.

Horsted Keynes (2/3C) *see* Ashdown Forest

Houghton (1/4D)

A hamlet on the B2139 north of Arundel with an interesting history, an ancient bridge and an industrial museum. It straggles along the busy road which runs down a chalk spur to cross the river Arun at Houghton bridge, the only road crossing of the river between Arundel and Greatham. Occupying such a strategic position, the hamlet has seen many distinguished travellers in its time, none more so than Charles II who came this way when escaping from the Parliamentary army after the Battle of Worcester. Disguised as the servant of his guide and protector, Colonel Gunter of RACTON, the King survived a narrow escape from an army patrol in Houghton Forest and crossed the river here *en route* for Brighton and safety in France. The King's journey is remembered today in the annual yacht race from Brighton to Fécamp known as The Royal Escape.

The village has a number of early 17th-century semi-detached cottages, each pair with a massive central chimney stack dividing the two dwellings and incorporating large, back-to-back inglenooks. There are many interesting old buildings in the village, especially in South Lane which runs down to the river from the crossroads and the estate village nature of the place is still reflected in the large number of houses painted in the Norfolk Estate dark red colour.

Situated in the midst of chalk country and with easy access to river transport, Houghton was for centuries an important centre for chalk quarrying and lime burning. Lime was first used extensively in the 17th century, to improve agriculture on the heavy clay soils of the Weald and, until alternative fertilisers became available, continued to be used in great quantities, especially for the cultivation of wheat. The legacy of this activity is the large number of chalk quarries and pits all over the Downs; they became particularly extensive where the lime could easily be moved inland by water, as at Houghton. Here, the complex of pits on the east side of the river developed into one of the largest of such sites in the country, with its own railway sidings connecting the works with the main line to London.

Today the old workings form the home of the Chalk Pits Museum, a fascinating museum of industrial history which uses the 36-acre quarry as an open-air centre for the display of historic industrial machines and tools. The museum reflects the industrial heritage of southern England and, while the massive lime kilns form the centrepiece, a number of working craftsmen demonstrate crafts such as potting, blacksmithing, printing and boatbuilding.

A short walk along the lane from Houghton bridge leads to the tiny settlement of **North Stoke**, which has a delightful Norman and Early English church with a small timber bell tower and medieval wall paintings above the chancel arch. The visitor with half an hour to spare should press on south on the public footpath to **South Stoke**, crossing the old course of the river by a charming suspension bridge recently restored by the County Council. South Stoke is an idyllic spot and the parish church of St Leonard has no electricity: on Christmas Eve the church is lit with candles for the annual carol service after which hot soup is served to the congregation.

Hove (2/2E)

Brighton's twin town, whose centre features no fewer than five conservation areas with examples of the best of English 19th-century architecture and estate development. By about 1820, the outward development of Brighton had brought building to the eastern boundary of the rural parish of Hove, which until that time had remained a small village on the road to Worthing. Further expansion outside the area for which the Brighton Town Commissioners were responsible resulted in the passing of the Brunswick Square Act 1830, which vested powers of building

Overleaf: Houghton from Bury Hill

control in the hands of the Brunswick Square Commissioners, the predecessors of the present Hove Borough Council. The development from which the Commissioners took their name, Brunswick Town, is the largest and most important conservation area in Hove and balances the Kemp Town development, to the east of Brighton, both designed by the architects Charles Busby and Amon Wilds.

Brunswick Square and Terrace were built between 1824 and 1840, and with Waterloo Street and other roads provided housing for servants and tradesmen. The estate included a market building, mews properties, a school and the Italianate St Andrew's church in Waterloo Street, designed by Sir Charles Barry, architect of the Houses of Parliament. Further west, Adelaide Crescent was designed in 1830 by Decimus Burton, but it was only partly built and the rest of the development was completed to a different design by Sir Isaac Goldsmid in 1850–60. An excellent walking guide to the area, *The Brunswick Town Trail*, is available from the Tourist Information Centre at Hove Town Hall, Church Road.

Hove's other conservation areas are The Avenues, Cliftonville, Denmark Villas and The Drive. The Avenues area extends from First Avenue to Fourth Avenue, between Church Road and the seafront and includes a variety of styles: Italianate and yellow brick in First and Second Avenues and Victorian domestic revival in red brick at the top of Grand Avenue. Edward VII spent holidays in a house in King's Gardens and the Electricity Board offices in Queen's Gardens are a good example of a restored listed building complemented by a sympathetic modern extension.

Cliftonville, in central Hove, has a distinct identity of its own, reflecting its development in the 1860s and 70s. A particularly attractive street is Osborne Villas, consisting of semi-detached villas and bay-fronted terraced houses. Denmark Villas was built in 1860–80 for the professional middle classes and the houses have yellow-brick fronts under slate roofs, without the rich detailing of earlier houses in the area. Finally, The Drive conservation area includes some of the best brick buildings in the town, large Victorian mansions with terracotta detailing, under plain tiled roofs. In Eaton Road is the superb All Saints parish church, designed by J. L. Pearson and built in 1890–1, of Horsham sandstone in 13th-century French style.

In addition to its rich architectural heritage,

Hove contains fine parks, lawns and promenades, the Booth Museum of Natural History in Dyke Road, the King Alfred sports and swimming centre, the Sussex County Cricket Club ground in Eaton Road and the British Engineerium. The Engineerium in Hove Park, off Nevill Road, is inside the 19th-century Goldstone Water Pumping Station and features hundreds of full-size and model steam engines, including an 1876 beam engine. The Engineerium is 'in steam' at certain times. Also of interest is

West Blatchington Windmill, an early 19th-century smock mill bought by Hove Borough Council in 1936 and now used as a small museum. The original machinery is intact.

The 11th-century nave of St Helen's parish church, **Hangleton**, is reckoned to be the oldest building in Hove. The nearby Manor House, now a pub, dates from about 1540 and features a splendid 17th-century dovecot which has been restored by volunteers with the support of Hove Borough Council.

Brunswick Square, Hove

To the west of Hove is **Portslade-by-Sea**, originally on the old Roman coast road. Today the area is dominated by the power station, with its attendant wires and pylons, and a rash of undistinguished housing, but the old village centre with the 12th-century parish church of St Nicholas and cottages date from the 16th century, is of interest and retains a charming rural atmosphere.

Danny Park, near Hurstpierpoint

Hurstpierpoint (2/2D)
A substantial village just to the east of the A23 London to Brighton road and close to the main line station at Hassocks. 'Hurst' is a common element in Sussex place names and means 'wooded hill'. Here, the name of the village reflects the association with the de Pierpoint family who originated at Pierrepont in Normandy. Robert de Pierpoint held the manor after the Conquest as a tenant of William de Warenne, lord of Lewes, and there is a memorial to one of his descendants in the parish church. The family continued to hold the estate until well into the 15th century, by which time the name of the village was firmly established.

The parish church of Holy Trinity was built in 1843–5 to the designs of Sir Charles Barry, architect of the Houses of Parliament. It replaced a smaller less elaborate one. Around the church there are a number of Georgian houses and, despite some recent development, the village has many attractive 18th and early 19th-century buildings. A house of particular interest is St George's, a villa built for the Hannington family who owned the Brighton department store of that name. Just outside the village is Hurstpierpoint College, one of the schools founded by Canon Woodard. The buildings at the College are of knapped flint, designed by R. C. Carpenter and erected in 1851–3. Near the College, in Malthouse Lane, is the Malthouse Theatre, a modern theatre in a converted 15th-century barn which seats 100 people.

South-east of the village under Wolstonbury Hill is Danny Park, an E-shaped Elizabethan brick mansion now converted into private apartments. The house was used during the First World War for meetings of the War Cabinet and it was here that the terms of the 1918 armistice was drafted.

To the west of the A23 is the village of **Albourne**, beside a stream which flows into the river Adur. The parish church of St Bartholomew, much restored in the 1850s, is just outside the village close to Albourne Place, a 17th-century brick house once the home of William Juxon. Although he was later to become Archbishop of Canterbury, Juxon was imprisoned during the Interregnum, apparently for refusing to disclose Charles I's dying words on the scaffold.

Ifield (2/2B) *see* Crawley

Iford (2/4E) *see* Rodmell

Jevington (2/5E)
A delightful Downland village near Eastbourne, on the inland route of the South Downs Way. The Saxon church of St Andrew was a victim of Victorian restoration and has lost much of its charm as a result. Even the fine old church bells were sold to finance the reconstruction, giving rise to a popular local verse:

> Jevington folk are very proud people,
> They sold their bells to mend their steeple
> And before they are left in the lurch,
> They would sell the steeple to mend the church.

A mile north of the church, on Combe Hill, is a series of prehistoric earthworks which include a large mound or barrow and, until modern intensive farming obliterated them, the characteristic terracing of medieval field systems.

Lancing (2/1E) *see* Sompting

Lavants, The (1/2E)
Two villages north of Chichester, on the road to Midhurst. The word 'lavant' is an old English name for a river, perhaps derived from a word meaning 'to glide'. In Sussex the word is used to describe a stream which rises from an underground reservoir in the chalk and whose flow is unpredictable. Thus, the little river which flows south from the Downs, through Singleton and Chichester to the sea at Dell Quay, was known from earliest times as the Lavant.

The village of **Mid Lavant** straddles the busy A286 road from Chichester to Midhurst. The buildings are of no special interest but the church of St Nicholas – where the road bends sharply as it crosses the old railway line – should not be missed. This is not because of the quality of the building itself, which is largely Victorian, but because of the important monument there to Lady Mary May. When the church was restored by the Victorians the unusual triple chancel arch was installed and, in the process, the 17th-century memorial to Lady Mary by the sculptor John Bushnell was destroyed. The reclining figure in her diaphanous robe probably offended Victorian susceptibilities and was consigned to a hole under the floor. The effigy was discovered only in 1982 during building works and has now been restored to a place of honour.

East Lavant, a short distance to the east, is a

Grocery shopfront, Hurstpierpoint

Lewes Castle

pretty village beside the river, consisting largely of mid 19th-century estate cottages. The parish church of St Mary was also restored in the Victorian period, but there are a number of good brick and flint cottages and the former rectory is 19th-century mock Tudor.

Leonardslee (2/2C) *see* St Leonard's Forest

Lewes (2/4D)

County town of East Sussex, set on a steep hill commanding the Ouse valley and with superb views in all directions. The town of Lewes, whose name derives from a Saxon word meaning 'hill', is built on a steep chalk promontory at a narrow crossing of the tidal Ouse, about 6 miles from its mouth, at the junction of overland and water communications routes. The Rape of Lewes was given by William the Conqueror to his trusted lieutenant William de Warenne, who later became Earl of Surrey and acquired land in Yorkshire, Norfolk and many other counties. At Lewes, de Warenne built a castle, unusual with its two mottes and, in atonement for the blood shed in the Battle of Hastings, the Priory of St Pancras (see *The Norman Heritage*, p. 28).

The layout of Lewes evolved from the early pattern of parallel lanes and twittens, or pedestrian alleys, running from the High Street by the castle down to the southern defences of the town. The town was reputedly walled but the wall is now visible only on the west side, in Keere Street and Pipe Passage, the one boundary not naturally defended. Beyond the walls two suburbs developed, at Cliffe and Southover. Southover grew rapidly after the foundation there in 1077 of the Priory by de Warenne and his wife, Gundrada. The Priory church was larger than Chichester Cathedral and after the dissolution of the monasteries its ruins provided a ready source of building stone for the town. The Grange in Southover, once the home of the diarist John Evelyn, is made of mellow Caen stone, raided from the Priory ruins.

The most important event in the history of the town was the Battle of Lewes, fought between the forces of Henry III and Simon de Montfort in 1264. The armies met on the Downs to the west of the town. The royal forces having been put to flight, the King was obliged to sign a treaty known as the Mise of Lewes, which acknowledged the political position of the barons and is regarded as the beginning of Parliamentary government in England.

At the time of the Reformation, the new Protestant faith struck deep roots in mid Sussex and Lewes developed a strong Puritan tradition encouraged by the burning, in the reign of Mary I, of 17 Protestant martyrs in the town. Not surprisingly, the Civil War found Lewes firmly on the side of Parliament and the centre of operations for the Parliamentary cause in Sussex. It was during this period of bitter religious strife that the association of the Protestant cause with the celebration of the anniversary of the discovery of the Gunpowder Plot developed. The Puritans in Lewes adopted 'No Popery' as their slogan and commemorated 5 November with great fervour. Lewes still makes far more of 5 November than any other town in England, its bonfire societies marching through the town with bands and flaming torches.

In the 18th century Lewes remained a centre of political dissent and argument. One of the most forceful orators at meetings of The Headstrong Club held at The White Hart was the local excise officer, Tom Paine, who subsequently wrote *The Rights of Man* and became a prominent figure in the American War of Independence. The end of the 18th century saw a golden age in Lewes, reflecting the prosperity of the large agricultural district of which the town was the centre. At the Lewes markets the surplus agricultural products of the sheep/corn economy of the eastern Downland were distributed and exchanged, professional services developed and the town became a centre of law, government and fashion.

The prosperity of the period is evident in the new building of the time, much of which remains today. Substantial houses, such as School Hill House and Lewes House, were built by successful doctors and lawyers and the old County Hall in the High Street (now the Crown Court) was erected in the early years of the 19th century. More modest citizens arranged for their old-fashioned timber-framed houses to be modernised and many of the apparently brick-built houses in Lewes are actually older buildings refaced with hanging tiles designed to resemble bricks. These 'mathematical' tiles, as they are called, are characteristic of Lewes and are found in such numbers nowhere else in the country. They enabled a timber-framed house to be updated in appearance by the addition of a lightweight and relatively cheap façade and could be used to achieve bow windows which were (and are) difficult to build in brick. They could be plain, painted or glazed and are not

High Street, Lewes

always easy to detect. One tell-tale sign is that they occur with white-painted wooden quoins designed to resemble stone, but clearly detectable when tapped.

The churches of Lewes are unremarkable, with the striking exception of the Nonconformist Jireh Chapel in the Cliffe. This Grade 1 listed building was the headquarters of the principal Calvinist congregation in Sussex and drew adherents from a wide area. The Chapel was founded in 1805 by William Huntingdon, one of the great evangelical preachers of the early 19th century. It seated over 1,000 on Sundays and there were 300 children in its Sunday school, looked after by 30 teachers and six superintendents. Sadly, it is now disused. The church of St Michael, in the High Street, is one of only three in Sussex with a round tower. (The other two are at Piddinghoe and Southease).

Lewes Castle, Barbican House and museum and Anne of Cleves House in Southover High Street are owned by the Sussex Archaeological Society; visits to these properties will enhance the visitor's understanding of Lewes and of the county. In addition, the Society and Lewes Town Council have recently established the Lewes Town Model and Living History Centre in the High Street, which is already proving an essential first port of call for visitors.

From its hill, Lewes looks out to the heights of Mount Caburn to the east and over the water meadows of the lower Ouse valley to the south. The sea and the open coutryside are within easy reach, Glyndebourne is near by and the town's traditional role as legal, administrative and commercial centre, combined with its proximity to the modern University of Sussex, provide many opportunities for local employment. Lewes continues to charm visitors, as it has since William de Warenne and his wife arrived here from Normandy more than 900 years ago. The excellent walking guide to the town by Dr Colin Brent, *Historic Lewes and its Buildings* is published by Lewes Town Council and is essential reading for the discerning visitor.

Lickfold (1/3C) *see* Lurgashall

Lindfield (2/3C)
Although only a mile away from Haywards Heath, Lindfield has retained its separate identity and has one of the most distinguished village

High Street, Lindfield

THE
BENT ARMS
FREE
LINDFIELD
HOUSE
THE
TIGER

streets in the county. Approaching from the south, the visitor follows the extensive and well-maintained Common past the famous village pond and into the High Street. Lined with brick pavements and shady trees, the street is a delightful mixture of timber-framed and Georgian brick buildings, most of them listed. Of particular interest are the Manor House, Barnlands, Malling Priory and Bower House.

At the top of the street is The Tiger, formerly an inn and now used as the church house. Local legend has it that, at the time of the defeat of the Spanish Armada, it served so much strong ale to the bellringers in the church next door that they broke the ropes and cracked one of the bells. The building got its name from the crest of the old family of Michelbourne and in the 18th century was the headquarters of the Benefit Friendly Society, a political and mutual aid association founded by Thomas Finch in 1757.

The parish church of St John the Baptist dates from the 14th century and has a tower at the west end with a shingled broach spire. North of the church is Church Cottage, a 15th-century timber-framed house, and behind it is Old Place, also timber-framed and with brick nogging. Old Place was the home of Charles Eames Kempe, the famous artist in stained glass who restored the house and built the pavilion in the garden where he worked. Near by is The Thatched Cottage, another 15th-century house which was used as a hunting lodge by Henry VIII when he visited the Wealden forest. Later houses at this end of the village include the 18th-century red brick Lindfield House and Lindfield Place.

Lindfield once had many small workshops making pianos, gloves, candles and paper and was on the old coach road from London to Brighton. Today, its quiet beauty and nearness to the main line station at Haywards Heath make it a popular choice for retired people and commuters.

Litlington (2/5E) *see* Alfriston

Little Bognor (1/4D) *see* Pulborough

Littlehampton (1/4E)

A family resort and minor port at the mouth of the River Arun, south of Arundel. There are many 'hamptons' in England, the name meaning 'home farm'. Spelled as two words until quite recently, Littlehampton possibly acquired its diminutive affix in order to distinguish it from

other towns with the same or similar names. There is evidence of a Roman settlement here and Domesday records that, at the end of the Saxon era, the manor was held by Countess Goda, an association remembered in a present day street name in the town.

When the Normans came, ports such as Littlehampton and SHOREHAM took on a new importance as gateways linking England and the Duchy of Normandy. Stone from the quarries of Caen was imported in large quantitites for new building works and much of it came through Littlehampton. Throughout the medieval period, although the principal port on the Arun was upstream at Arundel, Littlehampton benefited from the considerable trade with Normandy. It

Church and the River Arun at Ford

was here that Queen Matilda landed in 1139 when she came from France to try to seize the throne from her cousin, Stephen.

The old town developed on the east bank of the river, a little way back from its mouth. Although little of interest remains today, the line of flint cottages from the river to the church indicates the basic layout of the medieval town. Like New Shoreham and Newhaven, Littlehampton prospered as ports further up river – Arundel in this case – declined, although Arundel's fate as a port was finally sealed only in the 1930s when the installation of the fixed railway bridge at FORD prevented masted ships getting upstream. Meanwhile, the river had been improved for navigation and a direct cut made to the sea in 1732, assuring Littlehampton's position as the port on the River Arun.

Early 19th-century seaside development in Littlehampton was limited to Norfolk Place and South Terrace, near the sea and some half a mile from the old town. It was only during the late 19th century that the two parts were linked by new building, none of it very distinguished. The parish church of St Mary the Virgin was built in 1826 and substantially remodelled in 1934. Despite its lack of architectural charm, Littlehampton retains a salty air. Its extensive sandy beaches include West Beach, an area of unspoiled natural coastline accessible from the

Bathing huts at Littlehampton

town by passenger ferry, and the river is popular with fishermen and sailors, whose base is the Arun Yacht Club on the west bank. Cruises may be taken up the river to Arundel and Amberley from the jetty on the east bank. When the weather is not so good, Smarts Amusements on the front is popular and other attractions include the excellent museum in River Road, which features local history with a maritime flavour, and the Swimming Centre in Sea Road at the eastern end of the front.

To the east of Littlehampton is the surburban area of **Rustington**. With associated areas such as East Preston and Angmering on Sea, Rustington has developed from a small coastal settlement in the 19th century set in fields beside the sea, to a large residential and retirement area. Rustington has few buildings of any interest, other than the late 12th-century tower of the parish church of St Peter and St Paul and an 1879 Norman Shaw house in Sea Lane which for 37 years was the home of the composer, Sir Hubert Parry. Here he composed his famous hymn tune, 'Jerusalem', whose words had been written by William Blake at FELPHAM.

East Preston has a few old cottages and a generally well-heeled air. The East Preston Poor Law Union workhouse was demolished in 1969, having thankfully outlived its usefulness.

West of Littlehampton, on the River Arun to Arundel, is **Ford**, a tiny settlement of some historic interest. The derivation of the name is self-evident and the 12th-century spelling of Fordes suggests that there was more than one river crossing at this point, possibly one over the main river and another over a tributary stream. The crossing of the River Arun subsequently moved to Arundel, but in the early years of the 19th century Ford again became important as a junction on the inland navigation system that linked London with Portsmouth: 'London's Lost Route to the Sea'. The French Wars prompted the Government to seek a safe inland route for transporting supplies to the Fleet at Portsmouth which avoided the use of the Channel; the improvement of the Wey and Arun Navigations and the construction of the Wey and Arun Canal were followed, in 1823, by the opening of the Portsmouth to Arundel Canal.

Ford has a tiny parish church, dedicated to St Andrew, which stands alone in the fields. Next to it is Lock Cottage and the remains of the first pair of locks at the entrance to the old canal. More modern building includes the former Fleet Air Arm station, now used as an open prison. The Ship and Anchor operates a useful touring caravan and camping site. The County Council have produced a walking guide to the old canal, copies of which are available locally or from County Hall, Chichester.

Lodsworth (1/3C) *see* Lurgshall

Lower Horsebridge (3/1D) *see* Hailsham

Loxwood (1/4B)

A Wealden village close to the Surrey border, north-west of Billingshurst. It straggles out along the road to Guildford and has several good houses, some of them tile hung. The good building sandstone available from the ridge on which PULBOROUGH stands was transported some distance north into the Weald and was used to build a number of attractive farmhouses in this area. With nearby Plaistow, Loxwood shares the distinction of having had a medieval timber-framed church which survived into the 19th century. Both churches were recorded in the collection of drawings made between 1781 and 1783 for Sir William Burrell's projected History of Sussex. Loxwood's was replaced in 1895 but some of the pews from the old building have been preserved in the new.

Until the 17th century the King required that, to protect the timber supplies of the shipbuilding industry, iron and glass furnaces might not be established within 12 miles of the coast. Loxwood, with good local supplies of wood, lay just outside this boundary and therefore a number of furnaces were established in the area from medieval times. This modest industrial base and the presence of a class of independent artisans and small proprietors perhaps explains the enthusiasm which Loxwood showed for an independent religious sect which arrived from London in 1850. Its members were known as the Dependents and in a short time they had established considerable support in the villages and surrounding countryside. The sect emphasised industry and thrift and set up their own shop, staffed by female adherents. Other chapels and shops followed in Northchapel, Kirdford and Warnham. Today, the shop at Loxwood has gone and there are few Dependents left.

The Wey and Arun Canal once ran through the village. A stretch survives beside The Onslow Arms, named after one of the chairmen of the Wey and Arun Junction Canal Company. The route of the old canal can be followed on foot from here with the help of *Wey South Path*, published by the Canal Restoration Trust. The path is marked on the OS 1:50,000 Landranger series.

Lullington (1/5E) *see* Alfriston

Lurgashall (1/3C).
In deepest north-west Sussex, a classic English village north-west of Petworth with many good buildings, mainly of stone. The village is grouped around a triangular green and lies below Black Down, at 918 ft the highest point in the county. Black Down is a high sandstone ridge and its 600 acres owned by the National Trust provide fine opportunities for walking, riding and enjoying the wide views across the Weald. Alfred Lord Tennyson lived at Aldworth House on Black Down from 1867 until his death in 1892. In the village below, many of the houses are built of the local sandstone and some are tile hung, indicating the nearness of Surrey. The parish church of St Lawrence, with its simple 16th-century lean-to timber gallery, is noteworthy as is the Rectory, near the church and now mainly 19th-century.

A mile away from Lurgashall is the hamlet of **Lickfold**, which contains many pretty cottages and, to the south, closer to Midhurst and Petworth, is **Lodsworth**. The village lies on the River Lod, a tributary of the River Rother. The church of St Peter occupies a superb site with views across a wooded valley. Unfortunately, the building does not live up to its position. The village contains many attractive cottages and of particular note are the early 18th-century Dower House, the later Great House and the Manor House, near the church whose origins go back to the 13th century.

Church and thatched well, East Marden

Lyminster (1/4E) *see* Arundel

Mardens, The (1/1–2D)

Four settlements in the western Downs, close to the Hampshire border. The name means 'boundary hill' and is common to the four communities of North, East, Up and West Marden. Towards the summit of the Downs above North Marden is one of the best Neolithic long barrows or burial mounds in Sussex. Known as Bevis's Thumb after the fabled giant, the Marden barrow is 150 ft long by over 20 ft wide. West Marden is now the largest of the four settlements but is the only one without a church. St Mary's at North Marden is one of the smallest churches in Sussex, while St Michael's at Up Marden, approached through a farmyard, has a beautiful unspoilt 13th-century interior and is worth going a long way to see. The village of East Marden has a very small centre, with a well-known thatched well. There is a good round walk from East Marden through Wildham Wood, one of the largest beech woodlands on the Downs, now owned by the Forestry Commission.

Maresfield (2/4C)

A large village on the A22 London to Eastbourne road, north of Uckfield and once an important junction for coaching routes. Maresfield can truly be described as having been beyond the pale of civilisation until the 18th century. The huge parish, which includes much of ASHDOWN FOREST, formed part of the remote, inaccessible Weald, which was tamed only gradually as roads began to cut through the dense woodland separating London from the sea. In early times, the area was populated only by the sturdily independent iron-masters and by bands of outlaws who hoped to escape the King's justice in these remote and wooded hills. The name of the place is thought to be derived from an old English word meaning a pond or pool. As all iron workings had nearby ponds for cooling the smelted iron, this once important industry must have had very ancient origins.

The Chequers Inn, built during the Georgian period, is one of the oldest buildings in the village and was an important coaching inn for travellers on their way to London. It is assumed that the inspiration for inns of this name was the chess board: they are often found in market places, suggesting that some form of chequer board or abacus was used for recording transactions and making calculations. There is another inn called The Chequers in STEYNING High Street, for example. Alternatively, it is equally possible that The Chequers at Maresfield was named after the chequer tree, once prevalent in this part of the country before a terrible blight, worse even than the modern Dutch elm disease, wiped them out.

Maresfield Park is derelict: only the Gothic gatetower with its gargoyles still remains. Just outside the village the old army camp is now used by the County Council as a Fire Brigade training centre and as a caravan site for gypsies and travelling people. The milestone on the boundary of the village dates from coaching days and shows the way to London. It is not, in fact, made of stone but, appropriately for this area, of whitewashed cast iron. Another reminder of the importance of the iron industry in this part of Sussex is a 17th-century iron tomb slab in the parish church.

Mayfield (3/1C)

A large Wealden village in north-east Sussex with one of the best High Streets in the county, famous for the legendary conflict that took place here between St Dunstan and the Devil. It was in Saxon times that a hardy saint by the name of Dunstan came to Mayfield to deliver the people of the village from the grip of paganism. His challenge to the forces of darkness was taken up by the Devil himself, who sought to tempt Dunstan and thereby destroy his reputation. Dunstan, a blacksmith by trade, was working at his anvil one day when he was approached by a beautiful young woman who tried to compromise him. Fortunately he noticed the cloven feet beneath the girl's dress and recognised her as the Devil whom he seized by the nose with a pair of red-hot pincers. Lucifer let out a blood-curdling scream and vanished. Later, he returned in the form of a weary traveller seeking new horseshoes for his mount. Again the saint saw through the disguise and beat the Devil until he vowed never to enter a house with a horseshoe above its door. This popular folk tale is recalled in the splendid village sign.

Puritanism flourished in the remote Weald and, during the reign of Catholic Mary I in the 1550s, four Protestant martyrs were burned at the stake at Mayfield. Their deaths were not forgotten and the village still boasts one of the oldest and most successful bonfire societies in Sussex, second only to the august societies of Calvinist LEWES. The parish church, dedicated to St Dunstan, had to be rebuilt, together with most of the village, after a terrible fire in the 14th century caused widespread destruction. In 1621 the building was again damaged, this time by lightning. The present church has an impressive ceiling with moulded beams, a Jacobean pulpit and a font bearing the date 1666 with the initials of the church wardens.

Like BURWASH and LINDFIELD, Mayfield has a distinguished High Street with many attractive buildings and a raised red brick pavement. At the east end of the High Street is the Convent of the Holy Child, now a Roman Catholic girls' school. It enshrines the remains of a palace of the Archbishops of Canterbury with a magnificent medieval hall. Few inns in Sussex have received more praise than The Middle House in Mayfield High Street. A glorious Tudor building with oak beams, it was originally a country house. During the early part of the 19th century, one landlord with misogynist tendencies kept his wife locked away in a secret room in the attic. There she languished for several years, until at last she overcame him with a sharp blow on the head and was able to make her escape.

On Argos Hill overlooking the village is an old post mill, now a museum. It is however open on only a few days during the summer and visitors are advised to check for details first with the district council at Crowborough. During the Second World War the hill provided a good view of the dog-fights of the Battle of Britain and, later, of the sinister unmanned flying bombs, which passed this way *en route* for London.

Michelham Priory (2/5E) *see* Dickers, The

Midhurst (1/2C)

A comfortable and peaceful town on the sandstone ridge north of the Downs above Chichester. The town's Saxon name suggests that it stood in the middle of a wood, perhaps a clearing in the Wealden forest whose elevated position beside the River Rother attracted early settlers.

Midhurst's many fine sandstone and timber-framed buildings lend it a prosperous air. The parish church of St Mary Magdalen is unremarkable but the market square, repaved for European Architectural Heritage Year in 1975, forms the focus for a particularly attractive group of houses. Elizabeth House is an unusual example of a four-storeyed timber-framed house, The Spread Eagle Inn dates from the 17th century but includes earlier work and in Knockhundred Row a 17th-century cottage contains the county library. There are many places to eat and drink and the town has good local shops. There are also fine walks in the surrounding countryside, by the Cowdray ruins, over the sandy heaths and commons and beside the River Rother which, in the 19th century, was navigable by barge from the River Arun at Pulborough, connecting Midhurst with the inland waterway system.

Midhurst's development was unremarkable until the 16th century when what was probably the most magnificent Tudor house in Sussex was built at **Cowdray**, just east of the town. (The name is derived from the old French *coudraie*, 'a hazel hedge'). Cowdray House was built in the reign of Henry VIII by the Earl of Southampton and reached its full glory under Sir Anthony Browne, later first Viscount Montague. The house emulated the style of the royal palace at Hampton Court, although it was built in local sandstone rather than brick.

Montague entertained Elizabeth I at Cowdray in 1591. The Queen and her party stayed for a week, consumed three oxen and 140 geese for breakfast and dined at a table 48 yards long. The second Viscount Montague wrote a *Book of Orders and Rules* for the household at Cowdray which provides a fascinating insight into life in an Elizabethan country house. The house was burned to the ground in 1793 and a week later the last Viscount Montague was drowned. The land was bought by the Earl of Egmont and in 1909 sold to Sir Weetman Pearson who the following year was created Baron Cowdray. The 17,000 acre estate remains in the Cowdray family today and is one of the largest private estates in Sussex. The ruins are very picturesque and provide a unique backdrop to the town's cricket field. The park is famous for polo and contains a fine golf course.

Separated from Midhurst by the mill stream which joins the River Rother to the north-east is **Easebourne** (Ezbourne), the Cowdray Estate village, famous for its yellow-painted estate cottages and farm buildings. Easebourne was the site chosen in the 13th century for the foundation of a convent of Augustinian nuns. The nunnery flourished for 200 years until, in 1478, the Prioress and two of the nuns were accused of gross immorality and of squandering the nunnery's resources in hunting and extravagant entertaining. The nunnery was later dissolved and the remains of the buildings now form part of the parish church of St Mary and the

Overleaf: Ruins of Cowdray Castle

Great Dixter, house and garden

adjoining vicarage and garden.

Sir Anthony Browne, who built Cowdray House, benefited enormously from the dissolution of the monasteries under Henry VIII. In addition to Easebourne Priory, his family acquired BATTLE and Bayham Abbeys in Sussex, Waverley Abbey in Surrey and a London nunnery, possibly to preserve them in Catholic hands.

Another interesting building in Easebourne is Budgenor Lodge, now used by the district council but originally built in 1793 as the parish workhouse for the Easebourne 'union'. In its day the workhouse was a model of its kind, built under an Act of 1782 which enabled parishes to unite to make provision for the poor. It included workrooms and was solid and well built, attracting visits from representatives of poor law unions elsewhere in the country anxious to see what could be achieved.

Mid Lavant (1/2E) *see* Lavant

Newhaven (2/4E)
The site of Sussex's cross-Channel ferry port at the mouth of the River Ouse, south of Lewes. The Ouse originally entered the sea at Seaford, east of Newhaven. Improvements to the course of the river to prevent flooding and a new cut engineered in the 1530s created the New Haven at a place on the coast previously called Meeching. Over the years it developed into a thriving port and a fast-expanding town emerged around it. Recent excavations have indicated the site's prehistoric origins, several shards of Roman pottery have been discovered and it has been suggested that a Celtic hill fort may once have existed on Castle Hill.

The modern harbour works were undertaken towards the end of the 19th century and today Newhaven provides a cross-Channel link with Dieppe, some four hours away. Connections with France have always been important; Louis Philippe landed here in 1848 on his escape from revolutionary forces. He stayed at The Bridge Hotel, one of the most prominent buildings in the town. The church, dedicated to St Michael, is largely Victorian. In the churchyard are several curious gravestones including one to Thomas Tipper, brewer of Tipper Ale, with a carving of Newhaven's old bridge as its central theme. There are good views from the churchyard to the Downs around Lewes.

Until it closed in 1977, The Jolly Sailor was Sussex's last surviving beer house. These were premises licensed to sell only beer, not wine or spirits. Beer houses were at one time extremely popular and convivial, but modern standards of decor and variety brought about their demise. One of the best-known beer houses in West Sussex, now a popular country pub, was The Royal Oak at Hooksway, near HARTING.

Newick (2/4C) *see* Chailey

Newtimber (2/2D) *see* Pyecombe

North Common (2/3C) *see* Chailey

Northiam (3/4C)
On the border between Sussex and Kent, Northiam's delightful collection of white, weatherboarded cottages and large timber-framed houses make it one of the finest large villages in the county. The Hayes Arms Hotel, Wellhouse, Strawberry Hole Farmhouse and Silverden Manor all date from the late medieval period and are exceptionally well-preserved. A puritan vicar who lived at the other fine house in the parish, Brickwall House, during the 17th century, demonstrated his devotion by calling his two sons 'Accepted' and 'Thankful'. Thankful Frewen presented the altar rails to the church in 1683 and is buried in the churchyard. This use of complicated, pietistic names was common among Sussex Puritans during the Civil War and Interregnum and other

examples from the Lewes area include Redeemed Compton, Fight-the-good-fight White and Fly-fornication Richardson.

The parish church of St Mary is of no outstanding merit, though it does boast one of the few remaining stone spires in Sussex. The mausoleum to the Frewen Turner family of Brickwall was added in 1846. In 1822, a 9th-century Viking ship was discovered in the mudflats of the river. It was 60 ft long and had a cabin and forecastle. Until fairly recently, barges laden with timber and coal used to navigate up the Rother to this point and 'Norjem', as the village was referred to in dialect, became quite a meeting place for tradesmen and craftsmen.

Great Dixter, just under a mile north-west of the village dates from about 1450 and is a fine, large timber-framed and tile-hung house. It was restored by Sir Edwin Lutyens for Nathaniel Lloyd, the great historian of English houses, and the result is regarded as one of the master's most successful pieces of work. The gardens, containing a wide variety of interesting and unusual plants, are open to the public from April to October. Plants may be bought in the nursery. The current owner, Christopher Lloyd, is a gardening writer and regular contributor to *County Life*.

Northiam was the home of the novelist Sheila Kaye-Smith, who was born in HASTINGS. She spent most of her life in this part of Sussex, which is the setting for her novels *The End of the House of Alard*, *Joanna Godden*, *Susan Spray* and *Sussex Gorse*.

North Stoke (1/4D) *see* Houghton

Nutley (2/4C) *see* Ashdown Forest

Nymans (2/2C) *see* Cuckfield

Nyetimber (1/2F) *see* Pagham

Pagham (1/2F)

A seaside village west of Bognor Regis and on the edge of one of the most important nature reserves in the county. In the days when the manor was owned by the Archbishop of Canterbury, Pagham must have been a delightful spot. Today, following a rash of inter-war and later development, a sense of its past may be recaptured only in the area around the parish church and, fleetingly, in parts of the old settlement of **Nyetimber**.

Pagham suffered from the violent storms of the 13th and 14th centuries which altered the face of the Sussex coast. At SHOREHAM half the Norman town was lost to the sea and at Pagham some 2,500 acres of farmland disappeared under water, forming a wide estuary stretching inland to **Sidlesham**. In the 19th century the area was drained and returned to agriculture, but the experiment was not a success: the sea broke through the defences and today Pagham Harbour is a complex of tidal mudflats and shingle banks of great importance for wildlife. Over 1,000 acres are managed by the County Council as a local nature reserve and particular attention is paid to the conservation of birdlife: the reserve is an important breeding area for the little tern and a safe haven for migrant species.

Saltdean Lido, near Peacehaven

The information centre at Sidlesham Ferry, north of Selsey on the B2145, has an interesting exhibition about the nature reserve and guided walks are led by the warden and voluntary helpers. Pagham Harbour has recently been designated a wetland of international importance and a special protection area for birds. Its future conservation seems assured.

There are three buildings of interest in the area: the parish church of St Thomas à Becket, Nyetimber Barton, an early medieval house much altered and extended and, beside the Harbour and accessible from the road to the church, the old Salt House, restored by the Pagham and West Sussex Wildfowling and Conservation Association.

Parham (1/4D)

One of the best Elizabethan houses in Sussex, occupying an incomparable position in the lee of the Downs near Storrington. At Domesday, the manor of Parham was held by the Abbott of Westminster and the place remained in the possession of the Abbey until its dissolution in

1539. That this was their only manor in the county shows how attached the Abbey must have been to Parham. Since the manor regularly supplied Westminster with venison from its extensive deer park, its loss must have been felt especially keenly. After some 600 years of church patronage Parham was granted in 1540 to Robert Palmer of London, whose son laid the foundation stone for the present house in 1577, when he was just two years old.

The east wing of the house incorporates part of the original monastic farm buildings dating back to the 14th century, but with this exception the house is an entirely Elizabethan creation, restored in the early 20th century. It follows the traditional E plan, supposedly in tribute to the virgin Queen, with projections and gables. The main room is the Great Hall, still entered via a passage and screen; above, instead of a gallery, is the steward's room, from which he could look into the hall through two wooden mullioned windows. The other notable room is the Long Gallery at the top of the house. 160 ft long, it provided a place for relaxation and exercise when the weather was too unpleasant for outdoor activities. The wide oak floorboards and wainscotting are original but the much admired painted ceiling by Oliver Messel is relatively modern.

Queen Elizabeth dined at Parham in 1593 on her way to Cowdray from Sutton Place in Surrey. A few years later the house was sold to Thomas Bishop of Henfield, whose family lived here for 11 generations until, in 1922, Lord Zouche sold the property to the second son of the first Viscount Cowdray, the Hon. Clive Pearson. His eldest daughter, Veronica Tritton, now lives at Parham, but responsibility for the house and gardens has been transferred to a charity.

The house contains many fine paintings, but two are of particular interest. The first is in the Great Hall, an equestrian portrait, attributed to Robert Peake, of Henry Frederick, Prince of Wales, dated about 1610. The figure of *Winged Time* and the rest of the background were revealed only when the picture was being prepared for a recent exhibition in Washington DC. The other painting of interest is that of a kangaroo by George Stubbs in the Green Room. The room is associated with Sir Joseph Banks who accompanied Captain Cook on his voyage round the world in the *Endeavour* in 1768–71. He brought back a skinned kangaroo from Australia and asked Stubbs to make a picture of the animal as best he could. Stubbs is said to have cleverly inflated the skin and the result is the delightful picture in this room.

In the grounds, close to the house, is the little church of St Peter, which was largely rebuilt (with an added tower) by Sir Cecil Bishop in 1800–20. A feature of the church is its set of high box pews in 19th-century pitch pine. The private pew has its own fireplace and it is said that the rector knew that his sermon was overrunning when the squire began to shovel coal noisily on to the fire.

Patching (1/4E) *see* Clapham

Peacehaven (2/4E)

The bungalow town on the cliffs between Brighton and Newhaven which everyone loves to hate, and with good reason. Peacehaven is, for those who love the Sussex landscape, the ultimate symbol of what can happen if private greed is given its head. For here, on the unspoiled Downs where they march beside the English Channel, grew up in the 1920s and 30s a frontier settlement of bungalows and shacks providing, it was alleged, homes fit for the returning heroes of the First World War. The land was bought up during the war by the enterprising developer Charles Neville, who saw its potential for cheap housing in a bracing and healthy climate. Having divided the land into small plots, he launched a national competition in 1916 to choose a name for his projected 'garden city'. The competition attracted 80,000 entries, from which the name 'New Anzac-on-Sea' was selected in honour of the Australian and New Zealand troops stationed in the area. With the ending of the war this name was abandoned in favour of Peacehaven and many ex-servicemen, former colonial employees and others who could not afford anything better bought plots and began to put up houses in the new settlement.

Although the development was 'planned' in the sense that the area was marked out on a map and divided up into plots in grid-iron fashion, no thought was given to the provision of roads or drainage, plots were sold on a piecemeal basis and building took place in a random fashion, with new houses separated by unkempt, undeveloped land. Peacehaven, like similar plotland developments at SHOREHAM and PAGHAM, was eventually taken over by the local authorities: proper services were provided and the development was made regular and respectable, if undistinguished. But there is no doubt that

Petworth House, west front (National Trust)

Peacehaven remains a gross affront to the principles of good town and country planning which acquired legal status too late to stop the spoilation of what must have been a particularly beautiful stretch of the Sussex coast. The best thing to come out of the experience was the formation in 1923 of The Society of Sussex Downsmen, determined that this should not happen again.

Petworth (1/3C)
A feudal town due east of Midhurst set high on a sandstone hill with a large number of important houses, clustering around the former seat of the Percy, Seymour and Wyndham families. Petworth is undeniably one of the most important small country towns in Sussex, its character determined by its dependence on Petworth House. The town lies on the sandstone ridge north of the Downs where promontories provide natural routes, both north/south (along the

River Shimmings, a tributary of the western Rother) and east/west across the valley. These topographical features explain both Petworth's position at the crossroads of three busy modern routes (the A283, A285 and A272) which results in considerable traffic congestion, and the use of local sandstone for many of the town's buildings.

Petworth House, which descended from the Percy Earls of Northumberland to the Dukes of Somerset and then to the Wyndhams in the 18th century, was enlarged from an existing manor house after licence to crenellate was granted in 1309. In the late 16th century the 8th and 9th Earls of Northumberland enlarged the house, and it was rebuilt in the late 17th century by Charles, 6th Duke of Somerset, who married a Percy heiress in 1682. This complete remodelling followed a distinctly French style and the design has been attributed to Daniel Marot, who is known to have worked on royal palaces during this period. The house turns its back on the town and looks out over the park and pleasure grounds designed by Capability Brown. It is from here that Petworth is seen at its best, with the magnificent west front for which the house is famous. Inside are paintings by Van Dyck and Turner (whose patron was George O'Brien Wyndham, 3rd Earl of Egremont), carving by Grinling Gibbons and a sculpture gallery. Both house and grounds are now owned by the National Trust. The 700-acre deer park is a good place for walks and the National Trust has provided a free car park for visitors on the A283 to the north of the town.

The principal feature of the parish church of St Mary, close to Petworth House, is the tower built of stone below and brick above. Between 1827 and 1947 the tower was surmounted by a tall brick and stucco spire which must have been visible for miles around. By the 16th century, Petworth had acquired a reputation as a cloth town and evidently drew much of its wealth from local landowners who lived in town in the winter and returned to their country estates for the remainder of the year. As a result, the town contains a large number of important gentleman's houses, including Tudor House opposite the church, Daintrey House in East Street and North House in North Street.

The Market Place, dominated by the Town Hall of 1793, has some fine buildings, including the wisteria-clad solicitors' office in the north-east corner and the 1901 National Westminster Bank. Another interesting building is Somerset Hospital, originally built as a grand private residence in the early 17th century and bought by the Duke of Somerset in 1728. In 1747 the Duke endowed the property to found an alms-house, the original endowment being for 12 widows each to receive £10 a year. Cobbled Lombard Street leads off the Market Place towards the church and there are a number of good antique shops in East Street and New Street.

Petworth is in good walking country and, in addition to walks in the park, a favourite stroll is

Moonrise at Pevensey Castle

from the Billingshurst road at the north end of the town, through the Shimmings valley, emerging by the Roman Catholic church on the Fittleworth road. South of the town, the hamlet of Byworth is well worth a visit, as is Coultershaw water wheel and beam pump, 2 miles south of the town on the Chichester road. The machinery was installed in 1790 to pump water from the River Rother to Petworth, thus providing one of the earliest pumped public water supplies. The water wheel and pump have been restored by the Sussex Industrial Archaeology Society and operate on open days.

Quite close to Coultershaw bridge is Burton Mill Pond, a local nature reserve managed by the County Council and the Sussex Wildlife Trust. There is a nature trail which follows public footpaths around the reserve and which can be extended north across public footpaths across private farmland and through woodland. The

30-acre pond, which was created to serve the old Sussex iron industry, is noted for its fish – tench, pike, roach, perch and carp are all fished on a day ticket basis. Tickets are available from the mill.

A mill at Burton is recorded in Domesday but the present building was erected in 1780. The mill is now powered by a water turbine, originally installed around 1900 to generate electricity for St Michael's, Burton Park (now a girls' school). The arrangement was not wholly satisfactory as the house lights grew brighter and dimmer by turns, nearly driving the inhabitants distracted. The mill and pond were bought by the County Council in the 1960s and the machinery restored by the Sussex Industrial Archaeology Society. In 1978 it was let for flour milling provided it was repaired by the tenant.

West of Petworth towards Midhurst are the villages of **Tillington** and **Selham**. Tillington is an estate village and consists of many fine small houses. The parish church of All Hallows is famous for its Scots Crown tower, presumably intended to be an eyecatcher for Petworth. The church of St James at Selham combines Saxon and Norman elements and has an outstanding Saxon chancel arch.

Petworth was the home of George Garland, the celebrated photographer, and several collections of his photographs showing life in rural West Sussex in the 1920s and 30s are available for sale locally. The whole collection of his negatives (some 60,000) is now owned by the West Sussex County Record Office.

Pevensey (3/2E)

One of the most remarkable places in England, Pevensey is dominated by its castle and its streets are lined with outstanding medieval buildings. Only the through traffic from Hastings to Eastbourne can spoil this historical gem. Pevensey has consistently taken centre stage in the unfolding drama of English history. The Roman legions landed here and built a vast fortification which, although added to and restored over the centuries, still remains one of the most enduring monuments of Roman Britain. In 491, after the departure of the Romans, the Anglo-Saxon tribes moved into England. Although modern historians now tend to regard this migration as largely peaceful, there is little doubt that the inhabitants of what was to become Sussex put up considerable resistance. The Anglo-Saxon Chronicle records that: 'Aelle and Cissa beseiged Anderida, near Pevensey, and killed all who were inside, so that there was not one Briton left'. Aella and his son had landed near SELSEY and Cissa gave his name to the city of CHICHESTER.

In 1066 it was the Saxons' turn to endure the horrors of invasion. William the Conqueror established a temporary headquarters within the ruins of the Roman fort; subsequently, following the defeat of the Saxons at the Battle of Hastings, a formidable Norman Castle was erected by the Count of Mortain, to whom

William had entrusted the Rape of Pevensey. The castle is now in the care of English Heritage and is open to the public. The Normans never over-looked the importance of Pevensey and during the time of the Plantagenets it became one of the Cinque Ports, providing men and ships for the defence of the realm in the era before the establishment of a Royal Navy. During the Tudor period Pevensey developed as a port and the massive walls of the castle acted as a demarcation line between old Pevensey and neighbouring Westham. Iron from the foundries of the northern Weald was brought down here for export to the Continent. Unfortunately the erection of dams and sluices for drainage only helped to speed up the natural eastward drift of shingle and the harbour gradually silted up. The area known as Pevensey Bay is a modern development and has no link with the old harbour.

At one time Pevensey had its own Royal Mint, on the site of which now stands the Old Mint House. Further along the road is Court House, the town hall of the incorporated town of Pevensey, where local justice was dispensed. The village has so many fine houses that it is impossible to pick out a few for special attention. The old inns are, of course, accessible to the public and Glyndley Manor with its famous colony of herons looks like the ideal setting for a horror film.

The string of Martello Towers on the **Pevensey Levels** reminds the visitor of the threat of invasion during the Napoleonic Wars. A folk-song of the time had a verse which ran:

> If Bonyparte should have the heart
> To land on Pens'ny Levels,
> Then English sons with English guns
> Will blow him to the Devil.

Pevensey Castle was refortified during the Second World War when these islands were again threatened with invasion; Pevensey thus fulfilled its traditional role of almost 2,000 years.

The Marsh known as the Pevensey Levels was probably a wide bay in early times, studded with islands. Gradually, the area was reclaimed from the sea for agriculture, changing from saltmarsh to meadows and, ultimately, arable fields. An important activity here in medieval times was salt-making, the retreating sea water being collected in shallow pans or depressions for evaporation, prior to boiling in salt houses.

Piddinghoe (2/4E)

A village directly north of Newhaven, over-looking the Ouse valley. Of the only three churches in Sussex with round towers, two are in neighbouring parishes, Piddinghoe and SOUTHEASE slightly further north. The third is St Michael's in the High Street, LEWES. It is something of a surprise to venture round the back of the churchyard at Piddinghoe to find oneself staring over the wide expanse of the Ouse, across which are the lush water meadows of the river valley. In early times, when the water level was higher, the little villages of the lower Ouse valley were accessible by boat and served as subsidiary ports to the principal harbours of Lewes and Newhaven. Close to the church is one of the few bottle-shaped brick

kilns to survive in Sussex. Painstakingly restored, it stands in the grounds of Kiln Cottage and was last operated commercially in 1912. It was common for brick and lime kilns to be situated beside rivers, providing a means of transport into the interior or along the coast, an outstanding example being Pepper's Lime Works at AMBERLEY Chalk Pits on the River Arun.

Piddinghoe was the source of many rhymes and folktales, perhaps partly because of its comical name and partly because its people kept themselves to themselves, avoiding too many questions about their involvement in smuggling, a popular and profitable local sideline. If someone in Sussex was asked where he was going and gave the answer: 'Down to Piddinghoe to shoe

Medieval stone bridge at Stopham

magpies', it meant he didn't want to be pressed too closely on his activities.

Playden (3/5C) *see* Rye

Plumpton (2/3D) *see* Ditchling

Poling (1/4E) *see* Arundel

Portslade by Sea (2/2E) *see* Hove

Pulborough (1/4D)
A diffused village straggling along a sandstone ridge and looking south over the Amberley Wild Brooks to the Downs. Pulborough developed at

the point where the Roman road from London to Chichester crossed the River Arun. The modern A29 closely follows the old road north to Billingshurst and the southerly route can be traced on foot over Bignor Hill from Eartham. The first section of the road was built on an alignment from Chichester to Pulborough Hill; near the river crossing the Romans built a *mansio* or staging post for the benefit of travellers. Despite its strategic position, however, Pulborough did not grow into a major settlement and today, apart from a pleasant group of houses around St Mary's church, it is a somewhat unsatisfactory collection of indifferent buildings, lacking a central focus.

It is Pulborough's connection with the river and the Arun valley which explains its attraction for visitors. Accessible by the Arun Valley railway line from London and the coast, Pulborough has much to offer the fisherman, walker, cyclist and canoeist. The Arun (and its tributary the western Rother, which joins the Arun here) has long been a favourite haunt of anglers and eel was once a local delicacy. Fishing permits are available in the village. Walkers and cyclists find Pulborough a good base for exploring the Arun and Rother valleys: a favourite walk is from St Mary's, through sandy Pulborough Park to Stopham Bridge, returning through the water meadows via Hardham.

For canoes and small boats, a public slipway is provided adjoining the old (1787) bridge and there is also access to the river near Stopham Bridge. **Stopham**'s stone bridge of 1423 is generally regarded as the best medieval bridge in Sussex and, now that cars and lorries are diverted to another, can be quietly enjoyed by the visitor on foot. Of particular interest are the raised centre arch of 1822, designed to enable masted vessels to proceed upriver to join the Wey and Arun Canal, and the inscribed stone tablet on the western end of the bridge recording the association with the Barttelot family of Stopham House. The Barttelots came over with William the Conqueror and the early Norman church of St Mary contains a number of family monuments, including memorial brasses of some 12 of them with their children. The brasses are among the best in the county and can be rubbed for a small fee.

To the west of Pulborough and Stopham is **Fittleworth**, a pretty sandstone village on the River Rother, popular with fishermen and artists. The great attraction for the family visitor is the high sandy heath of Hesworth Common, just off the main A272 road, a splendid place for gentle walks, picnics and adventurous games, with views over the river valley to the Downs.

Just south of Pulborough is the Saxon church of St Botolph at **Hardham**. The church is unique in having the earliest nearly complete series of wall paintings in the country. They date from the early 12th century and belong to a small group associated with artists connected with the Priory of St Pancras at LEWES. The paintings at Hardham include vivid depictions

12th-century wall paintings at Hardham

of *Adam and Eve after the Fall* and *St George on horseback*. They should be compared with those at CLAYTON and at COOMBES, which are thought to be by the same artists. Close to the church is Hardham Priory, originally a small house of the Augustinian canons, and from the nearby public footpath it is possible to spot the overgrown southern portal of Hardham tunnel, built to provide a shorter route for barges on the Arun by avoiding the wide loop which the river takes to the east.

The hamlet of **Little Bognor** about a mile to the north of Fittleworth contains a group of old cottages and what was once Crowshole Mill, where members of an evangelical free church were baptised in the millpond. An isolated cottage, Brinkwells, was for a while the home of Sir Edward Elgar, who composed some of his work here and occasionally played the organ at St Mary's, Fittleworth.

The South Downs Way

MILES JEBB

The South Downs Way extends along the ridge of the South Downs from Eastbourne for seventy miles to the Hampshire border, from where it continues for thirty miles more to Winchester. It includes a further ten miles on an alternative route from Eastbourne to Alfriston by way of the coast. Apart from this alternative, the route is also a bridleway throughout.

Although not as wild or dramatic as many of the other official walking trails in Britain, it has a strong claim to being the most charming and delightful of them all. It provides a terrace from which to survey the greater part of the county of Sussex, and a means of physically experiencing the meaning of Kipling's couplet that 'The Weald is good, the Downs are best – I'll give you the run of 'em, East to West'.

Its charm derives, in the first instance, from the small scale of the scenery. The South Downs are, in truth, a range of only very small hills, whose highest point in Sussex is only 255 metres and from a distance of ten miles or more they appear negligible. But, once in them, their lines become impressive and their panoramas extensive, and from their steep and straight northern scarp they give a distinct illusion of size. The effect of this geography is that the views from the South Downs Way are constantly changing and the impression is rendered all the more varied by the fences and hedges, the copses and the clumps, that cross the Downs. To the north is the complex and ancient pattern of the Weald and to the south the ever changing colour of the sea.

Closely associated with this scenery, the record of human habitation is always present on the South Downs Way. Up on the top is a succession of burial mounds, hill-forts and cross-dykes, which bear witness to prehistoric societies. The Way itself follows the line of the ancient drove-way along which men and animals moved before the Weald was cleared or inhabited. Down below are the old villages, whose churches evoke the spirituality of the Middle Ages and whose pubs provide for the material needs of long-distance walkers.

In addition to these features, a special attraction of the South Downs Way is that it is on chalk, that purest of limestones. Chalk is porous and so its surface remains firm in rain, a fact of prime importance for walkers, especially in winter. Its crumbly, crunchy texture is good to feel underfoot. Its white colour adds brightness to the scene on the dullest day. It is due to the soft chalk that the Downs present their rounded, feminine, appearance, the result of eons of imperceptible erosion, so that nothing is precipitous among the humpy hills and gentle combes and the only cliffs to be seen are where the present sea encroaches, or at former chalk quarries. It is thanks to the chalk that the thin topsoil, or renzina, is non-acidic and so supports the beautiful downland flora. Within living memory the Downs were largely open sheep pastures, covered with a finely-matted and close-cropped natural turf, broken only by clumps of thorns or brambles and sprinkled with many wild flowers, of which the scabious and the rampion, known as the Pride of Sussex, are the two most evocative. Today, sadly, this habitat is confined to the steepest slopes and some isolated patches, although the flowers do border the path for much of its length.

With all these special characteristics, the South Downs Way provides a wealth of interest. Even though it can be followed without a guide-book because so well waymarked (by concrete plinths in East Sussex and by wooden signposts in West Sussex), walkers should study one before they start their journey, for true appreciation only comes from understanding and not merely physically experiencing the route. The Way undoubtedly becomes very crowded on summer weekends, especially in its eastern sections, but fortunately the attractions of autumn, winter and spring are great and much more bracing. There are plenty of access points by car; public transport is still convenient at several places; no given point on the route is more than three miles from a pub; and accommodation is available throughout for those prepared to walk fifteen miles or so in a day.

There follows a general description of the Sussex South Downs Way in four sections, east to west.

Eastbourne to the Ouse

The rolled scarp rises from the edge of Eastbourne and the South Downs Way kicks off with a climb up to the ridge. But it is more satisfactory to begin at Eastbourne Pier and walk along the promenade and thence by quiet streets to the official start.

For the first couple of miles along the ridge the view extends eastwards over Eastbourne towards the Pevensey Levels and their multitude of water

View towards Windover Hill from near Lullington

channels. A golf course alongside precedes a more natural stretch where, among the bushes, there are three circular barrows, or burial mounds.

The scene changes on the brow of Willingdon Hill where the route turns down into the dry valley of Jevington, the start of the descent ceremonially marked by two carved stones. At this point, on the adjacent slopes of Combe Hill, the lines of lynchets, or very early field systems, can be detected. After Jevington a second climb brings the Way up to Lullington Heath where the chalk is mixed, unusually, with a sandy, heather-bearing soil.

Next comes Windover Hill, one of the prime archeological sites on the South Downs. Within a single acre are to be found a fine bowl barrow and a less prominent but much older long barrow, as well as the refuse humps of Stone Age flint mines and a steep terraced track that may date back to Romano-British times. And just below, out of sight, is the famous Long Man of Wilmington, etched on the steep hillside by means of white-washed concrete blocks. His origins are quite uncertain, so if one is cynical one can imagine him only some 2–300 years old; if romantic, some 2,500 years old and the image of a Bronze Age sun god.

The valley of the Cuckmere now unfolds, the first of four that cut through the Downs to the sea, making use of the great furrows in the hills through which the higher soils of the Weald had once drained away.

Just before Alfriston is the point where the alternative footpath route from Eastbourne rejoins the main South Downs Way. For seven of its ten miles it goes along the top of the dramatic white cliffs of the coast, and is unquestionably the finest stretch of coastal path in South East England. From the promenade at Eastbourne it mounts 163 metres to the top of Beachy Head, a fine vantage point with the sea visible in three directions. From there on it is gradually downhill to Birling Gap, near sea level, before tackling the rises and falls of the famous Seven Sisters. This is the most elemental part of the South Downs Way, completely different in character to all the rest. The sight, sound and smell of the sea; the swoops and cries of the gannets and the fulmars; the broad sweeps of grass cut sharply at the cliff's edge; and the roller-coaster nature of the walk – all these make it remarkable enough. And contemplation of the inexorable erosion, as the sea gradually encroaches through the millennia, makes it even more so.

At Cuckmere Haven, where the river enters the sea in an entirely natural setting, the Way turns inland along the valley past marsh, wood, fields, village and riverside to Alfriston.

Long Man of Wilmington

From the Cuckmere to the Ouse the South Downs are at their most bare, their lines unbroken by any woods or clumps. For many this is the finest section of the Way. The sea is only a few miles off and visible almost throughout. To the north the scene is enhanced by the isolated group of hills around Mount Caburn. The track is mostly free from close-restraining fences and there are good displays of flowers, especially on Itford Hill. Furthermore, a very pleasant circular route can be devised by making use of the underhill lane, the ancient route linking the villages along the foot of the scarp. The underhill lane remains, in some form or other, as a parallel route to the entire South Downs Way, but it is now mostly a road and hence not so good for walking. In this section, however, it takes the form of a hedge-lined track running from back at Jevington to Alfriston and then on past Berwick, Alciston and Firle. From it Firle Beacon, flanked by the attendant Bostal and Beddingham Hills, gives the suggestion of a great elephant's head with its trunk probing forward into the woods of Firle Place.

The Ouse to the Adur

From where it crosses the Ouse near Southease, the Way has to gain the northern ridge west of Lewes, which it does by eight miles of rather circuitous routing. The largely arable slopes of Swanborough Hill are succeeded by the turf on Castle Hill. The ancient cart track between Brighton and Lewes, known as Juggs Road (the fisherfolk, who carried their produce along it, were known as 'Juggs') is succeeded by the rushing A27 road. Back on the ridge, Plumpton Plain precedes Ditchling Beacon, once lit to warn of the Spanish Armada; from there it is gradually downhill to Pyecombe.

Between Plumpton and Pyecombe there are three notable points of interest. The first is a late Bronze Age settlement site, where a group of men and women once eked a living by keeping some cattle and goats, growing a little barley, trapping wild animals and collecting wild fruit. The second is the natural turf around Ditchling Beacon, where sheep still safely graze among the tufts and bushes, reminiscent of the not-so-distant past when shepherds daily drove their flocks of black-faced Southdown sheep to these pastures, returning them every evening to their close-confined hurdled enclosures in the fields around the villages. The third point of interest is the pair of windmills, Jack and Jill. As the Ordnance Survey Landranger Series map correctly specifies, the former is disused and the latter is in use, for Jill has been lovingly restored to her former functional glory, grinding the wheat between her stones into warm nourishing flour, by means of medieval machinery. Once there were scores of windmills up on the Downs and their harsh silhouettes dominated the scenery like watch-towers.

The Way now cuts behind the outcrops of Wolstonbury Hill and Newtimber Hill (Wolstonbury is the site of a major Iron Age fort) and goes through the village of Pyecombe, once the remote abode of shepherds where their distinctive crooks were hammered out at the blacksmith's forge, but now uncomfortably close to the main Brighton road and the very opposite of remote. More evocative of the past is the small hamlet at Saddlescombe, with its cottages and flint farm buildings: a place reminiscent of the farming life of the past century, when labourers were paid one pound a week and black Pembroke oxen were worked in pairs.

Next comes the Devil's Dyke, the steepest and strangest of the South Downs combes. Although entirely natural it gives the appearance of being man-made, hence the legend about the devil trying to dig a trench through the Downs to flood the Weald from the sea. He had nearly succeeded

in his fiendish plan when he was disturbed by an old woman carrying a candle, which he mistook for the dawn; since he could only operate in darkness, he had to leave the job unfinished. It is thickly bushed and still a place of mystery, despite the brash Devil's Dyke Hotel at its top end. Dyke Hill, beyond it, is the site of another Iron Age fort and now a prime site for hang-gliders.

There follows a pleasant sequence of little hills: Fulking Hill, Perching Hill, Edburton Hill and Truleigh Hill all pass in quick succession within only one and a half miles. As with most of the hilltops of the South Downs these do not bear names of their own, but merely those of the villages below them. Along the northern ridge the normal pattern for each parish was to comprise a section of downland to the south and another of the Weald to the north, which was progressively cleared and planted through the centuries.

The Downs around here were one of the last remaining habitats of the great bustard, the largest native bird of its day, which was hunted by greyhounds. Meanwhile the little wheatear was killed in large numbers by the shepherds, who trapped it in narrow turf-covered trenches. Happily the lark is still amazingly populous on the Downs and under no threat from man.

After the strategically placed Youth Hostel at Tottington Barn, the Way descends across Beeding Hill to the valley of the Adur.

Devil's Dyke

The Adur to the Arun

A cement works, a busy road and overhead pylons briefly clutch at the South Downs Way as it crosses the Adur. But once over the footbridge the quiet and solitude are soon resumed, exemplified almost immediately by the sight of a disused railway line and the burial mounds of the shrunken village of Botolphs. Botolphs's Saxon church shares with the churches at Jevington, Alfriston, Pyecombe and Houghton the distinction of being plum on the line of the Way, although of course there are many others lying within a mile or two of it. In medieval times the whole appearance of this river basin would have been utterly different because the sea encroached as far as Bramber and Botolphs was a prosperous fishing village and a centre for the salt industry.

By way of Annington Hill the Way ascends on to Steyning Round Hill and thence by a sinuous track up to Chanctonbury Hill, crowned with its famous clump of beeches. The plantation of clumps of deciduous trees at prominent points on the hills of lowland England was one of the most genial aspects of the 18th-century passion for landscaping; nor was it always easy, because the saplings needed watering during the dry summers. Charles Goring of Wiston Park fostered his clump well, and it has for long constituted the principal

Barn at Southease (see Rodmell)

landmark of south-central Sussex; but such were the ravages of the 1987 storm that many years will pass before it can regain its former glory. Besides the beeches some Scots firs, evergreen oaks, sycamores and ashes have insinuated themselves into the charmed circle and excavations on the site of a Romano-British temple have also formed a gap within the grove. The clump is known as Chanctonbury Ring, though the ring is really the bank and ditch around them, the remains of an Iron Age fort. The wood bends away from the prevailing south-easterlies which sweep up to it from the coast.

A few hundred metres beyond the Ring the Way passes a curiosity – a dew pond. Before water was first pumped up on to the Downs half a century ago the only supply was from pits such as this. Once dug, they were then lined with layers of compacted clay, straw and rubble and were extremely efficient in capturing and retaining rainwater. Despite their name, the dew had precious little effect in producing water.

Chanctonbury Hill is also the centre for several circular walks. Once again the underhill lane provides a parallel traffic-free path at the foot of the scarp from Steyning through Wiston Park to Washington; while on the dip slope a network of bridleways leads southwards to the seaside conurbations, some of them converging at the impressive earthworks of Cissbury Ring. This massive Iron Age fortification, the greatest on the entire South Downs, is two miles off course from the Way but well worth the diversion.

From the Washington gap (cut by the A24) to the Arun the Way is once again straight, as it presses along the brows of Barnsfarm, Kithurst and Rackham Hills. Just past the summit of Rackham Hill are some formidable cross-dykes known as the Rackham Banks. Standing on these, a splendid panorama is revealed. Back to the right is Parham House in its wooded parkland. Half right are the Amberley Wildbrooks, a large area of natural water-meadows. Ahead is the Arun flowing between the villages of Amberley and Bury and beyond it the continuing Downs. And to the left is the aforested hillside of Arundel Park, with the castle silhouetted at the furthest extremity.

Finally, the Way descends over a shoulder of Rackham Hill known as Amberley Mount, which is full of interest. The archeologist will find a Bronze Age settlement site and the naturalist a fine display of flowers, including the very rare Fly Honeysuckle and the Lady's Tress Orchid.

The Arun to the Hampshire border

From Houghton the route regains height by way of Bury Hill and Westburton Hill on to Bignor

Hill. On its brow is a contemporary grave, contrasting with all the scores of prehistoric graves – some still visible but others destroyed by plough – that line the South Downs Way.

The saddle between Bignor Hill and Burton Down is yet another place of mystery, this time associated with the era of Roman rule, for a Roman road from Noviomagus (Chichester) to Londinium here crossed the line of the Downs. The embankments of Stane Street (as the Saxons subsequently called it) still look impressive; a modern signpost, slightly off course, points the way to the two Roman cities, as well as to Bignor at the foot of the hill, with its Roman mosaics. Resting on the bank among the vipers bugloss and the marjoram one can easily imagine the scene as marching legionaries or shuffling slaves came past along the flint-paved road.

The Way next takes a short cut across the gap near Upwaltham to Littleton Down, behind the promontory of Duncton Down: it descends between zigzagging hedgelines and ascends through the middle of a cornfield. It then heads straight along the ridge to the Cocking gap. By now the differences between this section and the previous three will have became evident. From Eastbourne to the Arun the South Downs are narrow and decline directly on to the coast: they display much exposed chalk, are largely arable and treeless and the Way itself is confined mostly between fences. From the Arun westwards they are broader and are separated from the coast by a plain: they bear a thicker topsoil, support large plantations of trees and there are many more hedgelines. Individual preferences may differ, but the long stretch between Littleton and Harting Downs is truly magnificent and makes for some splendid walking.

Not all the plantations are felicitous: the beech forest that borders the Way on Graffham and Heyshott Downs, for instance, should never have been brought so close to the ridge. But there are fine hanging woods on the escarpment, with many spreading beeches as well as ashes, oaks and hawthorns. Before the plantations this area of open land was once the territory of the Charlton Hunt, one of the earliest packs of foxhounds, founded by a group of noblemen over 300 years ago.

Just before the crossing road near Cocking the Way goes past a timber yard and a tap for drinking water placed here in memory of a boy who died at the age of 14 but not before he had walked the South Downs Way.

There follow four hill-tops – Linch Down, Treyford Hill, Beacon Hill and Harting Down. Linch Down lies near the border of two large estates, the Cowdray estate to the north and the West Dean estate to the south, and from it can be seen the spire of Chichester Cathedral rising from the valley of the Lavant. Treyford Hill has, near its summit, a group of the largest and most pronounced Bronze Age burial mounds in Sussex, known as the Devil's Jumps. The flat plateau of Beacon Hill bears extensive earthworks, as well as the site of the beacon: near it is Telegraph House, where the naval semaphores connecting Portsmouth and London once operated. The area around here and to Harting Down is unenclosed grass and bush, thankfully preserved from the plough.

The Way passes through the woods below Tower Hill, topped by the ruin of Uppark Tower, an octagonal Gothic folly (Uppark itself is only half a mile off course) and then heads towards the border between luxuriant hedges of hawthorn, blackthorn, field maple, dogwood, briony, dog-rose, spindle, elder and suchlike.

Hilaire Belloc, that great Sussex patriot, referred to 'the Hampshire border, beyond which there is nothing.' There isn't nothing, of course; there's a great deal: keen walkers will continue over Butser Hill and on to Winchester. But for those who only want Sussex there are plenty of circular trails, long and short, in this fourth section of the Way, through villages such as Chilgrove, Singleton, Charlton, East Dean, Eartham and Slindon where one can walk extensively among the high woods of the South Downs.

Wild orchids growing on Harting Down

Pyecombe (2/2D)
A village north of Brighton on the busy A23 London road, where it squeezes between Wolstonbury Hill and Newtimber Hill. In the past it was a staging post and The Plough still has the look of a coaching inn. Today, heavy traffic thunders by and walkers and riders on the South Downs Way take their lives in their hands when they try to cross the road. The old centre of the village has now been bypassed, however, and a visit to the Norman church reminds the traveller of calmer days gone by.

The churchyard is entered through a tapsel gate turning on a central pivot. (There is a similar gate at COOMBES.) The church, dedicated to the Transfiguration of Our Lord, is built of flint and pebble-dash. It contains an unusual leaden, drum-shaped font, painted white during the Civil War to save the lead from being requisitioned by Parliamentary troops and melted down for bullets. Opposite the church is the old forge, no longer working but, for 200 years, the place where the best shepherds' crooks in the county were made until shepherding died out after the Second World War. This association is remembered in the village sign erected by the parish council.

Below Newtimber Hill is the hamlet of **Newtimber**, consisting of the Victorian parish church of St John the Baptist, the Old Rectory and the 17th-century Newtimber Place, a flint and brick house with a moat.

North-east of Pyecombe, on the road to Burgess Hill, is the village of **Clayton**. Like Pyecombe, Clayton is associated with travel from London to Brighton but this time by railway rather than by road. The one and a quarter mile long Clayton tunnel, matching that through the North Downs at Merstham, was built in 1846 and was one of the great engineering triumphs of the London, Brighton and South Coast Railway. Its northern portal boasts a splendid castellated tunnel-keeper's cottage, towering above the trains far below.

The Norman parish church of St John the Baptist is renowned for its wall paintings. Discovered in 1895, they covered every wall in the church and were probably completed about 1140. They are contemporary with those at HARDHAM and COOMBES and like them were the work of artists associated with the great Priory of St Pancras at LEWES. The paintings which include scenes depicting the *Last Judgment*, may be identified with the aid of a guide available in the church.

Jack and Jill windmills near Pyecombe

Above the village on Clayton Hill are two windmills known as Jack and Jill. As a pair, they are unique in the country. Jack is a black-painted tower mill, now part of a private house once lived in by the golfer Henry Longhurst. Jill is a much smaller wooden post mill which was originally sited in Dyke Road, Brighton, and in 1821 was towed here by a team of oxen.

Both mills continued working into the 20th century and Jill has recently been restored by a dedicated band of volunteers. When the wind is in the right quarter flour is ground and the mill is open to visitors at certain times. The car park adjoining Jill is a good starting point for downland walks in the area and is within 100 yd of the South Downs Way. A series of walks between here and DITCHLING Beacon are way-marked: a descriptive leaflet is available from County Hall, Lewes.

Racton (1/2D) *see* Stoughton

Ringmer (2/4D)
A large village to the north-east of Lewes on the B2192, which has been expanded considerably in recent years. Despite considerable development in recent years, Ringmer still retains many reminders of its past. In the parish church of St Mary is a memorial to the members of the prestigious Ringmer cricket team who lost their lives in the First World War. It declares: 'They played the game' and it is sobering to reflect that, of the 34 men who joined up, only six returned. The church dates from the 13th century but was greatly restored by the Victorians, who rebuilt the tower and much of the nave. The lectern is believed to be the largest in the county and was carved by a young sculptor from Lewes in 1975.

Tapsel gate in Pyecombe churchyard

The tortoise depicted on the village sign recalls the time when the naturalist Gilbert White used to visit his aunt and sit in her garden, watching her pet tortoise called Timothy. White found it strange that a creature with so little apparent enthusiasm for life should live to such a great age. When his aunt died White adopted Timothy, whose remains are now preserved in the British Museum.

It could be argued that no village in Sussex had a greater influence on the early development of the United States of America than Ringmer, as both the statesman William Penn and the scholar John Harvard married girls from the village. Penn came from Warminghurst, near COOLHAM and his wife was the posthumous daughter of Sir William Springate of Broyle Place, Ringmer, joint governor of ARUNDEL Castle on behalf of the Parliamentary army in the Civil War. During the early years of the 18th century Daniel Defoe stopped in Ringmer and commented: 'I travelled through the dirtiest, but in many respects, the richest and most profitable country in England'. Modern visitors are unlikely to agree with the first element of his description. Perhaps Defoe stayed at the 16th-century Cock Inn, which has provided for the needs of travellers for hundreds of years. Wagons on their way north would pause here to hitch up an additional 'cock-horse' for extra pulling power up the long hill towards Tunbridge Wells, returning the horse to the landlord when they reached the top.

Ripe (2/5E) *see* Alciston

Robertsbridge (3/3C)

Home of the cricket bat and of one of England's oldest pubs, Robertsbridge is situated off the A21 due north of Battle. Gray-Nicolls have been making cricket bats from English willow at Robertsbridge for several generations and have supplied specially commissioned bats for many leading cricketers. The workshops are not open to the public. They also make the rounded bats used for stoolball, a game more or less unique to Sussex. It is believed to have originated when dairy maids played an improvised game of cricket, using an upturned milking stool instead of stumps; today the bowler aims at a board on a post. Stoolball has remained not only a Sussex game, but also largely a women's preserve. Many teams still compete for a coveted championship every summer.

The Seven Stars pub at Robertsbridge is reputed to date back to the days of Richard I. Although this seems doubtful, there are certain very interesting features of the building. The curved counter of the public bar is said to be the longest in Sussex and the giant oak beam which supports the roof can have few equals anywhere. Horace Walpole stayed here for a night in 1752 and was disturbed to find that he was sharing the place with prostitutes and smugglers. It goes without saying that the clientele today is somewhat more respectable. The Congregational

Fore Hill and Fore Farm near Telscombe

Church has been much criticised but the tile-hung George Hotel, with its delightful bay windows, is a gem. It was here, drinking port and staring into the fire, that Hilaire Belloc conceived the idea of the journey across Sussex which forms the subject of one of his best-known books, *The Four Men*.

Outside the village are the remains of Robertsbridge Abbey, a Cistercian community founded in 1176 by Robert de St Martin. During the reign of Henry VI, an official report accused the monks of indulging in all kinds of misbehaviour. The Abbey was dissolved following Henry VIII's break with Rome and the remains of the buildings are incorporated in Abbey Farm. The Abbey and the village are situated on the eastern River Rother and the name of the place may a corruption of 'Rotherbridge'. Alternatively, it may derive from that of the founder of the Abbey.

Rock Mill (1/5D) *see* Washington

Rodmell (2/4E)
A charming brick and flint village in the Ouse valley between Lewes and Newhaven, once the home of the writer Virginia Woolf. She and her husband Leonard lived at Monk's House for 20 years until her tragic suicide in 1941. Today the house is owned by the National Trust and may be visited by the public in spring and summer. It is not large and, when the Woolfs bought it, was extremely primitive, with no hot water or proper sanitation. Not surprisingly, they often preferred to stay in their more comfortable London house, especially during the winter. Virginia was troubled by depression and increasingly severe mental illness throughout her life and eventually drowned herself in the River Ouse.

Just north of Rodmell is the delightful hamlet of **Iford**, with a Norman flint church dedicated to St Nicholas, the patron saint of sailors, and the largely 15th- and 16th-century Swanborough Manor, now the official home of the Vice-Chancellor of the University of Sussex.

Downstream from Rodwell is **Southease**, with its famous round-towered church. Historians now believe that the greater part of the church is Norman rather than Saxon and that the original building, constructed during the reign of the Saxon King Edgar, was largely rebuilt in the 11th century. Nevertheless the round tower, one of only three in Sussex, is of considerable interest. One theory is that the round church towers of the lower Ouse valley (the others are at PIDDINGHOE and LEWES) may have served as beacons to guide mariners safely into the wide, tidal estuary of the Ouse with its many small wharves and anchorages. The church also possesses medieval wall paintings. One shows the *Passion of Christ*, the other the *Life of St Christopher*. The church bells date from the 13th century. Southease once had its share of seafarers and fishermen but their prosperity, tied as it was with the fortunes of nearby Seaford, declined as that town lost its primacy to neighbouring Newhaven.

Close by is **Telscombe** an enchanting little village in a hollow of the Downs, now mainly owned by Brighton Borough Council and protected from development, unlike the cliff top to the south which was a victim of urban sprawl in the interwar years. The flint church of St Lawrence dates from Saxon times, although the greater part of the building is Norman. The tower has a distinctive Saxon cap of clay tiles and on the south-west corner there are two Mass dials or sun dials which, in the days before clocks and watches were commonplace, informed the villagers when it was time for the service. At the foot of the tower is an Ordnance Survey bench mark which gives the height above sea level at 219.2 ft. In the parish registers, now kept in the County Record Office at Lewes, there is an entry relating to the death of John Lulham of Telscombe in 1819, with the marginal note in a later hand and prefaced by a question mark: 'Last man hanged for sheep stealing'.

Rogate (1/2C)
In the far north of West Sussex, in the wooded valley of the River Rother, close to the site of Durford Abbey. The name of the village may signify its position at the gateway to wooded countryside populated by wild deer; in early times it was a centre for timber production, shipbuilding and charcoal burning. Today the charm of its location is diminished by the busy A272 road from Midhurst to Petersfield, but Rogate remains worth exploring. The exterior of the church of St Bartholomew looks quite new, as it was restored in 1875, but the interior has been retained. A mile or two to the west is the site of Durford Abbey, founded as a community of Premonstratensian canons in the 12th century. The Abbey was never rich and life was always a struggle. When the community was dissolved under Henry VIII the commissioner sent to assess Durford reported to his master, Thomas Cromwell: 'The poorest abbey I have seen – far in debt and in decay'.

Nevertheless, the canons of Durford have left a priceless legacy in the three medieval stone bridges across the River Rother which they built and maintained. The provision of bridges was a religious duty in the Middle Ages: other Sussex bridges – such as those at ARUNDEL and Upper Beeding near BRAMBER – owe their preservation to religious communities. Here in the Rother valley, the canons of Durford built the Habin bridge south of Rogate on the road to Harting and Maidenmarsh bridge close to the site of the Abbey. The remaining bridges, with their round-headed arches and massive cutwaters are well worth visiting; it is refreshing to reflect on the peaceful lives of the monks who built and looked after them. Following the dissolution of the Abbey its lands were appropriated to the Crown and the maintenance of the bridges became a charge on the public purse.

A few miles south-east of Rogate is **Trotton**, a

Southease church

sandstone village in the valley of the western River Rother, which also has an important medieval bridge, carrying the busy A272 Midhurst to Petersfield road. The name of the village may indicate that it developed at a point where the river could be forded with the help of stepping or 'treading' stones, as the village was recorded as 'Tradyngton' in the time of Domesday. The sandstone landscape through which the river runs provides quite good building stone of a lovely honey colour; Trotton and other Rother valley villages have many examples of houses and cottages built of agreeable local materials. The bridge itself is of sandstone and was provided by the first Lord Camoys at a cost, it is said, of only a few pence less than that of the church, which he also built. The bridge is a fine structure of five semicircular arches with four massive cutwater buttresses on each side.

Dating from about 1300, the church of St George contains a memorial to the 17th-century dramatist Thomas Otway, who was born in the rectory and died aged 33 of unrequited love for the actress Mrs Barry. It also boasts some important monumental brasses, including that of Thomas, first Lord Camoys who was with Henry V at the Battle of Agincourt, and another of Margaret de Camoys, thought to be one of the earliest brasses in the country to portray a woman. The wall paintings at the west end of the church date from the late 14th century and depict the contrasting activities and eventual fates of *The Good Man* and *The Evil Man*.

Rottingdean (2/3E) *see* Brighton

Rustington (1/4E) *see* Littlehampton

Rye (3/5C)

At the eastern extremity of Sussex, Rye is the best preserved medieval fishing town in southern England. This, combined with its hilltop location and wealth of interesting buildings, makes a trip to Rye essential for most visitors to the county. Rye was one of the Cinque Ports, the group of Kent and Sussex seaports which were granted special privileges for providing ships and men for the defence of the Channel. It exported wool and iron to the Continent and had a large merchant sailing fleet. Its comparative prosperity in the Middle Ages was such that it is said to have exported the old shoes of its inhabitants to the poverty-stricken French, who rarely had any shoes to wear. The receding of the sea, after the centuries of erosion and fierce

Church Square, Rye

gales which often threatened Rye's very existence, led to an inevitable decline: the town that had resisted French raids and the full force of the elements could not withstand the loss of its harbour and commercial facilities. Yet this decline has been to our advantage, preserving Rye as in a time capsule. Its cobbled streets and timber-framed houses would never have survived had it continued to expand and prosper.

Of all the streets in Rye, none is more celebrated than Mermaid Street. The cobbled lane makes its way up a gentle incline, with timber-framed cottages on both sides. The Mermaid Inn has a series of information boards that chart the town's progress over the years. During the 18th century the most powerful and ruthless of all the smuggling gangs, the Hawkhurst Gang, used the Mermaid as its headquarters. In the 19th century the excesses of Rye's Bonfire Boys became notorious. They would march through the streets with patriotic banners and skull and crossbones flags. Lighted tar barrels were rolled down the streets and unpopular figures found themselves burned in effigy or their property attacked. During the 1870s and 80s serious attempts to stop the disorders led to terrible rioting. On one occasion the local police chief was thrown onto a bonfire by a resentful mob and later died a painful death from his burns.

The parish church of St Mary is proud and splendid, recalling the past prominence of the town. The golden quarter boys above the church clock are replicas: the originals date from 1760 and are now inside the church. The reproduction quarter boys still come out to chime each quarter of an hour. Lamb House, named after James Lamb, 13 times mayor of Rye in the early 18th century, was also the home of the novelist Henry James, who entertained writers such as H. G. Wells, Joseph Conrad and Ford Madox Ford in his beloved retirement home where he lived until his death in 1916. Subsequently Lamb House was owned by E. F. Benson, author of the Mapp and Lucia books which are set in Rye, lightly disguised as 'Tilling'. Today, the house is owned by the National Trust and is open to the public on certain days in spring and summer. The town museum is housed in the Ypres Tower which, in the 15th century, was the home of John de Ypres. It had previously been used as a courthouse and gaol. Other notable buildings include the Landgate and the 18th-century Town Hall, from whose balcony it is the custom for the newly elected mayor to throw hot pennies to the children below.

A useful walking guide to Rye has been produced by the County Council and may be bought at the public library and the excellent, long-established bookshop in the High Street has a good stock of books of local interest.

A mile north of Rye is the small hamlet of **Playden**, whose 13th-century church dedicated to St Michael has an elegant shingled broach spire. Leasam House, a fine, red brick house of about 1800, commands a good view over Rye. A country museum in a private house called Cherries has several agricultural and domestic implements on show as well as artifacts of the brewing trade. There is a fine monument to a Flemish brewer in the church. In translation, the inscription reads: 'Here is buried Cornelis Roetmans, pray for his soul' and beneath are two beer barrels and two crossed pitchforks. The inscription and the illustrations were once inlaid with brass.

16th-century monument to a Flemish brewer, Playden

Built as part of the country's defences against Napoleon, the Royal Military Canal runs from Rye to Hythe and provides a good 20-mile towpath walk, part of which is owned by the National Trust. Romney Marsh, with its isolated churches at **East Guldeford** and at Fairfield over the county boundary in Kent, has an atmosphere all of its own, its peace disturbed only by birdsong and the sounds of sheep. Visitors should avoid Camber, with its bungalows, holiday camps and grim military installations.

St Leonard's (3/4E) *see* Hastings

St Leonard's Forest (2/2B)

Nine thousand acres of heath and woodland between Horsham and East Grinstead, and the natural habitat of the Sussex dragon. The Forest is first recorded in 1213, taking its name from a chapel dedicated to St Leonard, the patron saint of prisoners. It lies on a sandstone ridge rising above the surrounding clay country and reaches a height of nearly 500 ft in the centre of an open undulating plateau much dissected by valleys. The characteristic trees of the Forest are pine, larch and birch, and its commons are covered with gorse and heather. It is bounded on the north-west by the A264 Horsham to Crawley road, on the east by the M23/A23 London to Brighton road between Crawley and Handcross and to the south by the road from Horsham to Handcross via Lower Beeding.

The Forest was owned by the de Braose family after the Conquest and later by the Dukes of Norfolk before passing into other hands. The woodland was speedily consumed as the Wealden iron industry developed, and a number of hammer ponds and other associations with the industry can be found in the area. The larger houses of the forge and furnace masters were often built beside the hammer ponds, a good example being the Barn House at Bucks Head near Mannings Heath. Such was the appetite of the furnaces that by Elizabethan times less than a third of the Forest was described as wooded. The 17th and 18th centuries saw attempts to improve the value of the land for agriculture: one pioneer, Sir Thomas Seymour, even dreamed of founding a new community in the Forest, anticipating by 400 years the establishment of Crawley new town. Attempts at agricultural improvement were foiled when the sandy soils proved too wet in bad weather for sheep folding, the principal source of manure, and a late 18th-century observer noted that the Forest was 'as bleak and barren as moorland in Yorkshire or Westmorland'. Reclamation had to await the introduction of tile-draining in the 1840s.

To the north of Horsham and on the edge of St Leonard's Forest, the village of **Faygate** is associated with a famous dragon which allegedly roamed the Forest. According to an account dated 1614, 'within three or four miles compasse are its usual haunts, often times at a place called Faygate, and it hath been seene within halfe a

River Cuckmere near Exceat

mile of Horsam; a wonder, no doubt, most terrible and noisome to the inhabitants thereabouts'. It was apparently about 9ft long with black and red scales and was a considerable nuisance to the local people. Dragon stories abound in the High Weald and more than one place in the area is known as Dragon's Green. It is therefore intriguing to find that it was in these woods that Dr Gideon Mantell, a distinguished geologist, discovered the remains of the iguanodon, the prehistoric creature which, it is conjectured, bore a striking resemblance to the traditional depiction of the dragon. Mantell lived in LEWES and wrote a number of valuable books on the geology of Sussex.

There is a memorable garden on the fringe of the Forest at **Leonardslee**, home of the Loder family, on the A281 south of Lower Beeding. This is a spring-flowering garden created in the early 19th century in a natural valley with a string of small lakes which form one of the principal sources of the River Adur.

Seaford (2/4F)
A coastal town east of Newhaven, Seaford still retains some old streets and buildings and provides access to the open Downland at Seaford Head. During the Middle Ages, the River Ouse entered the sea here and the town became an important harbour and commercial centre, linked with the historic Cinque Ports. But engineering works in the 1530s affected both the shoreline and the course of the river and a new harbour was established at Newhaven, along the coast to the west. To the east of the town is Seaford Head, where archaeologists have discovered prehistoric remains as well as a number of Roman graves. The cliffs here rise to 300 ft above the sea and a popular walk is through Seaford Head nature reserve to Cuckmere Haven, near Exceat. The parish church of St Leonard is of no particular interest, though it was the scene of a macabre discovery during the early years of the 19th century when workmen found a great stone coffin containing 16 skulls and no other bones.

The tiny hamlet of **Exceat** (Excet), although little more than a collection of farm buildings on the A259 east of Seaford, is of considerable interest to the visitor. In the 1340s the village was ravaged by the Black Death, which killed most of the inhabitants. The community recovered to prosper again, only to suffer more destruction and loss of life at the hands of French raiders in 1460. In 1913 the vicar of FRISTON led an excavation which unearthed remains of the old village, including the church. Some years later, Exceat was back in the news when the last team of working farm oxen in Sussex was retired. For many centuries oxen rather than horses were used to plough the Downs: a popular photograph shows an ox being shoed at Saddlescombe Farm, below Devil's Dyke.

The modern visitor to Exceat can visit the Seven Sisters Country Park and the Living World centre. The centre contains living examples of rare and strange insects and crustacea, while the Country Park, established in 1971 by the County Council, has an information centre in a converted 18th-century barn, from which maps and guided walk leaflets may be obtained. The centre and adjoining car park are a good base from which to explore the 700 acres of cliff top and Cuckmere Haven, the tranquil and undeveloped estuary of the Cuckmere River, all contained within the Country Park. Walkers may also explore the South Downs Way and the paths through Friston Forest, to the north of the information centre.

The Seven Sisters (there are actually eight but the alliterative seven has always been preferred), is a Heritage Coast and the whole area is now owned by either the County Council or the National Trust, guaranteeing its preservation for the public. Below the impressive range of chalk cliffs has been established one of the first voluntary marine nature reserves in the country. The Seven Sisters area represents the very best in English chalk coastal scenery.

Sedlescombe (3/3D)
Situated on the A229 to the north-west of Battle, Sedlescombe is famous as the home of the Pestalozzi children's village. The settlement dates from the time of the iron industry and would no doubt have declined with that industry had it not been for the abundance of hop gardens in the area. Although hop fields and oast houses are normally more associated with Kent, the eastern part of Sussex has also traditionally been the home of the Englishman's favourite perennial climbing plant. The parish church of St John the Baptist was restored by the Victorians and most of the exterior dates from the 1860s. Durhamford Manor House, half a mile to the west of the village, is the oldest building in the parish and is believed to have been built about 1450. There are a number of attractive houses round the village green, including the well-known Brickwall Hotel.

This Sussex village became the focus of international attention during the 19th century when the Swiss educationalist, Johann Heinrich Pestalozzi, established an experimental system of learning here, based on the assumption that children learned best in the conducive atmosphere of the country and that the young of all nationalities should be educated together. The Pestalozzi children's village now educates children from Third World countries, whose improved skills help them to contribute to their countries' development.

Selham (1/3C) *see* Petworth

Selmeston (2/5E) *see* Alciston

Selsey (1/2F)
A bright and breezy village south of Chichester

Sedlescombe village green

with an important past, the remains of which are now mostly buried beneath the sea. Over the centuries the coastline of Sussex has changed considerably. This is illustrated particularly clearly at the eastern and western extremities of the county. At Rye and Winchelsea the sea has receded, leaving once thriving ports high and dry. Here at Selsey the coast has been eroded by the sea and places which played a significant part in national and local history have disappeared beneath the waves.

It was to a spot on the coast some distance seaward of the present shoreline that the Saxon invaders came in the 5th century. At that time, the area that is now Selsey was an island (known as Seal Island) and it was here that the Christian missionary St Wilfrid landed, a hundred years later. He founded a monastery which later became the seat of the diocese. In 1075 the centre of Christian operations in Sussex was moved to the new cathedral at Chichester, in line with a decision of the early English Church to transfer certain sees from villages to towns, and the cathedral at Selsey was abandoned.

Seal Island, connected to the mainland by a ferry at Sidlesham, originally had two settlements, one at the south end of the island (Sutton) and one to the north (Norton). The church at what is now known as **Church Norton** was built in the 13th century to replace the cathedral but only the chancel of that building now survives *in situ*, the nave having been removed and re-erected to form the centrepiece of the new church of St Peter in the village of Selsey. Church Norton is well worth visiting, the old church nestling beside an ancient castle mound on the banks of Pagham Harbour. Another interesting building in the area is the windmill at Medmerry. This is a circular, brick-built tower mill constructed in about 1750 at West Sands Leisure Centre, west of Selsey village.

St Wilfrid taught the pagan Saxons to fish and fishing has always been a major activity here. Cockles, prawns, lobsters and crabs were once extensively gathered; oysters, too, were taken in large quantities. The village may have lost its cathedral and its position as one of the most important places in the old kingdom of the South Saxons, but its fishermen still go to sea and a Selsey crab, dressed in the traditional way, is a popular local delicacy which no visitor should miss.

Literary Sussex

MICHAEL BIRKETT

Sussex is a joyous anthology of writers and artists, not a long serious tome. So many have loved Sussex, or praised it, or found moments of inspiration there, or simply been happy. But no-one has immortalised it – not like the counties almost recreated by Hardy and the Brontës, or the London of Charles Dickens where the detail seems richer and sharper than real life. Even Hilaire Belloc loves Sussex better than he describes it and Kipling is more evocative of India than of Burwash. No painter can claim Sussex as his own, as Constable could Suffolk or Samuel Palmer of the Shoreham Valley in Kent. I do not forget the breathtaking Turners at Petworth, but these were born more of an old friendship than of any sense of belonging. Turner was a house-guest of genius, not a man of the very soil. His pictures breathe the life of Petworth and its incomparable Park, not the life of Sussex.

Why is it, I wonder, that Sussex should have attracted such transitory, if powerful devotion? Can it be that London itself has proved too powerful a magnet? Artists of all sorts thrive on the stimulus and applause which capital cities provide in the fullest measure. The literary recluse is usually an old recluse, who has grown out of the need for such things.

At all events, Sussex has seen great beginnings. John Evelyn, diarist and gardener extraordinary, was educated at Lewes Grammar School next door to his grandmother's house. John Fletcher (how unlucky to be remembered as the second half of Beaumont and Fletcher) was born in Rye. In 1579 of course it was a flourishing port; the receding of the sea, which has left it stranded today, had only just begun. Another dramatist, Thomas Otway, author of one of the few remembered Restoration Tragedies *Venice Preserv'd*, spent his youth in his father's rectory at Woolbeding where the Rother valley sweeps lyrically down to Midhurst. Midhurst Grammar School was responsible for a spell of schooling, and later a spell of school-mastering, for H. G. Wells, with apprenticeship to a chemist in between. In *Tono-Bungay* he calls Midhurst Wimblehurst and seems to have liked the town itself. He is, however, extremely scathing about its inhabitants. George Orwell and Cyril Connolly were friends at school in Eastbourne. Both wrote reminiscences of those days and Connolly spent the last four years of his life in Eastbourne. Can their school-boy conversations, I wonder, have been as formidably intelligent as their reputations would suggest? The most productive childhood Sussex can claim must surely have been Daisy Ashford's. *The Young Visiters* [*sic*] was written when she was nine, at the Priory in Haywards Heath. The energy and determination of the writing make it joyfully immortal. It is now 100 years since the book was written yet it dates less than most of its grown-up contemporaries. Most prestigious of all, Shelley was born and bred at Warnham (near Horsham); not schooled there, though, unless one misappropriates Sir Osbert Sitwell's celebrated entry in *Who's Who*: 'Educated: in the holidays from Eton'.

From beginnings to endings. Several literary giants spent their last years in the county: Conan Doyle in Crowborough (though the great days of Sherlock Holmes were already over); Malcolm Lowry in the tiny village of Ripe not far from Glyndebourne; Gibbon, for his last months only, with his friend Lord Sheffield at Sheffield Park; and George Crabbe nearly ended his days in Hastings, where he was knocked down by a phaeton at the age of seventy-five.

As if to emphasise the reluctance of the great and the gifted to submit for too long to the seductions of peaceful Sussex, the list of visitors is long and distinguished. Distinguished and sometimes sad. Francis Thomson spent four years in the Pentasaph in the care of the monks of Storrington Priory. Indeed he wrote or at least finished his most famous poem 'The Hound of Heaven' there. The care was necessary, for he had been what today would be called a down-and-out.

> Come on the following Feet
> And a Voice above their beat –
> 'Naught shelters thee, who will not shelter Me.'

Keats spent his last night in England at Bedhampton between Portsmouth and Chichester, after a stay which had included not only Chichester itself but a visit to Stansted Chapel for its dedication in 1819. The house and chapel seem to have provided what might be called the decor for 'The Eve of St Agnes'.

> The sculptur'd dead, on each side, seem to freeze,
> Emprison'd in black, purgatorial rails:
> Knights, ladies, praying in dumb orat'ries . . .

Keats certainly started the poem in Chichester and the much scribbled-over and suddenly-altered manuscript bears out Keats's remarking that he had taken with him paper of exceptional thinness.

Lewis Carroll spent his holidays from Oxford in Eastbourne, Virginia Woolf her weekends in Rodmell on the Ouse and Cobbett's *Rural Rides* took him through many parts of Sussex, always in search of the shameful and exploitative – then, as now, not difficult to find. And Alexander Pope managed to find West Grinstead (a long way west, and south, of East Grinstead) so sympathetic that he composed *The Rape of the Lock* there:

> Fair tresses man's imperial race insnare,
> And beauty draws us with a single hair . . .

Visits beget visits. Virginia Woolf entertained T. S. Eliot and when W. B. Yeats rented a cottage at Coleman's Hatch for a couple of years in 1912 his guests included Ezra Pound. Indeed when Henry James acquired Lamb House in Rye at the very end of the last century his visitors were often as talented and distinguished as himself. H. G. Wells and G. K. Chesterton, of course, but also Stephen Crane, author of *The Red Badge of Courage*, that most powerfully tragic document of the American Civil War, and Joseph Conrad, for whom the tiny, almost land-locked, harbour must have given off at best a very faint whiff of the scents of the ocean and the Far East which he distilled more potently than anyone before or since.

Of course visitors to the famous and seductive seaside towns were legion. Hastings knew Byron and Keats and the Lambs, Thomas Carlyle and Thomas Campbell, and Rider Haggard. It also knew Rossetti and Elizabeth Siddal, archetype of the 'Stunners', the models immortalised by a whole generation of Pre-Raphaelite painters as hapless maidens, usually in mortal peril and frequently bereft of clothing. Brighton has an even longer list. Not merely Harrison Ainsworth, (historical novelist and Sussex traveller) Surtees (the almost acceptable face of the hunting set) A. E. Coppard (the most prolific short story writer) and John Cowper Powys (the slightly less complex of two mystical hedonistic brothers). But even Dr Johnson, Wordsworth and Dickens who wrote much of *Dombey and Son* there. Can it really have been our domesticated Channel just beyond the pier that was in the mind of little Paul as, dying, he spoke those doom-laden words to his sister:

> How fast the river runs, between its green banks and the rushes, Floy! But it's very near the sea. I hear the waves. They always said so.

Clive Bell's study, Charleston Farmhouse

Enough of visits, except perhaps to reflect that there must be enough tactfully unchronicled visits to Brighton to create a whole research department at an American university. (Do not be misled by John Betjeman's poem 'Original sin on the Sussex Coast.' It's as touching as you'd expect but not much to do with Sussex, or sin.) What a pity that the Nonesuch Press, developing so variously its successful *Week-End Book*, never got as far as *The Dirty Week-End Book*.

This has not up to now been much of a celebratory essay. More of a complaint from a proud but disappointed county that it has not been uniquely, magisterially, unforgettbly celebrated. Perhaps it has, though. Richard Jeffries, more famous as a naturalist than a novelist, spent his last year in Sussex and wrote of it with the detailed affection which nature always inspired in him, whether the deep countryside of Sussex or that London suburbia which was already burgeoning at the end of the last century. An even more celebrated and passionate naturalist can be half-claimed by Sussex: Gilbert White is remembered as Gilbert White of Selborne, in Hampshire, but much of his *Natural History* is

Ringmer's village sign

really of Ringmer, where his aunt's house was a regular holiday home and the abode of Timothy, surely the best-loved tortoise in history. (His shell is preserved in the British Museum.)

There are several major figures for whom Sussex has been not just a home but an inspiration. Not necessarily for long – the theme of transience keeps returning – but the effect is clear. D. H. Lawrence, who hired a couple of converted cowsheds at Greatham for a season in 1915 and wrote much of *The Rainbow* there, ventured as far as the coast and was so bowled over by the light that he felt 'like Persephone come up from Hell'. Henry James settled permanently at Lamb House in Rye and wrote as well as ever. It is a ravishing house, perfect architecturally, poised over the sloping town yet as indirect of access as the prose of that elegant, passionate, misunderstood American.

Galsworthy lived in a valley of the Arun which promises the sea and glories in dramatic swoops of the Downs. The windows of his solid stone house at Bury command as dramatic a view as the county can offer. That nothing indelibly stained with Sussex life should have emerged from his pen is sad but not surprising. His country house was essentially a retreat from the pressures of the London theatrical world. He bought the house in 1920 and *The Forsyte Saga* was published in 1922. We should be wary, though, of claiming for Sussex too large a share in its creation.

Coventry Patmore lived for 25 years (in Temple Grove and Hastings) in Sussex contentment. It would be nice to think that 'Magna Est Veritas' owes its inspiration to the coast there.

> Here in this little Bay
> Full of tumultuous life and great repose,
> Where, twice a day,
> The purposeless, glad ocean comes and goes,
> Under high cliffs and far from the huge town
> I sit me down.
> For want of me the world's course will not fail:
> When all its work is done, the lie shall rot;
> The truth is great, and shall prevail,
> When none cares whether it prevail or not.

But Patmore's poetry was written before he reached Sussex – the insights into family love and

King's windmill at Shipley, home of Hilaire Belloc

tragedy all set down in London. Nowadays, in any case, the experience will be hard to reproduce: the high cliffs are still there, but none of them is any longer far from the huge town. I recall Michael Flanders, 'at the drop of another hat', saying cheerfully 'they're thinking of building a new suburb for South London . . . they're going to call it Brighton . . .'

Kipling is usually regarded as the most famous son of 'Sussex by the Sea', to use his own song. But although he spent the second half of his life at Batemans, his house at Burwash (still to be visited, and the county's most important literary pilgrimage), most of his best loved books were already written. At least *Puck of Pook's Hill* is a real product of Sussex and redolent of it. The gratitude that Kipling felt for his 'fair ground', 'beloved over all', is here alive and breathing.

But not even Kipling can compare as a celebrant of Sussex with Hilaire Belloc. Singing the praises of 'the southern hills and the south sea' came as naturally to him as wine and religion. True he also sang the praises of countless corners of Europe and made ballads out of forgotten battles, but he had a trick of rhyme and rhythm which never fails to quicken the pulse and stir the heart. Shipley was his home for close on half a century (1906–53) and his delight in the South country is as infectious today as it must have been in his hey-day between the wars. The rollicking and roistering can become a little wearing, but his moments of melancholy and nostalgia are as real as can be.

I never get between the pines
But I smell the Sussex air;
Nor I never come on a belt of sand
But my home is there

But it is the theme of regret for the lost and forgotten beauties of his homeland that touch him most. There is more than an echo of the despair of Crabbe's *The Village* in his lament over Halnacker:

Sally is gone that was so kindly
Sally is gone from Ha'nacker Hill.
And the Briar grows ever since then so blindly
And ever since then the clapper is still,
And the sweeps have fallen from Ha'nacker Mill

Ha'nacker Hill is in desolation:
Ruin a-top and a field unploughed.
And Spirits that call on a fallen nation
Spirits that loved her calling aloud:
Spirits abroad in a windy cloud.

Spirits that call and no one answers;
Ha'nacker's down and England's done.
Wind and Thistle for pipe and dancers
And never a ploughman under the Sun.
Never a ploughman. Never a one.

Halnaker Hill and windmill

Best of all though I like the accidents, the curious corners of Sussex literary history: H. E. Bates finding himself stationed at RAF Tangmere in 1942 and writing his short stories of the war in the air under the most evocative of war-time pen-names: Flying Officer X; the visionary William Blake, staying at Felpham near Bognor Regis in a cottage of his friend the poet William Hayley, writing his strange and lofty poem on Milton and prefacing it with the immortal lines: 'And did those feet in ancient time . . .' One day he threw an obstreperous part-time gardener off the property and found himself arraigned on a charge of high treason. The man, one John Schofield, was a Private (a 'disgraced sergeant') in the Dragoons and fabricated a whole diatribe of seditious libels which he ascribed to Blake. The perjury was patent and Blake was duly acquitted, to tumultuous applause in the Chichester court room. But he was badly shaken.

And for one moment in 1839 the little village of Donnington near Chichester was swept by the searchlight of literary history: the curate of nearby Earnley proposed in Donnington Rectory to Charlotte Brontë. He was instantly refused.

Sheffield Park (2/4C) *see* Fletching

Shipley (1/5C)
A large rural parish to the south of Horsham, once the home of the writer Hilaire Belloc, in whose memory the famous Shipley Windmill has been restored. The name means 'sheep clearing', indicating that the area once provided pasture in the Wealden forest for flocks belonging to settlers on the coastal plain. The animals were brought up into the Weald on wide drove roads and, in the case of Shipley, it is still quite possible to follow the drove way which starts at Dragon's Green, to the north of the parish, through the village and southwards to Ashington towards the Findon gap in the Downs. The village also lies on the River Adur, here a quiet stream but later the mighty river that we see at Bramber and Shoreham.

The strategic importance of Shipley was quickly realised by the Norman lord, William de Braose. He established his principal military headquarters at Bramber but built several subsidiary castles throughout the Rape, including one at Knepp, in Shipley parish. Knepp comes from a Saxon word meaning 'the crown of the hill' and the remains of the castle, standing on a grassy mound and surrounded by a moat, can be seen beside the A24 Horsham to Worthing road.

The Adur was navigable up to Shipley at this time and communications between Knepp, Bramber and the sea at Shoreham could be maintained by river. Knepp was used as a hunting lodge and was a favourite residence of King John, who kept over 200 greyhounds here for hunting deer. After 1216 it ceased to be a fortified place but remained a residence until the end of the 13th century when it gradually became a ruin. In 1762 nearly all the remaining stone was taken away and used for the construction of the new Horsham to Steyning road. Today, with its weathercock and sprouting buddleia, the remaining fragment of Knepp Castle is one of the most evocative ruins in the county.

The Knepp estate came into the hands of the Burrell family towards the end of the 18th century when William Burrell married Sophie, daughter of Sir Charles Raymond. Sir William, as he became, was a distinguished antiquarian who wrote an uncompleted History of Sussex, now in the British Library. The two estates of Knepp and WEST GRINSTEAD were united in 1831 under Sir Charles Merrik Burrell MP, and the family have played a prominent role in the political life of the county ever since. Sir Charles built the modern Knepp Castle to the designs of Nash, architect to the Prince Regent, in 1809. The house was partly destroyed by fire in 1904 but rebuilt to the same designs.

The church and lands of Shipley were given by the de Braose family to the Knights Templar in about 1126. This order of fighting monks had been formed a few years earlier by a group of French knights to protect pilgrims on their way to the Holy Land. They took the name Templars because they had their headquarters on the site of the old Temple at Jerusalem. At Shipley the Templars owned an extensive agricultural estate. Water, power and transport were provided by the river and the community would have been fairly self-sufficient: the inhabitants would have grown most of their own food and kept pigs, sheep and other animals for meat, clothing and leather. The abundance of wood in the area would have satisfied their needs for cooking and heating.

The Templars built the parish church of St Mary the Virgin to replace an earlier structure. The present church therefore dates from the early 12th century and is contemporary with CHICHESTER Cathedral (see *The Norman Heritage*, p. 28). The west doorway has a good example of Norman carved stonework and the church contains a number of fine memorials. The alabaster tomb of Sir Thomas Caryll and his family in the chancel dates from 1616 and can be compared with the Gage tomb at West FIRLE. Look in particular for the three kneeling figures of Sir Thomas's daughters and his baby son in a cradle. Another memorial is to the composer John Ireland, whose grave in the churchyard overlooks Chanctonbury Ring. The 1914–18 war memorial shows that 20 men from this remote corner of Sussex died in action, including Hilaire Belloc's eldest son, Louis.

Belloc bought King's Land, Shipley, shortly after his election to the House of Commons in 1906 and lived here until his death in 1953. Best remembered today for his comic verse, Belloc loved Sussex and a number of his most important works – for example *The Four Men* and *The South Country* – celebrate the landscape of the county. King's Land is a grand old house with a Horsham slab roof and Belloc enjoyed cultivating his 5-acre plot.

The house, and the windmill in the grounds, are still owned by the Belloc family and the house is occupied by his descendants. The windmill, which was built in 1879, is the best preserved example of a smock mill in Sussex. It is now looked after by a charitable trust who face the continuous challenge of raising money to restore and maintain the complex wooden structure. The mill is open to the public on certain days and group visits are welcome at other times by appointment. From the mill the Downs, crowned by Chanctonbury Ring, can be clearly seen far away to the south, while walkers on the Downs who know where to look can make out the sun shining on the white-painted sails of the county's most famous windmill. Over the door of the mill there is a memorial tablet to Belloc, designed by his friend Edmund Ware. It reads: 'Let this be a memorial to Hilaire Belloc who garnered a harvest of wisdom and sympathy for young and old'.

Shoreham by Sea (2/2E)
The port at the mouth of the River Adur, west of Brighton, from which Charles II escaped to France after the Battle of Worcester.

Like the rivers Arun and Ouse, the Adur has had a port at its mouth for centuries. There is some evidence of a Roman settlement on the Adur estuary and the river was given its present name in the 16th century to support a supposed, probably inaccurate, identification of the Roman town of Portus Adurni with Shoreham. Historically the river had been known as BRAMBER Water and was much deeper and wider than it is now, enabling boats to navigate upstream to Bramber castle.

By the beginning of the 11th century, the silting up of the estuary resulted in the village and port being moved nearer the mouth of the river. Old Shoreham, with its parish church of St Nicholas and its wooden toll bridge crossing the estuary, was abandoned by the Normans in about 1100 in favour of New Shoreham, which they planned and built as a new town.

Although New Shoreham has been much changed and the historic core is now surrounded by undistinguished modern development, enough remains to make a visit worth while. The late Norman parish church of St Mary de Haura (of the harbour) is essentially of about 1130 and is a very fine building indeed. It is only half its original length, the nave having fallen down in 1720, and remains of the rest of the church can be seen in the churchyard. The splendid tower, 81 ft high, is visible for miles, and once a year members of the public can climb to the top and enjoy the view (see *The Norman Heritage*, p. 28).

Around the church are a number of lanes and flint walls and some attractive brick and flint cottages, but the most interesting building in Shoreham after the church is The Marlipins in the High Street, a rare example of a Norman building which is neither religious nor military in origin. It was the customs house from which the administration of the harbour was conducted, and has an attractive chequerboard front of alternate flint and stone panels. It now houses a fascinating museum owned by the Sussex Archaeological Society and is open to the public. As the displays in the Marlipins Museum explain, Shoreham was one of the leading English ports in the medieval period, but by the late 16th century the harbour entrance had become blocked and the port had fallen into comparative obscurity. The fixing of the mouth of the river in 1818 enabled Shoreham to grow extremely successful again and also encouraged the development of a very important shipbuilding industry. A reminder of this period in Shoreham's development is the picturesque

Tomb of Sir Thomas Caryll, Shipley

Overleaf: Ruins of Knepp Castle, near Shipley

Singleton village seen from The Trundle

stone lighthouse, built in 1846. Today, the port handles nearly 3m tons of cargo a year, including sand, coal, gravel, oil, timber, stone and wine.

Across the river from New Shoreham there developed in the early decades of the present century an unplanned collection of bungalows, railway carriages and shacks used originally for holidays and known as 'Bungalow Town'. The area, which acquired a somewhat raffish reputation, has now been tidied up by the local authorities and comprises a respectable housing estate known as Shoreham Beach. At the eastern end of the beach is a Napoleonic brick-built fortification, Shoreham Fort, the remains of which have been consolidated by the County Council. The Fort is open to the public at all times, free of charge.

Sidlesham (1/2F) *see* Pagham

Singleton (1/2D)
A charming village of brick and flint cottages in the valley of the River Lavant, between Chichester and Midhurst. The manor of Singleton, one of the largest in the county at the time of Domesday, was owned before the Conquest by Earl Godwin of Wessex, father of Harold, the last Saxon king. The parish church, dedicated to St Mary the Virgin, served a wide area and traces of Saxon work may be seen in it today. From Singleton priests went out to care for other, smaller churches in the area and it is thought that they were accommodated in the tower of St Mary's and in an upper room above the nave. This would explain the window high up over the chancel arch and the doorway halfway up the tower. The nave and chancel walls date from the 13th century but follow the foundations and outline of the Saxon church.

The church contains a number of interesting monuments and tombs; they include the Cobden family tomb made of Petworth marble, a local stone with a profusion of small snail shells (winkles) in its composition and sometimes known as 'winklestone'. St Mary's also contains two tombs in Purbeck marble thought to be those of Thomas and William, Earls of Arundel, who died in 1542 and 1544 respectively.

Singleton was situated on the high road from Chichester to London, so coaches and heavily-laden carts would labour over Trundle Hill and down Town Lane to the village. As is often the case in Sussex, Singleton has stories of smugglers; the fine 18th-century house north of the village on the Midhurst road, now called Drovers, allegedly has smuggling connections. There are two pleasant old inns in the village and a large number of attractive cottages. Most of the latter are brick and flint but a few are still thatched. On the village green is a well-known cricket field and a fine Sussex barn which has been removed from its original threatened location and now serves as an admirable pavilion.

The removal and re-erection of old buildings is, of course, a speciality of Singleton, the home of the famous Weald and Downland Museum. Founded in 1971 at the initiative of Mr J. R. Armstrong and the generosity of the West Dean Estate, the Museum consists of a large number of fascinating buildings which would otherwise have been lost and is also a centre for the study of vernacular building in the south-east of England. The buildings – farmhouses, cottages, a mill, a toll house and many more – are most attractively displayed in a magnificent 40-acre site to the south of the village. Special events – including demonstrations of building crafts such as thatching and flint-walling, sheep-shearing and ploughing – are held regularly and the Museum is highly recommended for every visitor to Sussex.

Slindon (1/3E)

A brick and flint village mainly owned by the National Trust on the south slope of the Downs between Arundel and Chichester. In early times the sea came inland as far as the foothills of the Downs between Arundel and GOODWOOD and nowhere is this seen more clearly than at Slindon, which stands on the edge of a raised beach of flint and pebbles some 200 ft above present sea level. For some reason the beach was not covered, as it was elsewhere, when the layers of chalk were laid down and it can still be seen today in Slindon woods.

The vantage point attracted early settlers and, judging from the quantity of flint tools found here, Slindon must have been quite important in the Stone Age. Today the village consists of a square of lanes, whose focus in the north-west corner, near the church, is a small open space where the roads meet and a tree stands in the middle. The houses are almost without exception charming and unspoiled, thanks partly to the care of the National Trust who own much of the village and adjoining estate, but also to the

A Sussex cow and the medieval 'Bayfleet Farm' at the Sussex Weald and Downland Museum, Singleton

Sussex Weald and Downland Museum, Singleton

attention of the residents. The use of brick to divide the flintwork with vertical lines rather than the conventional horizontal string course is a feature of the flint walling in Slindon.

Slindon House, now a boys' school, was originally a palace of the Archbishops of Canterbury, although only a ruined tower remains of the original building. The house was rebuilt by the Kemp family in about 1560 and then again at the end of the 18th century. The present house and estate buildings, in squared flints, owe much to the inspiration of nearby Goodwood House. Other major buildings in the village include the restored parish church of St Mary and the Roman Catholic church of St Richard, built in 1865 by C. A. Buckler, the architect of Arundel Castle. This substantial and long-established Catholic church in a small village reflects Slindon's role as a Catholic centre. The family at Slindon House remained loyal to the

old religion and during the 17th century, when the celebration of Mass was forbidden, built into the house a series of concealed chambers where priests could be accommodated and services held. It was the Catholic atmosphere of the village which attracted the mother of the Sussex writer Hilaire Belloc, who lived here as a child. The house and 3,500 acre estate eventually came into the hands of a successful businessman, who gave it to the National Trust. Today Slindon is one of the Trust's largest properties in Sussex and includes magnificent beech woods (sadly damaged by the 1987 storm), open downland and a substantial section of Stane Steet, the Roman road which ran from Chichester to London. The Trust has provided a car park for visitors to the beech woods. A good short walk is to the Nore Folly, which was built for shooting parties on a hill half a mile north-west of the village.

Near by is Fontwell Park racecourse, a most attractive course used mainly for national hunt racing. Also at Fontwell is Denmans, a very fine garden open to the public, where plants and shrubs are also on sale.

Slinfold (1/5B)

A pretty village west of Horsham, just off the Roman Stane Street from Chichester to London, Slinfold lies in an area long famous for the quarries which produced Horsham stone, the laminated sandstone used for roofing tiles and flagstones throughout south-east England. The stone was transported away from the quarries by barges on the River Arun. In the village street are many examples of good timber-framed houses – such as Little Hammers and Old House Farm – with roofs of Horsham slabs. The church of St Peter dates from 1861 and one of its rectors was James Dallaway, the historian of western Sussex. He lived, however, in Surrey, holding the rectory of Slinfold as a sinecure.

The junction of the A281 Horsham to Guildford road and the A29 London to Bognor Regis road is known as 'Roman Gate'. Lying on Stane Street, the junction marks the location of a staging post or *mansio* built by the Romans to provide rest and shelter for travellers. This *mansio* is at the point where the road crossed the River Arun at Alfoldean Bridge and is just 10 miles north of the lower crossing at PULBOROUGH, also the site of a *mansio*. It was the Roman's practice to provide these roadside 'service stations' at intervals of about 10 miles, the distance which might be covered in an easy day's march.

Modern walkers may join The Downs Link bridleway at Slinfold and follow the course of the old railway line either north to Guildford or south to STEYNING and the South Downs Way. A car park for walkers has been provided at the end of Station Road, adjoining what was once the old station and is now a touring caravan site.

Overleaf: Oak and beechwoods, Slindon estate

Sompting (2/1E)
A village in the foothills of the Downs, east of Worthing, with a famous parish church and a central street which has retained its brick and flint character. The settlemement has Saxon origins and, after the Norman Conquest, became part of the Rape of Bramber. It was later divided into three manors: Lychpole, Sompting Abbots owned by the Abbey of Fécamp in Normandy and Sompting Peverel owned by the Peverel family for some centuries. The parish church of St Mary's, to the north of the A27, is famous for its four-gabled Saxon tower, known as a 'Rhenish helm', a design popular in Germany but unique to Sompting in this country.

In 1154 the church was granted to the Knights Templar, an order of fighting monks who had a large agricultural estate further up the Adur valley at SHIPLEY. They rebuilt the nave and added both the north transept with two vaulted chapels and their own private chapel on the south side. When the Templars were suppressed in 1307, Sompting passed to the Knights Hospitaller of St John of Jerusalem (see *The Norman Heritage*, p. 28).

Over the centuries the ownership of Sompting passed to the Croft and Lancing Manor estates. With the break up of the latter in 1920, the Cokeham area was sold to the speculative builder and gradually merged into **Lancing** to form a continuous urban area. To the north of what is now the A27, what had been the Croft estate (now the Sompting estate) remained mostly rural with flint walls, older houses and cottages. Today it is a conservation area, with good access to the Downs. South Lancing has little to commend it; it was built to house workers in the railway carriage works which was transferred to Lancing from BRIGHTON in 1910 and provided considerable local employment until its closure in the 1960s.

High above the Adur valley on Lancing Hill is Lancing College, the public school founded in 1848 by Nathaniel Woodard who was then the curate at New Shoreham and later lived at Henfield. His aim was to found a comprehensive and classless federation of schools and by the time of his death in 1891 there were 15 of them (including ARDINGLY and HURSTPIERPOINT). Woodard instructed R. C. Carpenter to design his new college at Lancing and the result is universally admired by architectural historians. The crowning glory is the great chapel, only recently completed, in French Gothic style, to serve all the schools in the federation. Soaring

up to 90 ft, the chapel is floodlit at night and is a well-known local landmark.

Just north of Lancing College is the tiny hamlet of **Coombes**, consisting of a farm, some cottages and a small, unrestored church with notable wall paintings. The paintings are thought to be by artists of the same Lewes school which produced murals at HARDHAM. They probably date back to the 11th century and include a *Nativity* series and *Christ in Majesty*. Access to the churchyard is by a tapsel gate. This is a

particularly Sussex style which involves a central pivot, and about half a dozen examples are to be found on the Downs, including one at PYECOMBE. Church Farm, Coombes welcomes visitors and offers a 1½ hour tractor and trailer tour for school parties, clubs and other groups, which should be booked in advance. There are also splendid walks on the Downs in this area.

Southease (2/4E) *see* Rodmell

Lancing College Chapel, viewed from across the River Adur near Sompting

South Downs Way *see* p. 132 feature article

South Stoke (1/4E) *see* Houghton

Stanmer (2/3E) *see* Brighton

Stansted Park (1/1E) *see* Stoughton

Steyning (2/1D)
An attractive country town on the A283 about 5 miles north of Worthing with a large number of timber-framed buildings. Steyning lies on the west bank of the River Adur, about 4 miles from its mouth. In ancient times, the Adur was a wide and navigable estuary and boats could travel up river at least as far as Steyning, where they moored in an inlet to the north of the site of the present parish church. The area provided good arable lowlands and pastures on the Downs and building materials were available in ample supply: timber from the Weald, sand and reeds for thatching from the river, flints and lime for mortar. Shortly after the Norman Conquest, SHOREHAM became the main harbour on the Adur, but Steyning had already developed sufficiently to maintain itself as a self-sufficient community, owing allegiance to the Abbey of Fécamp, to whom the manor had been given by Edward the Confessor.

The present High Street extends north-west to south-east across the summit of a promontory formed between two tributary streams of the Adur; Church Street extends northwards from the High Street to the Norman church of St Andrew, which probably stands on the site of a yet earlier building. The earlier church and the port of Steyning were known as St Cuthman's, after a shepherd boy who, legend has it, was possessed of divine powers. On the death of his father he travelled across the country bearing his crippled mother on a simple cart which broke down on reaching Steyning, where he settled. The playwright Christopher Fry used this story as the basis for his play *The Boy with the Cart*.

St Andrew's parish church is very fine and is not to be missed. The late Norman nave, with massive round columns and robustly carved arches, makes this, along with St Mary's New Shoreham and St Mary's Climping, one of the most memorable early churches in the country (see *The Norman Heritage*, p. 28). There are examples in Steyning of the hall type of house of the 14th and 15th centuries, among the best being Penfold Cottage and the Post Office in the High Street. A splendid example of the Wealden type of hall house with two-storey sections, curved braces in the central recessed section and a jetty at each end is Workhouse Cottage in Mouse Lane. In due course, the jetty became a continuous feature along the front elevation – for example on 61 to 65 High Street – providing increased accommodation on the first floor.

Horsham stone, a laminated sandstone which is laid in diminishing courses, has been used for roofing since medieval days and still covers many Steyning buildings, although many roofs are now covered with plain clay Sussex tiles. Tile hanging is also one of the many forms of wall cladding which make the town so attractive, mixing well with timber-framing, brickwork, timber weatherboarding and, in a few cases, stone.

Of particular interest is the Brotherhood Hall in Church Street, the original building of the Steyning Grammar School founded in 1614 by William Holland, who was born here and made his money in business in Chichester. Near by was the house of the registrar in which the Irish Nationalist MP, Charles Parnell, married his mistress Kitty O'Shea, thus delaying progress towards Irish Home Rule in the late 19th century. The Old Market House in the High Street, whose clock tower came from the stables of Michelgrove House, Clapham, has been used for many purposes, including the holding of Parliamentary elections when Steyning was a rotten borough returning two MPs. George Fox the Quaker addressed a meeting here in 1655, when he stayed at William Penn's House.

There is a small but well devised local museum which gives the visitor a good idea of the history of Steyning. Copies of the excellent conservation area guide and walking trail produced by the Steyning Society can be purchased here. Walkers and riders may enjoy the Downs Link path which follows the old railway line to CHRIST'S HOSPITAL and Guildford. Indeed, Steyning is a particularly good walking centre with easy access to the South Downs Way long-distance bridleway and many other downland walks. An early 19th-century visitor noted that: 'Upon the hills, within one mile of the town, is a good four mile [race] course, where plates are often run for. The air hereabouts is very healthy and the people are generally long-lived. The town is supplied with water from a great hill, not half a mile off, which drives two mills'. One of these, Court Mill, now a private house, can be seen in Sir George's Place; the street is named after the local tanner, George Breach, who was known to his friends as Sir George and built the cottages here for his workpeople.

Stopham (1/4D) *see* Pulborough

Storrington (1/4D)
A large village, north of the Downs, between

The Old Market House, Steyning

Pulborough and Steyning. Storrington lies on the River Stor or, perhaps more accurately, the River Stor flows through Storrington, for the river takes its name from the village, rather than vice versa. The names of the rivers which flow through Arundel and Lewes (the Arun and the Ouse) are also examples of what students of place names refer to as 'back formations'. Storrington probably derives its name from the storks, herons and other large fish-eating birds which were attracted to the nearby marshes of the Arun valley.

The most famous event in Storrington's history was purely fictional, for Storrington was the model for Tillingfold, the setting for the village cricket match in Hugh de Selincourt's minor classic named after the game. Tillingfold, according to the novel, 'lies in a hollow under the Downs, and climbs up the sides of the hill, like a pool rising to overflow its banks'. It was here, on 4 August 1921, that Paul Gauvinier led out the Tillingfold side against their traditional rivals, Ravely. Sir James Barrie described *The Cricket Match* as 'the best story about cricket or any other game' and John Arlott has commented that the charm of the book lies in the fact that 'cricket is a universal; that through it, major emotion may be expressed to those to whom the ingredients of the game itself are a foreign language'.

Storrington today has grown considerably from the original settlement clustered round the parish church of St Mary, part of which probably dates from the 11th century. Much of the church was rebuilt in 1750 and then again in 1876. Church Lane has one or two cottages of interest and the Roman Catholic Priory and Priory Church of Our Lady of England, built in the late 19th century but with many later additions. A cattle market was once held in The Square and something of the flavour of that time is provided by the plain 18th-century building which now houses a firm of estate agents. From the village the motorist can gain access to the Downs at either Chantry Post or Kithurst Hill, both of which provide good starting points for walks. The composer Arnold Bax spent the last years of his life at the White Horse Inn in Storrington.

East of the village, just off the sandstone ridge, lies **Sullington**, consisting of little more than a church and a farm. The sandstone regions of Sussex provide several examples, including Sullington, of simple 11th-century churches which have survived in more or less their original form because the communities they served did not expand during the 12th century and suffered from increasing poverty in the agricultural recession of the later medieval period. As a result Sullington church, also dedicated to St Mary, provides us with a good example of what many of our country churches would have been like when first built by the Normans.

In addition to the church, Sullington has a very fine barn, attached to Manor Farm. 115 ft long, it is of tarred weatherboarding under a tiled roof. The interior, one of the finest in Sussex after the tithe barn at ALCISTON, features aisles and a braced tie-beam roof. The barn is private and may be visited only by appointment. To the north of the main road is Sullington Warren, a sandy area used historically for the breeding of rabbits and saved from development by the combined efforts of local people and conservationists which enabled it to be bought by the National Trust.

Two or three miles north of Storrington is **West Chiltington**, a popular residential area

Overleaf: Interior of the tithe barn at Sullington

Lutyens's Little Thakeham, near Storrington

which combines the old village centre around a crossroads and more recent, leafy development on West Chiltington Common. The parish church, another St Mary's, is a showpiece, a particularly attractive unspoiled old village church with interesting wall paintings uncovered in 1882. These include a 12th-century series over and around the arch at the end of the south aisle featuring *Christ in Majesty with angels*, in red and ochre. On both sides of the nave there is a 13th-century series showing scenes from the Passion of Christ and the Life of the Virgin. The church has an unusually long squint, or hagioscope, from the south aisle to the chancel, possibly to enable a bell-ringer to know when the climax of the Mass was reached.

West Chiltington stands on rising ground above the River Arun. At one time the area was famous for its glass making; in addition iron was smelted in a forge beside the river, oak was harvested for ship building and the woods were coppiced for hurdles. The village has a windmill which was last worked in the 1920s and has now been converted into a house. Smock Alley may refer to this smock mill. These and other aspects of village history are reflected in the museum in the old village reading room in Church Street, open at any reasonable time, free of charge.

The other village in the vicinity of Storrington is **Thakeham**. This consists of an attractive street leading to the parish church, which shares the dedication to St Mary with its neighbours. Thakeham means 'settlement of thatched dwellings' and there are still some thatched roofs to be seen here today. The White Lion Inn has interesting cellars and passages and Church House is a fine 16th-century building. Thakeham was the centre of a poor law union set up to administer poor relief in the 19th century; the union workhouse stood on the site of Rydon School.

South of the village is Little Thakeham, now a private hotel, designed by Sir Edwin Lutyens and described by him as 'the best of the bunch'. Built in 1902 of local sandstone which has now mellowed gracefully, the house features a number of individual touches, including enormous inglenooks and, in the nursery, a special window through which the nanny could check that the children were behaving. The gardens are by Lutyens's collaborator, Gertrude Jekyll.

Stoughton (1/2D)

A village in the Downs north-west of Chichester,

set in a superb landscape with many prehistoric associations. The church of St Mary just north of the village has a fine 11th-century chancel arch. Stoughton's most famous son was the fast bowler George Brown ('Brown of BRIGHTON'), who was born in the village in 1783. He could throw a 4½ oz cricket ball 137 yd. Bow Hill to the south-east is, at over 600 ft, a major vantage point, clearly visible from the creeks of Chichester Harbour. It was the site chosen by early man for the construction of an important group of barrows or burial mounds, some of which are still over 12 ft high today.

Perhaps the best-known feature of the area is Kingley Vale National Nature Reserve, which includes what is described as the finest yew forest in Europe. The forest is in a valley formed by erosion of the chalk over a long period and the first yew trees, possibly planted by man, grew on the rich soil of the valley bottom 500 years ago. About 20 of these ancient trees remain, with girths up to 16 ft. The rest of the forest originated from seed spread by birds and the yew woodland on the steep valley slope varies in age from 50 to 250 years. The site is managed by the Nature Conservancy Council and a car park and nature trail are provided for visitors.

To the south east of Stoughton in the Ems valley north of Emsworth lies **Racton**, which comprises a few scattered houses and a church. The hamlet is close to Stansted Park, seat of the Earl and Countess of Bessborough. Racton's small and mainly 13th-century church contains two monuments. The 17th-century memorial to Sir George Gunter and his wife follows a standard pattern of kneeling figures in painted stone and the later monument to Sir Charles Nicholl is in marble.

Half a mile away, on an isolated site with good views, is Racton Tower, a folly built in 1772 by Theodosius Keene. It was Colonel Gunter of Racton, possibly the son of Sir George, who helped Charles II to escape from Shoreham to France after the Battle of Worcester in 1651. Gunter met the King on the county boundary and, with the King disguised as his servant and leading his horse, they travelled through Sussex to Shoreham, following what is now the south Downs Way and eluding the Parliamentary controls at the two unavoidable river crossings of Houghton Bridge and Bramber.

Just north of Racton is **Stansted Park**. The original house was designed by William Talman, the architect of UPPARK, but following a fire at the turn of this century the main part was rebuilt in a neo-Wren style. The splendid grounds feature one of the best beech avenues in England, 1½ miles long, laid out in the early 18th century and replanted in 1820. The avenue was badly damaged – though fortunately not destroyed – in the 1987 storm. Stansted Park also has a theatre museum which, with the house and gardens, is open to the public in summer. Cricket matches are played in front of the house on most Sundays during the season, including epic confrontations between the actors of the Chichester Festival Theatre and the Royal Shakespeare Company.

There is also a car park to the north of Stoughton, provided by the Forestry Commission to enable public access to Wildham Wood, one of the largest beech woodlands on the Downs.

Strettington (1/2E) *see* Goodwood

Sullington (1/5D) *see* Storrington

Sutton (1/3D) *see* Bury

Telscombe (2/4E) *see* Rodmell

Thakeham (1/5D) *see* Storrington

Three Bridges (2/2B) *see* Crawley

Ticehurst (3/2B)

At the junction of the B2087 and the B 2099 and within walking distance of Bewl Bridge Reservoir. The parish church of St Mary dates from the 14th century and was restored by the Victorians. The church features a splendid front cover, octagonal with doors that fold back. The Baptist chapel in the village was built in 1820 and, in common with most other vernacular buildings in this part of the county, is tile hung. Two other buildings in the village of special interest are Furze House and Dunsters Mill House. The former was once the local workhouse while the latter should, by rights, be several fathoms under the waters of the reservoir. When the Southern Water Authority created Bewl Bridge Reservoir in 1975, many acres of farmland and many farm buildings were lost. The Authority agreed, however, to save the 500 years-old mill house and transport it, brick by brick, to its present site, where it was re-erected. Some of the best of the other buildings rescued from the reservoir site may be seen at the Weald and Downland Museum at SINGLETON.

Stanstead Park

Tillington (1/3C) *see* Petworth

Trotton (1/2C) *see* Rogate

Treyford (1/2D) *see* Harting

Uckfield (2/4C)
An expanding commuter town on the A26 to the north-east of Lewes, now provided with a bypass. The church of Holy Cross was designed by William Mosely in 1839. Some older buildings remain: The Maiden's Head Hotel is Georgian and marks the start of modern Uckfield's growth; Hook Hall is slightly earlier and has some attractive chequered brickwork. Much of what survives has been due to the efforts of the Uckfield Preservation Society, which in 1984 was awarded a European Heritage Award for its work in restoring nearby Nutley windmill, the oldest working post-mill in Sussex. Uckfield station was lit by gas until as recently as 1977. The railway used to continue to Lewes, but was closed south of Uckfield in the 1960s.

Uppark (1/1D)
Formerly one of the loveliest country houses in Sussex, one mile south of South Harting on the B2146 road, Uppark was all but destroyed in a

Bewl Lake Reservoir, near Wadhurst

disastrous fire in September 1989. In about 1690 Edward Forde, an engineer who gave London its first public water supply, commissioned William Talman, an architect of Dutch origin, to design a country house for him at Uppark on the crest of the Downs with sweeping views to the Solent and the Isle of Wight. The house Talman built reflected his Dutch background and had many features which would not be out of place in old Amsterdam. It was built of two storeys of mellow red brick, a steep hipped roof with a pronounced cornice, and simple stone architraves, quoins and string course. It was Forde's skill as an engineer which enabled the construction of a country house on top of a hill, with water pumped up from below.

Forde's descendants sold Uppark in 1747 to Sir Matthew Fetherstonhaugh, who altered and improved the house considerably. A magistrate, Member of Parliament and Fellow of the Royal Society, Sir Matthew was involved in various financial schemes, including a project to found a colony to be called Vandalia in West Virginia. The project came to nothing and the only tangible result is the Vandalian Tower erected on Tower Hill. In 1771 Sir Matthew's 21-year-old son Harry succeeded to the estate. Rich, sociable and extravagant, and a friend of the Prince Regent, Sir Harry brought the 15-year-old Emma Hart, later Lord Nelson's Lady Hamilton, to live briefly at Uppark as his mistress. His vigour undiminished, Sir Harry married his 20-year-old dairymaid Mary Anne Bullock in 1825, when he was in his 70th year. Mary Anne and her sister lived on at Uppark after his death and ensured that nothing was changed, thus sparing the house from the damage which might have been caused by Victorian 'restoration'. H. G. Wells spent his childhood at Uppark, where his mother had become housekeeper in 1880, and as a boy attended MIDHURST Grammar School. The fire in late 1989 followed a year-long restoration programme, which had almost been completed.

Many valuable items, including paintings and a complete 18th-century dolls' house, were saved, but the roof and interior were destroyed. The National Trust, who now owns the house, hopes that it can be rebuilt; in the meantime it is not open to visitors.

Upper Beeding (2/2D) *see* Bramber

Wadhurst (3/2B)
Close to the Kent border south-east of Tunbridge Wells, an interesting Wealden parish with several buildings of architectural interest and close connections with the Sussex iron industry. Wadhurst was the last place in Sussex to keep alive the native iron industry. The local iron-masters refused to adapt to the new methods developed in the northern counties during the Industrial Revolution. As a result of their conservative ways and lack of competitiveness, they soon became redundant and the last Sussex furnace, traditionally at Ashburnham, was put out some time in the early 19th century. There are still many reminders of the iron industry in Sussex, not least in Wadhurst's parish church of St Peter and St Paul where a number of cast-iron memorials dating from 1617 to 1799 line the floor of the nave and the choir. These iron graveslabs are of considerable interest. Often the illiterate caster failed to understand the significance of individual words, leaving no spaces between them or splitting them unconventionally at the end of lines. Part of the church is late Norman and is therefore comparatively early for the district, which is not generally considered to have been 'civilised' until the mid-18th century.

Until the 19th century the parish was divided into six districts, known as 'quarters': Town quarter, Cousley Wood quarter, Bivelham quarter, Faircouch quarter, Riseden quarter and Weeke quarter. The investigative visitor may spend many hours trying to retrace these

View towards the church at Washington

divisions in surviving street names and the names of local woods and fields. Wadhurst itself means 'the clearing in a wood where Wada made his settlement'. This Anglo-Saxon inheritance suggests that the parish may be one of the oldest in the northern Weald.

During the Second World War Wadhurst lay in the infamous 'Bomb Alley', the route that German bombers and later flying bombs took on their way to London. Several buildings, including the school house, received direct hits. Churchgate House, which stands by the churchyard, is timber-framed and tile-hung and is one of many excellent examples in Wadhurst of 18th-century Wealden architecture. Even the railway station, built in 1852 in a Gothic style, is worthy of note. Out in one of the old 'quarters', Cousley Wood is a small but pretty chequer brick cottage, dated 1707. South of the village, Welland House is even older, dating from about 1600, and there are several 16th-century houses in the parish.

Wakehurst Place (2/3B) *see* Ardingly

Warminghurst (1/5D) *see* Coneyhurst

Warnham (1/5B) *see* Horsham

Washington (1/5D)
A village just off the busy A24 Horsham to Worthing road and in the shadow of Chanctonbury Ring. The name means 'the settlement of Wassa's people'. Now that the village has been bypassed Washington is a peaceful spot, with immediate access to the South Downs Way and superb downland scenery. It is situated below the Findon gap, at the point where the road to Worthing has always crossed the Downs and at the junction of the chalk country and the Weald. Its geological situation is reflected in the mixture of local building materials used, including chalk, sandstone, brick and flint. To the north is the Lower Greensand ridge, an important source of building sand where the extensive excavations are a prominent feature in the local landscape. The parish church of St Mary is disappointing, having suffered a severe restoration in 1867, but the tower is four-square and solid, providing a fine visual stop at the end of the village street.

The South Downs Way at this point follows the crest of the Downs but also includes an alternative route which descends into the village before climbing back up via Rowdell Farm. Walkers may leave their cars in the village in one

Hollygate Cactus Nursery at Ashington

Lawn mowers at West Dean Gardens

of the two public car parks, one near the quarry on the summit of Highden Hill, the other to the south of the A283 road to Steyning, under Chanctonbury Hill. A visit to the area should include the stiff climb up to Chanctonbury, for the grove of trees which graces the top of the hill is perhaps the most famous landmark in the county. On a clear day, the views in all directions are stunning.

Chanctonbury Ring is an Iron Age hill fort consisting of a small enclosure of less than 4 acres defended by a low bank and ditch. Within the fort are the remains of a Roman temple, for it was quite common for the Romans to make use of ancient sites for religious purposes. The hill and the fort were treeless until, in 1760, a clump of young beech trees was planted by Charles Goring of Wiston House, then a boy but later the owner of the estate, including Chanctonbury Hill. Charles tended and watered the young trees and, thanks to his care, they survived and prospered in this inhospitable environment, where the salt-laden winds whip in from the sea. In old age, he looked back on his work and wrote:

> Oh! could I live to see the top,
> In all its beauty dressed,
> That time's arrived; I've had my wish,
> and lived to eighty-five.
> I'll thank my God who gave such grace,
> As long as e'er I live.

The clump suffered severely in the storm of October 1987, when the uprooting of the trees uncovered quantities of Roman tiles and other material confirming the archaeologial importance of the site. Plans are in hand to replant the clump.

Just off the South Downs Way, to the west of the Ring, is a dew pond restored and maintained by the Society of Sussex Downsmen. There being no running water on the porous chalk downland, farmers had to construct artificial ponds to water their stock. The traditional Sussex dew pond had a puddled clay seal which prevented or delayed seepage of rainwater falling into the pond. Evaporation was matched by condensation which takes place within about 6 in of the surface, causing moisture to fall back from the air into the pond. In this way, the Sussex dew ponds were able to remain full of water, even in the driest season. The process was not fully understood by our ancestors: hence the traditional name by which the ponds are known. This pond at Chanctonbury is a favourite habitat of the crested newt, who spends his winters buried in the mud and clay of the pond floor.

Below Chanctonbury is **Wiston**, comprising Wiston House, seat of the Goring family, and the parish church of St Mary, another example of brutal Victorian restoration. The house was built for Sir Thomas Shirley in about 1575 and so rebuilt in 1830 that only the main front is original. The Shirley family, who lived here well into the 17th century, have a number of memorials in the church. The house is now owned by the Foreign Office and is used as a conference centre under the somewhat confusing title of Wilton Park.

Due north of Washington, above Washington Common and Warren Hill (both owned by the National Trust), is **Rock Mill**, a sailess windmill once the home of the composer John Ireland. He first came to Sussex in the 1920s and later made his home in the early 19th-century windmill, with its commanding views of the Downs. He said that much of his music was inspired by Sussex and its past, and one of his best-loved works is entitled 'Amberley Wild Brooks'. John Ireland is buried in the churchyard at SHIPLEY.

Further north is **Ashington**, an undistinguished settlement which nevertheless contains the interesting and unexpected Cactus Garden at Holly Gate Nursery with some 20,000 cactus and other succulent plants. Then to the east is **Ashurst**, a remote village deep in the agricultural Weald containing the pretty church of St James, a cheerful mixture of flint walls, Horsham stone roof and tile-hung nave gable. The village inn, The Fountain, is at least 300 years old and has a floor of huge stone flags.

Watersfield (1/4D) *see* Bury

West Burton (1/4D) *see* Bury

West Chiltington (1/4D) *see* Storrington

Westdean, *East Sussex* (2/5F)

Close to Seaford and best approached on foot from East Dean or Exceat via the South Downs Way, Westdean is a delightful Downland hamlet, unspoiled by the development that has taken place at neighbouring East Dean. The church of All Saints is remarkable for its broad, rectangular west tower, which has an oddly shaped half-hipped spire, a most unusual feature. The adjoining Rectory dates from the 13th century, while the nearby Manor House and dovecot are now in ruins. However, the 13th-century Charleston Manor, half a mile away to the north-east, has been described by Pevsner as 'A perfect house in a perfect setting'. Note that Charleston Manor is not to be confused with Charleston Farmhouse, the home of Duncan Grant near FIRLE.

West Dean, *West Sussex* (1/2D)

A downland village north of Chichester with associations with Edward VII and now the home of a flourishing arts and crafts college. The village was bypassed as long ago as 1810 when the new road from Chichester to Midhurst was built, leaving the village a quiet backwater. Shortly before, in 1804, West Dean House had been rebuilt for Lord Selsey by James Wyatt, the architect of GOODWOOD House. The house, in Gothick style, is largely of flint and the craftsmanship involved in knapping and shaping the irregular flints is particularly fine on the main elevation. Undoubtedly, however, West Dean suffers from the rather forbidding aspect of unrelieved flint over a large area and opinions on the merit of the house differ.

In 1893 West Dean was bought by the James family and became famous for its Edwardian house parties, especially during Goodwood races. When he suceeded to the family fortune Edward James devoted his life to the arts, becoming a major patron of the Surrealist movement. Through his generosity a highly successful college of arts and crafts was established at West Dean, where students of all ages may develop skills in antique furniture restoration, silver-smithing, bookbinding and many other activities.

The parks and gardens are open to the public, who may visit the 35 acres of lawns and gardens with many unusual trees and a unique collection of lawnmowers dating from 1850. There is also an exhibition showing the history of the gardens. Teas are served in the orangery. In the summer, open-air theatre is presented in the gardens as part of the annual Chichester Festivities. The parish church of St Andrew was burned in a disastrous fire in 1934 and a new church was sensitively built within the old walls by Frederick Etchells.

West Firle (2/4E) *see* Firle

West Grinstead (2/1C)

Comprises a park and two churches on the upper

reaches of the River Adur, south of Horsham, with very few houses except in the modern settlement of Partridge Green. West Grinstead was part of the estate of William de Braose, who rebuilt the church and dedicated it to St George, patron saint of England.

The River Adur flows to the south of the church and Knights Templar, on their way downstream from their estate at Shipley, would have passed by on their barges. Although there are very few buildings near the church, its location must have been determined by the nearby river crossing, which is also at the centre of a large parish. Even the development of the river as a commercial navigation with locks and considerable traffic failed to cause the expansion of the settlement and today there are still only a few buildings around the church. That St George's did, however, provide the spiritual focus for a large and far-flung community is graphically illustrated by the names of thëfarms and houses in the parish which appear in elegant early 19th-century lettering on the pews. For 150 years from 1695 members of the Woodward family were rectors of West Grinstead, a unique record of service which emphasises the continuity and stability of rural life at this time.

In the 17th century the estate came into the hands of the Caryll family, who also owned land at HARTING on the Hampshire border. The Carylls were Catholics and were related by marriage to almost all the prominent Catholic families in Sussex, including the Gages at FIRLE and the Shelleys at Michelgrove near CLAPHAM. As a result West Grinstead became, and has remained, an important Catholic centre and is home to the only Catholic community in Sussex east of the River Arun to have survived from the 18th century. This is particularly remarkable since after the collapse of the Caryll family in 1754 the community survived without the protection of a powerful Catholic patron. Under the Carylls West Grinstead represented a classic example of 'seigneurial Catholicism' whereby, after the Reformation, a Catholic squire and his estate rather than the parish church became the focus of parish life, providing security for their Catholic tenants and access to the Mass through their chaplains.

These chaplains were a succession of Benedictine, Jesuit and Franciscan missionaries, thanks to whom there was already a Catholic community in West Grinstead to welcome the remarkable Mgr Jean-Marie Denis the French

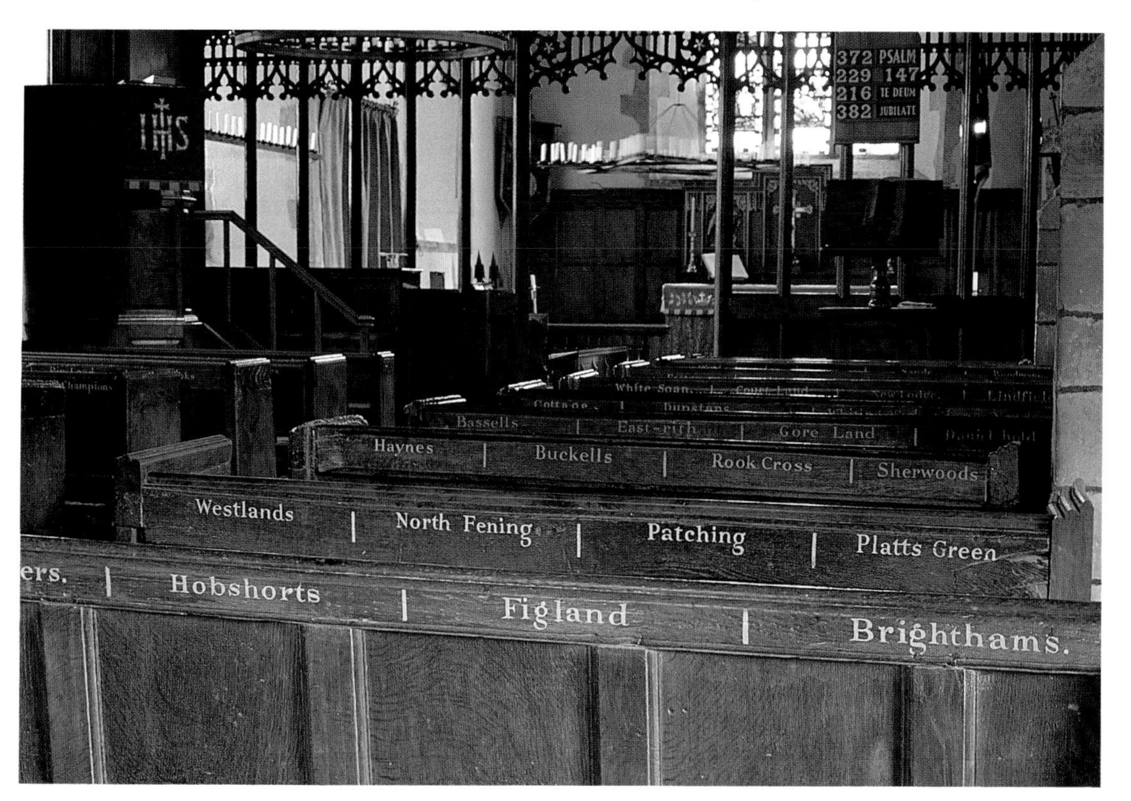

Farm names on pews in West Grinstead church

priest who served the mission from 1863 to 1900. He strengthened the community and the role of Catholicism in this part of Sussex and his legacy is visible today in the church of Our Lady of Consolation and St Francis (1876) and the adjoining building, originally a priory of Dominican nuns and now a school. In between is a delightful timber-framed house with a Georgian façade known as the Priest's House. This building is thought to be the oldest occupied presbytery in England and still has a secret chapel in the attic which was used regularly until the opening of the new church. The church was visited regularly by the writer Hilaire Belloc, who was influenced in his decision to settle at Shipley by the proximity of the Catholic centre at West Grinstead.

The estate was sold by the Carylls to the Burrells of Knepp Castle, who commissioned the Prince Regent's architect John Nash to build West Grinstead Park in 1806. The railway came to West Grinstead in the 19th century and a station was provided on the Horsham to Shoreham line north of the village on the A272. Since the closure of the line in the 1960s the track bed has been converted into a long-distance path known as The Downs Link, providing a route from Guildford to Steyning for walkers and horse-riders.

Westhampnett (1/2E) *see* Chichester

West Hoathly (2/3B) *see* Ashdown Forest

Westmeston (2/3D) *see* Ditchling

West Wittering (1/1F) *see* Witterings, The

Wilmington (2/5E)
Famous for the Long Man carved on the adjoining hillside and for its Priory, Wilmington is a small village north-west of Eastbourne. Many of the houses, once the simple homes of agricultural workers, have been restored by their owners, and the single village street is particularly picturesque.

Wilmington Priory has long been associated with ghost stories and folklore. It was founded in the 12th century by Benedictine monks from Grestain in Normandy and dissolved by Henry VIII some 400 years later. The Priory is now owned and maintained by the Sussex Archaeological Society and is open to the public. It is the Long Man of Wilmington, however, that most visitors come to see. The most curious thing about the great chalk carving is not so much its height – over 200 ft – but that whoever designed it took into account the elevation of the hill, so that the figure does not appear unduly foreshortened from the distance. As for its origins, many opinions have been put forward but none can be substantiated. Some say the Long Man is a surveyor; some see the Midsummer Man of pagan lore, opening up the doors to the underworld; others tend to identify him with a Saxon chieftain. Cynics put it all down to the mischievous monks.

Winchelsea (3/4D)
One of the ancient Cinque Ports, Winchelsea is historically one of the most important places in Sussex, with many attractions for the discerning visitor. Like neighbouring RYE, Winchelsea stands on a hill overlooking the coastal plain and the sea. From the fields to the south of the town, it is apparent that the grassy cliffs which now separate Winchelsea from the alluvial plain once received the full force of the sea. Old Winchelsea lay to the south and was destroyed by the encroaching sea in the early Middle Ages, to be replaced by the planned town of New Winchelsea which was laid out in 1283 by the Warden of the Cinque Ports and the Lord Mayor of London, with the intention of helping the wine trade with France. Ironically, the fickle sea then retreated, leaving the town stranded and its economy in ruins.

There are so many ancient buildings in Winchelsea that it would be impossible to mention them all. Fortunately there is a comprehensive information board on the green by the church, a useful walking guide published by the County Council and a good local museum in the old Court Hall. The Hall itself is one of the oldest buildings in the county and its museum is tiny but varied.

The parish church of St Thomas is large and spacious: a detailed guide explains its somewhat tempestuous history. It was built as part of the new town and, with its churchyard, occupies a large and important plot on the town plan. However, only the chancel and side chapels of the original building remain intact; the transepts and nave have disappeared, probably as the result of French raids. Look out for the three tomb recesses in the north aisle, with early 14th-century ogee arches. The effigies they contain are of Sussex marble and may have come from the church at Old Winchelsea. It was by a tree in the churchyard that Charles Wesley preached

The pond and the church at Wisborough Green

his last open air sermon, an event recorded by a plaque.

The grid street pattern of the medieval new town is easy to follow, as is the position of the town wall, built to protect the inhabitants against French raids. Three of the town gates still survive. Strand Gate, up on the hill, dates from the early 14th century. The Pipewell Gate was erected in about 1400 and gave access to the ferry and later the road to Rye. The New Gate is nearly a mile outside the present town and, despite its name, is of medieval origin. Winchelsea is an ancient borough and still elects a mayor, despite being no bigger than a village.

Wisborough Green (1/4C)
A classic Wealden village on the A272 a mile to the west of Billingshurst, with one of the largest village greens in the county. In the past the village was sometimes known simply as 'Green', which is not surprising as the most memorable feature of the place is the 9 acres of open space around which the church, houses, pubs and shops are grouped. The hill top site of the church and the unusually thick (4 ft 6 in) walls of the tower suggest that it was a Norman keep guarding the upper reaches of the Arun – a vital means of transport when the Weald was still thickly forested. It is certainly odd that the west door, normally the main entrance to a church, is not central and is much smaller than the north and south doors, both of which were built high enough to admit mounted men.

The church is dedicated to St Peter ad Vincula (St Peter in Chains), one of only a handful of such dedications in the country. The chains are those which bound St Peter when he was imprisoned by Herod Agrippa and which were thought to have miraculous properties. Slivers of them became much-prized relics in the Middle Ages and may well have formed part of the collection of treasures held at the church. According to an inventory taken in Henry VIII's time, these also included 'reliques of St Peter's hair and beard' and 'a crystall stone containing a lytyll of our Lady's milk'. Not surprisingly St Peter's church became a place of pilgrimage and was visited by pilgrims on their way to major national and international shrines. The church contains a good wall painting depicting *Christ on the cross* and *St James the Great with a group of pilgrims*. It disappeared when the chancel arch was rebuilt in the 13th century, and was rediscovered only during a major restoration in

1867. Two workmen were quarrelling over a local girl; in the fight which followed, a stone was thrown which dislodged the filling in the recess and revealed the painting.

Since the village was partly in the manor of BURY which Edward the Confessor had granted to the Abbey of Fécamp in Normandy, it is possible that the priest here was a Benedictine monk. Village legend has it that one of the houses near the church, the forerunner of the Three Crowns pub, was an inn called The Benedictine and it is interesting that three crowns on a blue sea form part of the arms of the Order. Perhaps the inn was once a guest house for pilgrims run by the priest.

The Arun Valley north of Wisborough Green contains a number of early agricultural settlements where wealthy absentee landlords moated large areas to protect their cattle from wolves and thieves. In 1256 the moat at Drungewick, still containing water, provided protection for a large stud farm containing cattle, sheep, goats and horses which the Bishop of Chichester bred for use on many of his Sussex manors. The Wealden glass industry flourished in this area and the introduction of new techniques from France caused further expansion in the 16th century. Jean Carée, a Huguenot, built a large furnace at Farnefold Wood near Wisborough Green in 1567; other centres were at Kirdford and at Plaistow, near LOXWOOD.

West of Wisborough Green, on the road to Petworth, are The Mens and The Cut woodlands which are managed by the Sussex Wildlife Trust. There are trees and shrubs here characteristic of ancient woodlands, such as the wild service tree and the midland hawthorn. These 400 acres therefore represent an important relic of the ancient Wealden forest and are a good indication of how the greater part of Sussex north of the Downs must have appeared in ancient times.

Wiston (1/5D) *see* Washington

Withyam (2/4B) *see* Ashdown Forest

Witterings, The (1/1F)
Twin seaside villages on the edge of Chichester Harbour, popular for holidays and as a residential area. East Head, the sand spit close to **West Wittering** village now owned by the National Trust, marks the western entrance to Chichester Harbour through which the Romans sailed when they came to capture the British tribal capital of Regnum. Local legend has it that they landed at Snow Hill Creek and that they brought elephants with them who were unable to negotiate the notorious Chichester Harbour mud. Access to East Head is by the large private car park managed by West Wittering Estate plc, from which it is possible to walk round the whole of the headland in under an hour with superb views out to sea, around the Harbour and inland to the Downs. The beaches at West Wittering, again with access from the car park, are probably the best in West Sussex for sunbathing and swimming. Beach equipment and take-away food may be found in cheap and cheerful **East Wittering**.

Notable buildings in West Wittering are the parish church of St Peter and St Paul, victim of a vicious Victorian restoration, and Cakeham Manor House. Originally a palace of the Bishops of Chichester, Cakeham is now an attractive medley of medieval, Tudor and Georgian elements, with a striking tall brick tower built in the early 16th century.

Woods Mill (2/2D) *see* Henfield

Woolavington (1/2C) *see* Graffham

Worth (2/2B) *see* Crawley

Worthing (1/5E)
The largest town and premier seaside resort of West Sussex, whose excellent shopping centre has been acquired at the expense of the town's architectural heritage. In ancient times the sea penetrated inland between Worthing and Lancing; even within living memory flooding was a feature of Worthing life. The extent of the tidal inlet is suggested by the name of the original nucleus of what was later to become Worthing: Broadwater. Here stands the late Norman parish church. Some idea of the flavour of the old settlement can be gained from the cottages to the north of the church in Broadwater Street East. At this time, Worthing was no more than an obscure fishing hamlet on the coast, at the mouth of what had been an inlet. The inhabitants scratched a living from mackerel fishing and subsistence agriculture. The settlements were isolated from the outside world, cut off from the road system and subject to flooding, particularly in the east.

Two factors contributed to the development

Cakeham Manor House near West Wittering

The Old Ice House, near Pagham

of the town in the late 18th and early 19th centuries: first, the construction of the turnpike road via Findon in 1804; second, the discovery of the therapeutic benefits of sea bathing. By 1750, the increasing popularity of the seaside as a health resort and the patronage of BRIGHTON by the Prince Regent began to influence the development of adjoining areas. Visitors started to arrive in the district and, in 1789, there opened at Worthing an exclusive apartment house which became known as Warwick House after its aristocratic patron. The position of Worthing as an alternative fashionable watering-place was confirmed when in 1798 George III sent his daughter, the Princess Amelia, here to recover from an unfortunate affair with one of his equerries. This sign of Royal approval, together with the delightful situation of the town beneath the Downs and the exceptionally mild climate for which the area became famous, combined to ensure a period of rapid expansion. Building took place in Montague Place, Bedford Row, The Steyne, Warwick Street and the east side of South Street. A circulating library was opened, followed by assembly rooms and a covered bath. In 1807 the opening of the threatre in Ann Street coincided with a second Royal visit, this time by the young Princess Charlotte, sickly daughter of the Prince Regent.

Building continued for another 10 years. St Paul's church, with its massive Doric portico, had been built in 1812 by J. B. Rebecca and 1830 saw the completion of the adjoining Ambrose Place, named after one of the contractors who worked on the project. The charming houses were provided with balconies so that their owners might better enjoy what was then an open view to the south. The best house in this attractive early Georgian terrace is probably number 14, which was occupied at one time by the playwright Harold Pinter. Other notable buildings of this period include Beach House, also by J. B. Rebecca, a stuccoed bow-fronted villa with gardens down to the sea; the unfinished Park Crescent by the Brighton architect Amon Wilds; and Liverpool Terrace, built by Henry Cotton in about 1830 and without doubt the finest architectural composition in the town. Like Ambrose Place, Liverpool Terrace was built to face open space and gardens, now filled with building.

By 1830 the bubble had burst. Large scale building ceased and the fashionable set departed, taking their patronage elsewhere. Throughout the rest of the 19th century, piecemeal development continued and the economy of the area was strengthened by the expansion of market gardening, taking advantage of the mild climate and frequent sunshine. Worthing produced grapes, figs, cucumbers and flowers; later, the Worthing tomato became famous throughout the country. The expansion of the urban area put pressure on this industry, however, forever pushing it to more peripheral locations. By the late Victorian period this process was more or less completed and the expanding town had incorporated the formerly separate settlements of Broadwater, West Tarring and Goring. In 1890 local government was reorganised and the new Borough of Worthing was created, with considerably extended boundaries.

And so Worthing settled down into its role as family resort and residential town – acquiring, in the present century, a respectable industrial base in pharmaceuticals and service industries such as banking, insurance and finance. In the 1950s and 60s much of old Worthing fell to the demolition contractor and even Beach House was once under threat. Too much was lost for the town now to be described as of high architectural quality, but it is to be hoped that remains will be carefully conserved. Worthing's past can be studied in the excellent museum in Chapel Road, winner of an important national award in the 1987 Museum of the Year competition, where a real attempt is made to place the town in its context of the Downs and the sea.

Literary visitors to the town include Oscar Wilde, who wrote *The Importance of Being Earnest* here and named his central character after the town; the naturalist W. H. Hudson, author of *Nature in Downland* and other minor classics, who is buried in Broadwater churchyard; and Arnold Bennett, J. B. Priestley and Sir Compton Mackenzie, all of whom stayed at Beach House during the heady days when it was the home of the dramatist Edward Knoblock. Pinter continues the tradition.

Apart from the museum and art gallery, visitors may enjoy over 100 acres of parks and gardens, the 960 ft long pier, bathing, a modern swimming pool, sports centre, the excellent and very comfortable Connaught Theatre and first-class shopping facilities.

On the outskirts of the borough but now engulfed in development is the old centre of West Tarring. The High Street includes an important group of 15th-century timber-framed

Avenue of Ilex oaks, Ferring

buildings with close-set timbers and overhang, known as Parsonage Row and restored by the Sussex Archaeological society. Also in West Tarring is the 13th-century Old Palace of the Archbishops of Canterbury, now a parish hall and used during the day by the neighbouring primary school. The gardens of the Old Palace were famous for their figs: tradition has it that one of the fig trees was planted by Thomas à Becket more than 800 years ago.

Further to the west is **Ferring**, another village which has been absorbed by the built-up area of Worthing, but which is nevertheless of some interest. Ferring occupies what must once have been a remote and isolated spot on the coast. In what remains of the old village there are a number of flint cottages and one or two agricultural buildings, now in different uses. An unusual feature here is the use of flint cobbles set in neatly bonded courses in house and garden walls, as in Church Lane. There is a fine avenue of ilex oaks joining Sea Lane, Ferring with Sea Lane, Goring. The avenue was originally one of the drives to Goring Hall, which was rebuilt in 1888 after having been destroyed by fire.

Between Ferring and Worthing lies **Goring by Sea** whose chief claim to fame is that the Sussex writer and naturalist Richard Jefferies spent the last years of his life here. He died in 1887 and is buried in Broadwater churchyard, Worthing, as

is his friend and fellow natural history writer W. H. Hudson. Jefferies's books include *The Story of My Heart*, *Nature near London*, and *The Life of the Fields*, all the result of his careful observation of the life of the countryside.

North of Ferring is the National Trust's Highdown Hill, whose most prominent feature is an early Iron Age hill fort dating from about 500 BC. The site has been excavated and the finds can be seen in Worthing Museum. An eccentric miller called John Olliver lived on the hill and built his tomb here many years before his death. When he died in 1793 he was buried head first so that when the world turned upside down on the day of judgment he would be the right way up.

Key to Maps

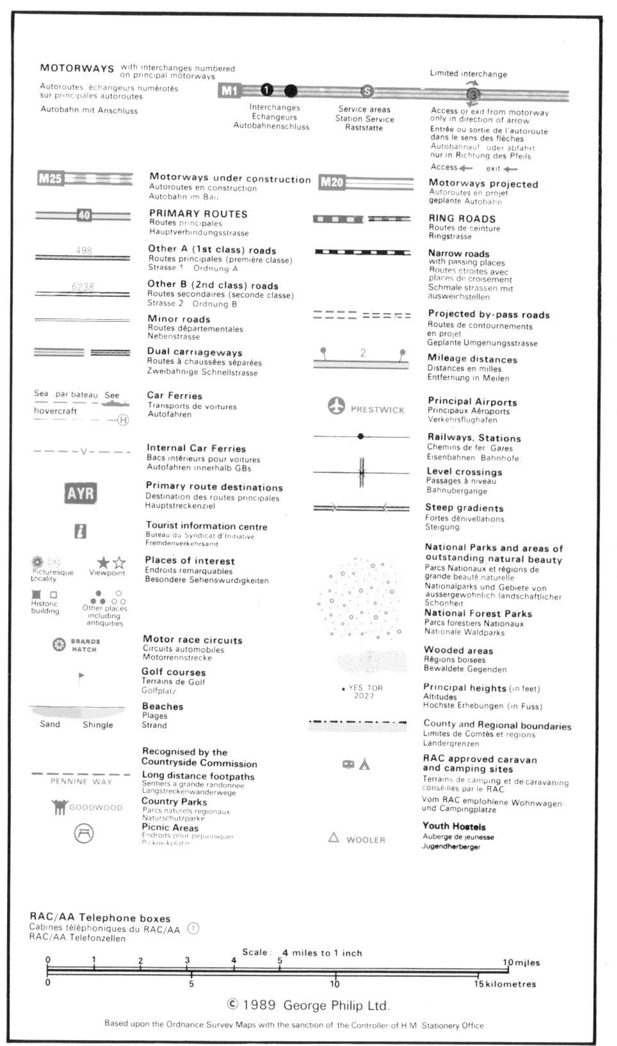

ALDERSHOT
FARNHAM
GUILDFORD
DORKING
Godalming
Haslemere
Hindhead
Grayshott
Liphook
Petersfield
Midhurst
Petworth
Pulborough
Billingshurst
Cranleigh
Storrington
Arundel
CHICHESTER
BOGNOR REGIS
LITTLEHAMPTON
WORTHIN
Rustington
Angmering
Ferring
Middleton on Sea
Selsey
SELSEY BILL
E. Wittering
Chichester Harbour
W E S T
S U S S E X
Odiham
Mill Lane
Crondall
Long Sutton
Well
Bentley
Froyle
Binsted
Wheatley
Kingsley
Bordon Camp
Oakhanger
Selborne
Blackmoor
Greatham
Liss
Liss Forest
Rake
Hill Brow
Steep
Sheet
Nursted
Buriton
E. Harting
Sth. Harting
Elsted
Treyford
Rogate
Trotton
Stedham
Iping
Chithurst
Woolbeding
Easebourne
Cocking
Heyshott
Graffham
Bepton
Didling
North Marden
Chilgrove
Compton
East Marden
W. Marden
West Dean
Singleton
Charlton
East Dean
Upwaltham
Forestside
Stoughton
Walderton
Funtington
Woodmancote
West Stoke
Lavant
E. Lavant
Halnaker
Boxgrove
Strettington
Westhampnett
Tangmere
Fontwell
Slindon
Eartham
Walberton
Norton
Nyton
Aldingbourne
Oving
Eastergate
Westergate
Woodgate
Barnham
Yapton
Ford
Climping
Tortington
Hambrook
Southbourne
Chidham
Bosham
Fishbourne
Broadbridge
Apuldram
Donnington
Hunston
Merston
Runcton
Colworth
Elbridge
Shripney
Flansham
Nth. Bersted
Sth. Bersted
Felpham
Ancton
Rose Grn.
Aldwick
Pagham
Nyetimber
Birdham
Somerley
Highleigh
Earnley
Bracklesham
Sidlesham
Street End
Church Norton
Norton
W. Wittering
Acre Street
Shipton Grn.
Itchenor
W. Thorney
Thorney
Lyminster
Wick
Poling
Hammerpot
Dorrington
Hangleton
E Preston
Angmering on Sea
Kingston Gorse
Goring by Sea
West Worthing
Broadwater
Salvington
High Salvington
Clapham
Patching
Findon
North End
Washington
Ashington
Sullington
Amberley
Rackham
Cootham
Greatham
Bury
Houghton
Nth. Stoke
Sth. Stoke
Burpham
Offham
Cross Bush
Arundel Park
Madehurst
Bignor
W. Burton
Sutton
Barlavington
Duncton
Coldwaltham
Waterstield
Hardham
Wiggonholt
Marehill
Fittleworth
Stopham
Byworth
Heathend
Tillington
Selham
Upperton
Lodsworth
Lickfold
Henley
Fernhurst
The Cylinders
Dial Grn.
Lurgashall
Northchapel
Fisherstreet
Kingsley Green
Camelsdale
Hammer
Shottermill
Linchmere
Milland
Milland Marsh
Borden
Fyning
Nyewood
Elsted Marsh
Cocking Causeway
W. Lavington
South Ambersham
Upr. Norwood
Bedham
North Hth
Codmore Hill
Nutbourne
W. Chiltington
Thakeham
Spear Hill
Goose Grn.
Broomer's Corner
Whitehall
Coolham
Shipley
Coneyhurst Common
Broadford Bridge
Gay St.
Adversane
Parbrook
Brooks Grn.
Southwater
Barns Grn
Itchingfield
Five Oaks
Slinfold
The Haven
Park St.
Broadbridge Hth
Strood Grn.
Bucks Green
Rudgwick
Rowhook
Warnham
Tisman's Common
Loxwood
Alfold Bars
Alfold
Alfold Crossways
Ellen's Grn.
Oakwoodhill
Walliswood
Ockle
Forest Grn.
Ewhurst
Rowly
Grafham
Plaistow
Ifold
Mackerel's Common
Kirdford
Balls Cross
Wisborough Green
Newpound Common
Roundstreet Common
Strood Grn.
Dunsfold
Chiddingfold
Combe Common
Grayswood
Hambledon
Loxhill
Hascombe
Witley
Wormley
Brook
Bowlhead Grn.
Thursley
Wheelerstreet
Hydestile
Milford
Tuesley
Thorncombe Street
Bramley
Wonersh
Shamley Green
Blackheath
Farley Green
Peaslake
Holmbury St. Mary
Hurt Wood
Abinger
Friday St.
Coldharbour
Sutton
Abinger Hammer
Wootton
Westco
Gomshall
Shere
Albury
Shalford
Compton
Puttenham
Onslow Village
Wanborough
Hog's Back
Flexford
Wyke
Normandy
Ash
Ash Vale
Willey Grn.
Stoughton
Wood Street
Burpham
West Clandon
Merrow
East Clandon
Newlands Corner
West Humt
Horsley
Tongham
Badshot Lea
Runfold
The Sands
Shackleford
Peper Harow
Hurtmore
Farncombe
Eashing
Elstead
Tilford
Millbridge
Rushmoor
Frensham
Churt
Bucks Horn Oak
Rowledge
Wrecclesham
Mt. Pleasant
Folly Hill
Upr. Hale
West Heath End
Blacknest
Wyck
E. Worldham
W. Worldham
Sleaford
Lindford
Arford
Headley
Standford
Bramshott
Conford
Longmoor Camp
Whitehill
Langley
Gibbet Hill
Black Down
Harrow Hill
Trundle Hill
Emsworth
Westbourne
Racton
Woodend
E. Ashling
W. Ashling

MAPS 187
DORKING
Reigate
Redhill
Horley
GATWICK
CRAWLEY
Horsham
East Grinstead
Haywards Heath
Burgess Hill
LEWES
BRIGHTON
HOVE
WORTHING
Shoreham by Sea
Newhaven
Seaford
Crowborough
Southborough
Edenbridge
Oxted
Westerham
Lingfield
Uckfield
THE WEALD
ASHDOWN FOREST
EAST SUSSEX
SOUTH DOWNS
Mickleham
Mersham
Limpsfield
Salfords
Copthorne
Three Bridges
Cuckfield
Lindfield
Hassocks
Hurstpierpoint
Ditchling
Keymer
Henfield
Steyning
Peacehaven
Rottingdean
Saltdean
Forest Row
Hartfield
Maresfield
Crowborough Town
St. Leonard's Forest
Balcombe
Handcross
Ardingly
Newick
Chailey
Rodmell
Glynde
Alfriston
Wilmington
Friston
Birling Gap
Seven Sisters (Cliffs)
Dieppe

Shipbourne
Nettlestead
Farleigh
Loose
Langley
Broomfield
Langley Hth.
Lenham
Stalisfield
West Peckham
Nettlestead Grn.
Coxheath
Boughton Grn.
Kingswood
Sandway
Oakhurst
Pitts Wood
Hadlow
Hale St.
Yalding
Linton
Hunton
Chart Corner
Warmlake
Boughton Malherbe
Lenham Hth.
Charing
Hildenborough
East Peckham
Benover
Chart Sutton
Sutton Valence
Ulcombe
Grafty Green
Charing Hth.
M20
Golden Grn.
Barnes St.
Beltring
Laddingford
Chainhurst
Rabbit's Cross
Gladdish
Egerton
Westwell Leacon
Medway
Whetsted
Collier Street
Beult
Cross-at-Hand
Hawkenbury
Southernden
The Forstal
Ram Lane
TONBRIDGE
Tudeley
Five Oak Green
Paddock Wood
Milebush
Marden
Headcorn
Pluckley
Little Chart
Hothfield
Southborough
Claygate
Staplehurst
Smarden Bell
Maltman's Hill
Pluckley Thorne
High Brooms
Matfield
Castle Hill
Marden Beech
Sinkhurst Grn
Smarden
Pembury
Brenchley
Frittenden
Wissenden
Petteridge
Horsmonden
Curtisden Green
Knox Bridge
Lashenden
Standen
Haffenden Quarter
Bethersden
ROYAL TUNBRIDGE WELLS
Hazel St.
Collier's Grn.
Cranbrook Common
Three Chimneys
Biddenden
Tanden
Lamberhurst Quarter
Goudhurst
Wilsley Pound
Sissinghurst
Woolpack
High Halden
Shadoxhurst
Bell's Yew Green
Lamberhurst
Kilndown
Cranbrook
East End
St. Michael's
Redbrook St.
Eridge Green
Frant
Hook Green
Hartley
Parkgate
Tenterden
Woodchurch
Platt
Sparrow's Grn.
Cousleywood
Bedgebury Forest
Benenden
Leigh Grn.
Kenardington
Mark Cross
Durgates
Wadhurst
Threeleg Cross
Flimwell
Gill's Green
Iden Green
Dingleden
Strood
Rolvenden
Reading Street
Appledore
Appledore Heath
Riseden
Bestbeech Hill
Union St.
Small Hythe
Rotherfield
Shover's Green
Wallcrouch
Ticehurst
Hawkhurst
The Horns
Four Throws
Rolvenden Layne
The Moor
ISLE OF OXNEY
Tidebrook
Stonegate
Swiftsden
Sandhurst
Linkhill
Newenden
Peening Quarter
The Stocks
Stone
Mayfield
Coggins Mill
Hurst Grn.
Sandhurst Cross
Ham Green
Wittersham
Rother
Etchingham
Witherenden Hill
Bodiam
Five Ashes
Salehurst
Ewhurst
Northiam
Beckley
Four Oaks
Iden
Paine's Cross
Burwash Common
Burwash
Northbridge St.
Robertsbridge
Staple Cross
Millcorner
Clayhill
Peasmarsh
Houghton Grn.
Burwash Weald
Horns Cross
Rye Foreign
East Guldeford
Broadoak
Cade St.
Brightling
Oxley's Grn.
John's Cross
Cripp's Corner
Playden
Heathfield
Punnett's Town
Three Cups Corner
Vinehall St.
Chitcombe
Broad Oak
Rye
Old Heathfield
Mountfield
Darwell Hole
Sedlescombe
Udimore
Lit. London
Maynard's Grn.
Rushlake Green
Dallington
Netherfield
Whatlington
Broadland Row
Rye Harbour
Warbleton
Brede
Horam
Vine's Cross
Canadia
Sedlescombe St
Winchelsea
Rye Bay
Penhurst
Icklesham
Winchelsea Beach
Foul Mile
Ponts Green
Battle
Kent St.
Westfield
Guestling Thorn
Gun Hill
Bodle St. Green
Telham
Three Oaks
Pett
Cowbeech
Catsfield
Baldslow
Guestling Green
Cliff End
Herstmonceux
Henley's Down
Hellingly
Magham Down
Windmill Hill
Ninfield
Crowhurst
St. Helen's
Fairlight
Fairlight Cove
Hollington
Lr. Horsebridge
Upr.
Boreham Street
Lunsford's Cross
Silverhill
Ore
Hailsham
Wartling
Hoe Common
Hooe
Bulverhythe
Little Common
Sidley
West Marina
St. Leonards
HASTINGS
Pevensey Levels
Cooden
BEXHILL
Polegate
Hankham
Norman's Bay
Westham
Pevensey
Stone Cross
Pevensey Bay
Folkington
Friday St.
Willingdon
Langney
Hampden Park
St. Anthony's Hill
Rose Lands
EASTBOURNE
Eastdean
Birling Gap
Holywell
BEACHY HEAD
Brookland
Walland Marsh
East Guldeford
Rye
Camber
Harbour
Rye Bay

Index

Numbers in italics refer to illustrations

Abbot's Wood 87
Adur, River/Valley 32, 38, 41, 43, 98, 106, 135, 148, 154, 155, 164, *164–5*, 166, 177
Ainsworth, Harrison 151
Albourne, Albourne Place 106
Alciston 15, 134; tithe barn 15, *15*, 167
Aldwick 36
Aldworth House, Black Down 115
Alfoldean Bridge: 'Roman Gate' 161
Alfred, King 23, 68
Alfriston 16–17, 132, 133, 134, 135; Clergy House 16–17; St Andrew's church ('cathedral of the Downs') 16
Amberley 17, 19, 31, 49, 114, 136; Castle 17, 19, 31; St Michael's church 17, 19, 31; The Thatched Cottage *18*
Amberley Chalk Pits: Pepper's Lime Works 129
Amberley Mount 136
Amberley Wild Brooks 17, 19, 50, 130, 136
Angmering 19
Angmering on Sea 114
Annington Hill 135
Ardingly 19, 24; South of England Show 19–20
Ardingly College 19, 98, 164
Argos Hill (Mayfield) 117
Arlington 87
Arun, River/Valley *11*, 17, 19, 20, 22, 31, 49, 62, 85, 99, 101, 112, 114, *114*, 117, 129, 130, 131, 136, 137, 152, 155, 161, 167, 169, 179, 180
Arun Valley railway 35, 130
Arundel 9, 20–2, 29, 57, 68, 92, 112, 113, 114, 167; Cathedral 20, 22; Maltravers Street 22, *22*; St Nicholas's church 22
Arundel bridge 142
Arundel Castle and Park 10, *11*, 20–2, *21*, 29, 85, 136, 140, 161; Swanbourne Lake 21
Arundel Festival 22
Ashdown Forest 14, 23–4, 74, 75, 116
Ashford, Daisy 150
Ashurst 176
Ashington 154, 176; Hollygate Cactus Nursery *174*, 176

Bailiffscourt Castle (Climping) 59
Balcombe 24
Balcombe Estate 24
Balcombe railway viaduct 24, *25*
Banks, Sir Joseph 123
Barcombe 24, 26
Barcombe Mills 24, 26
Barnsfarm Hill 136
Barrie, Sir James 167
Barry, Sir Charles 47, 104, 106
Bateman's, Kipling's home 10, 12, 48, 49, 153
Bates, H. E. 153
Battle 26–7, 64
Battle Abbey 8, 15, 26, *27*, 29, *30*, 120
Bayeux Tapestry 28, 40
Bayham Abbey 8, 81, 120
Beachy Head 44, 71, *71*, *72–3*, 74, 93, 133
Beacon Hill 137
Beddingham Hills 134
Bedhampton 150
Beeding Hill 135; *see also* Lower Beeding; Upper Beeding
Belaney, Archie, 'Grey Owl' 76
Bell, Clive 78, *151*
Bell, Quentin 78
Bell, Vanessa 78
Belloc, Hilaire 12, 14, 85, 88, 93, 137, 141, 150, *152*, 153, 154–5, 161, 178
Bell's Yew Green 81
Bennett, Arnold 183
Benson, E. F. 145
Berwick 78, 134
Betjeman, John 151
Bevis's Thumb (Neolithic long barrow) 116
Bewbush (Crawley) 61, 62
Bewl Bridge Reservoir 170, *172*
Bexhill 34, *34*, 88, 92; De La Warr Pavilion 34, 92
Bignor 10, 49–50, 137; The Old Shop 50, *50*; Roman villa 8, 19, 49–50
Bignor Hill 49, 70, 85, 130, 136–7
Billingshurst 34–5, 49
Birling Gap 74, 133
Bishopstone 17, 35–6; St Andrew's church 33, 35; Tide Mills 35, 52
Black Down 7, 115
Blake, William 36, 70, 114, 153
Blann, Michael 43
Bluebell Railway *23*, 24, 79
Blue Idol Meeting House, Coolham 35, 59–60, *63*
Blunt, Wilfrid Scawen 14, 64
Bodiam, Bodiam Castle 8, 36, *37*, 44
Bogarde, Dirk 52
Bognor Regis 7, 10, 36, 66, 91–2; The Dome 36, *38*
Bolney 36, 38
Bonfire Boys 78, 145
Borde Hill 75, 97
Bosham 38–40, 56, 88; church and millstream *39*; Holy Trinity chancel arch 28, *28*
Bostal Hill 134
Botolphs 43, 135; leper's window *42*, 43
Bow Hill 170
Boxgrove Priory (church of St Mary and St Blaise) 30, *31*, 40–1, 85; De La Warr chantry chapel *40*
Boxgrove village 41
Bramber 19, 41–2, 67, 99, 135, 154, 164, 170; Saint Mary's House *41*, 42
Bramber Castle 19, 29, 41, 42
Bramber Water 155
Brangwyn, Sir Frank 68
Braose, William de 41, 42, 99, 154, 177
Brede 43–4
Bridge, Frank 81
Brightling 36, 44; 'Mad Jack' Fuller's folly *43*, 44
Brighton 7, 9–10, 12, 44–8, 88–90, 91, 134, 153, 183; Chain Pier 12, 89; and Devil's Dyke 66, 67; Dukes Lane *45*; and Hove 101, 104–5; Kemp Town 47, 104; literary visitors 151; Madeira Drive *48*; Metropole Hotel 89; Palace Pier 89, *90*; Royal Pavilion 12, *46*, 47, 89, *89*; Victorian churches 47; West Pier 89
Brighton Festival 48
Brighton Rock *47*
Broadbridge Heath 99, 100
Broadfield (Crawley) 61, 62
Broadhurst Estate (Horsted Keynes) 24
Broadwater (Worthing) 180, 183
Bronze Age sites 71, 86, 87, 133, 134, 136, 137
Brown, George, fast bowler 170
Brown, Lancelot 'Capability' 79, 125
Browne, Sir Anthony, Viscount Montague 27, 117, 120
Buckler, C. A. 160
Bucks Head: Barn House 146
Budgenor Lodge (Easebourne) 120
'bungalow towns' 93
Burgess Hill 48–9
Burne-Jones, Sir Edward 48
Burpham 20, 22–3; St Mary the Virgin 22–3, 31
Burrell, William and Timothy (of Cuckfield) 165
Burrell, Sir William, historian 114, 154
Burrells of Knepp Castle 154, 178
Burton, Decimus 10, 90, 96, 104
Burton, James 96, 97
Burton Down 137
Burton Mill Pond (nature reserve) 126–7
Burwash 49, 97, 117, 150; Bateman's 10, 12, 48, 49, 153
Busby, Charles 47, 104
Butser Hill 137
Buxted, Buxted Park 50–1, 97
Byron, Lord 151
Byworth, near Petworth 126

Cade, Jack 79, 81
Cakeham Manor House 180, *181*
Camber 146
Campbell, Thomas 151
Canning, Sir Stratford 81
Canute, King 38, 88
Carlyle, Thomas 151
Carpenter, R. C. 47, 106, 164
Carroll, Lewis 151
Caryll, Sir Thomas 154, *155*
Carylls of West Grinstead 177, 178
Castle Hill 134
Catsfield 51
Chailey 51
Chailey Heritage 51–2
Chagall, Marc 54
Chanctonbury Ring/Hill 67, 76, 135–6, 154, 155, 174, 175–6
Chantry Post 167
Charles II, King 19, 42, 101, 155, 170
Charleston Farmhouse (near Firle) 78, 176; Clive Bell's study *151*; The Studio *79*
Charleston Manor (near Westdean) 176
Charlton 74, 85, 137
Charlton Hunt 74, 85, 137
Chesterton, G. K. 151
Chichester 14, 16, 19, 20, 29, 38, 52–6, 82, 87, 99, 127, 130, 137, 150, 151; Market Cross *54*; Pallant House Gallery *54*, 55; West Street, Clock Tower and Cathedral *55*
Chichester Castle 29
Chichester Cathedral 17, 29, 30, 31, 41, *53*, 54, 56, 76, 109, 137, 149, 154
Chichester Festivities 176
Chichester Harbour 38, 52, 55, 56, 88, 170, 180
Chiddingly 56
Chilgrove 137
Christie, John and Audrey 82
Christ's Hospital, Horsham 68, 98, *100*, 100–1, 166
Church Norton 149
Cissbury Ring Hill 76, 78, 93, 136
Civil War 10, 20, 36, 42, 55, 82, 109, 121, 138, 140
Clapham 56–7, 159; Michelgrove House 57, 166, 177
Clayton 49, 138; wall paintings 32, 131, 138
Clayton Hill: Jack and Jill windmills 138, *138*
Clayton tunnel 138
Climping 59; St Mary's church 30–1, 32, *58*, 59
Cobbett, William 12, 35, 151
Cocking gap 137
Coldwaltham 50
Coleman's Hatch 24, 151
Combe Hill (prehistoric site) 107, 133
Comper, Sir Ninian 52
Conan Doyle, Sir Arthur 64, 79, 150
Coneyhurst 59; Blue Idol meeting house 35, 59–60, *63*
Connolly, Cyril 150
Conrad, Joseph 145, 151
Coolham 59, 140
Coombes 138, 164–5; wall paintings 131, 138, 164
Coppard, A. E. 151
Cotton, Henry 183
Coultershaw water wheel and beam pump 126
Cowdray Castle 9, 27, 85, 117, *118–19*, 120, 137
Cowfold 60, *62*
Cowfold Monastery 60
Crabbe, George 150, 153
Crabbet Park 14, 64
Crane, Stephen 151
Crawley 14, 24, 61–3
Croft estate 164
Cromwell, Thomas 8, 142
Cross-in-Hand 98
Crowborough 64, 117, 150
Crowlink Valley 74, 81
Cuckfield 64–5, *65*, 97
Cuckfield Park 65, 97
Cuckmere, River/Valley 16, 17, 35, 68, 133, 134, *147*, 148
Cuckmere Haven 133, 148

Dacre, Lord 86–7
Dallington 44; 'Mad Jack' Fuller's folly *43*, 44
Danny Park 106, *106*
Darby, Revd Jonathan 74
Defoe, Daniel 140
Denis, Mgr Jean-Marie 177–8
Denmans 161
Dependents, The (religious sect) 115
Devil's Dyke 65–7, 134–5, *135*
Devil's Jumps, The (Monkton Down) 87, 137
Devonshire, Dukes of 70, 71, 92
dew ponds 136, 175–6
Dickens, Charles 151
Dickers, The 68
Dissolution of the Monasteries 27, 41, 68, 120, 122, 142, 178
Ditchling 68
Ditchling Beacon 7, *8*, 10, 14, 68, 134, 138
Donnington 153
Downs Link path, The 98, 100, 161, 166, 178
Dragon's Green 154
Drungewick 180
Drusilla's Zoo Park 17
Duncton Down 137
Duncton Hill 14
Durford Abbey 142
Durhamford Manor House 148
Dyke Hill 135

Earnley 153
Eartham, Eartham House 70, 85, 130, 137
Eartham Wood 70
Easebourne 27, 117, 120
Eastbourne, 7, 10, 70–1, *71*, 88, 92, 93, 132, 133, 137, 151; bandstand,

seafront and pier 7; Devonshire Park 70; The Redoubt: Sussex Combined Services Museum 70–1
East Dean (East Sussex) 74, 81, 176
East Dean (West Sussex) 74, 137
East Grinstead 64, 74–5, 146, 151; Queen Victoria Hospital 75; Sackville College almshouses 74, 75
East Guldeford 146
East Harting 87
East Head (near West Wittering) 180
East Marden *115*, 116
East Preston 114
East Sussex 10, 16, 33, 67, 74, 75, 109, 132
East Sussex College of Agriculture 70
East Wittering 180
Edburton 67, 75
Edburton Hill *66*, 135
Edward the Confessor, King 28, 180
Edward I, King 41
Edward III, King 23
Edward VI, King 100
Edward VII, King 104, 176
Edwardes, Revd Tickner 23
Egremont, George O'Brien Wyndham, 3rd Earl of 10, 12, 125
Elgar, Sir Edward 131
Eliot, T. S. 151
Elizabeth I, Queen 56, 117, 123
Elizabeth II, Queen 63, 70, 99
Elsted 87
Emsworth 170
English Heritage 26, 30, 41, 81, 128
English Wine Centre (near Alfriston) 17
Etchells, Frederick 176
Evelyn, John 109, 150
Exceat 81, 148, 176; River Cuckmere near *147*

Fairlight 75–6
Farnefold Wood 180
Faygate 146–7
Felpham 36, 114, 153
Ferring 184, *184*, 185
Findon 43, 183; sheep fair 76
Findon gap 154, 174
Findon Valley 76
Firle (West Firle) 77, 78, 134, 177
Firle Beacon 15, 78, 134
Firle Place 134
Fishbourne (Roman Palace), 8, 52–4, 56
Fittleworth 130–1
Fitzalans, Earls of Arundel 20, 74, 85
Flanders, Michael 153
Fletcher, John 150
Fletching 78–9
Fletching Common 79
Fontwell Park Racecourse 161
Ford 113, 114, *114*
Fore Hill and Fore Farm *140–1*
Forest Row 23–4
Forestry Commission 70, 87, 116, 170
Fox Hall, Charlton 85
Frant 81
Friston 81, 148; St Mary's church *80*, 81
Friston Forest 74, 81, 148
Frog Firle youth hostel 17
Fulking 67
Fulking Hill *66*, 135
Fuller, 'Mad Jack' *43*, 44

Gage, Sir John and Philippa 78
Gage family of Firle 78, 154, 177
Galsworthy, John 49, 152
gardens 19, 65, 75, 78, 79, 97, *120–1*, 122, 125, 147, 161, 176
Gatwick Airport 14, 61, 63, 75
George III, King 183
George IV (Prince Regent) 12, 46–7, 88–9, 154, 178, 183
George V, King 36
Gibbon, Edward 79, 150
Gibbons, Grinling 125
Gill, Eric 68, 87
Glynde 9, 20, 81–2; Palladian church 81, *82–3*
Glyndebourne opera 81, 82, 110, 150
Glynde Place 81–2
Glyndley Manor, Pevensey 128
Godwin, Earl of Wessex 40, 59, 82, 85, 158
Goldschmid, Sir Isaac 104
Goodwood House 56, 82–3, 85, 160, 176
Goodwood Racecourse 56, 83, 176
Goring, Charles 135, 175
Goring by Sea 183, 184
Graffham 86
Graffham Down 86, 137
Grant, Duncan 78, 176
Gravetye 10, 75
Great Dixter *120–1*, 122
Greatham 152
Grimes Graves, Suffolk 78
Gullege Farm East Grinstead 74

Habin Bridge (across Rother) 142
Haggard, Rider 151
Hailsham 40, 86
Halnaker 85
Halnaker Hill and Windmill 83, 153, *153*
Halnaker House 41, 85
Handcross 146; Nymans 65
Hangleton (Hove) 105
Hardham 131; St Botolph's wall paintings 31–2, 131, *131*, 138
Hardham Priory 131
Harold II Godwinson, King 28–9, 40, 59, 82, 158
Harting Down 87, 137, *137*
Harting Hill *86*, 87
Hartings, The 87, 177
Harvard, John 140
Hassocks 106
Hastings 7, 10, 88, 90–1, *94–5*, 96–7, 122, 150, 151, 152; Fishermen's Museum 96; net drying huts on beach *91*; Pelham Crescent 90, 96; St Clement's Caves 96
Hastings, Battle of (1066), 26, 27, 28–9, 40, 109, 127
Hastings Castle 29
Hastings Country Park 76
Hastings Embroidery 96
Hayley, William 70, 153
Haywards Heath 24, 65, 97, 110, 112, 150
Heaselands 97
Heathfield, Heathfield Park 97
Hellingly 86
Henfield 98, 164; 'Cat House' 98, *98*
Henry II, King 21, 74
Henry III, King 109
Henry V, King 143
Henry VI, King 141
Henry VIII, King 27, 68, 78, 112, 117, 120, 141, 142, 178, 179
Heron's Ghyll 23
Herstmonceux Castle 8, 9, 98
Herstmonceux, Royal Observatory 98, 99
Hesworth Common 131
Heyshott Down 137
Hickstead show jumping 36
High and Over Hill white horse 17
Highden Hill 175
Highdown Hill 76, 185
Hilton, Nathaniel 35
Hogge House, Buxted 51
Holland, Henry 46
Holland, William 166
Hooksway, Royal Oak pub, 121
Horselunges Manor, Hellingly 86
Horsham 49, 74, 75, 99–100, 146
Horsham Common 99
Horsted Keynes 24; Bluebell Railway terminus 24
Houghton 101, *102–3*, 135, 136; Chalk Pits Museum 101
Houghton Bridge 19, 49, 101, 170
Houghton Forest 101
Hove 44, 88, 90, 101, 104–5; Brunswick Square 104, *105*
Hudson, W. H. 33, 35, 183, 185
Hurstpierpoint 106, *107*
Hurstpierpoint College 19, 98, 106, 164

Ifield 61, 62
Iford 142
Ireland, John 154, 176
Iron Age sites 76, 81, 82, 134, 135, 136, 175, 185
Itford Hill 134

Jack and Jill windmills, near Pycombe 134, 138, *138*
James, Edward 176
James, Henry 90, 145, 151, 152
Jefferies, Richard 64, 74, 151, 184–5
Jevington 107, 133, 134, 135
John, King 41, 154
Johnson, Dr Samuel 46, 151
Juggs Road 134
Juxon, William, Archbishop of Canterbury 106

Kaye-Smith, Sheila 122
Keats, John 150–1
Kempe, Charles Eames 112
Keynes, Maynard 78
Kingsley Vale National Nature Reserve 170
Kipling, Rudyard 10, 12, 14, 48, 49, 67, 74, 93, 132, 150, 153
Kirdford 115, 180
Kithurst Hill 136, 167
Knepp Castle 99, 154, *156–7*, 178
Knights Hospitaller 23, 67–8, 164
Knights Templar 32, 67, 154, 164, 177
Knoblock, Edward 183
Knucker Hole, dragon legend of 23

Lancing 164, 180
Lancing College 19, 98, 164, *164–5*
Landmark Trust 85
Lavant, River/Valley 74, 83, 85, 137, 158
Lavants, The 107, 109
Lavington Common 86
Lavington Park (now Seaford College) 86
Lawrence, D. H. 152
Leith Hill, near Dorking 85
Leonardslee 147–8
Lewes 10, 14, 17, 20, 29, 43, 47, 67, 75, 99, 109–10, 116, 129, 134, 147, 150, 167; High Street 109, *110*; Jireh Chapel in the Cliffe 110; 'mathematical' tiles 109–10; Priory of St Pancras 8, 26, 29, 32, 50, 60, 87, 109, 130, 138; Prison 99; St Michael's church 33, 110, 128, 142; sheep fair 76
Lewes, Battle of (1264) 79, 109
Lewes Castle *108*, 110
Lickfold 115
Linch Down 137
Lindfield 97, 110, 112, 117; High Street *111*, 112
Litlington 17
Little Bognor 131
Little Halnaker 85
Littlehampton 7, 36, 92, 112–14; bathing huts at *113*
Little Thakeham 169, *169*
Littleton Down 137
Living World centre, Exceat 148
Lodsworth 115
Long Furlong, Findon 76
Long Man of Wilmington 133, *134*, 178
Lower, M. A. 49, 56, 75
Lower Beeding 42, 146
Lower Greensand ridge 174
Lower Horse bridge 86–7
Lowry, Malcolm 16, 150
Loxwood 114–15
Luffa, Ralph, Bishop of Chichester 17, 30, 31
Lullington 17, *17*
Lullington Heath, National Nature Reserve 17, 81, 133
Lurgashall 115
Lutyens, Sir Edwin 70, 85, 122, 169, *169*
Lychpole 164
Lyminster 23

Mackenzie, Sir Compton 183
Maidenbower, Crawley 62–3
Maidenmarsh Bridge (across Rother) 142
Mallydams Wood animal sanctuary 76
Malthouse Theatre, Hurstpierpoint 106
Manning Heath 146
Mantell, Dr Gideon 10, 147
Mardens, The 116
Maresfield 116; Chequers Inn 116
martello towers 8, 70, 75, 92, 128
Mary I, Queen 109, 116
Mayfield 116–17
Medmerry windmill 149
Michelgrove House, Clapham 57, 166, 177
Michelham Priory, near Hailsham 40, 68, *69*
Middleton Manor, Westmeston 68
Midhurst 74, 117, 150, 172
Mid Lavant 107, 121
Minoprio, Anthony 62
Mise of Lewes (1264) 109
Monkton Down: The Devil's Jumps 87
Montfort, Simon de 79, 109
Montgomery, Roger de, Lord of Arundel and Chichester 20, 29, 31, 59, 87
Morley, Colonel William, of Glynde 20, 82
Mortain, Robert, Count of 29, 127–8
Mount Caburn 26, 81, 110, 134

Nash, John, 47, 154, 178
National Gardens Scheme 97
National Trust 16–17, 36, 40, 42, 49, 59, 65, 67, 68, 74, 75, 78, 79, 86, 87, 115, 125, 142, 145, 146, 148, 159, 161, 173, 180, 185
Nature Conservancy Council 170
Nelond', Thomas, Prior of St Pancras, Lewes, 60
Nepcote 76
Neville, Charles 123
Neville, Ralph, Bishop of Chichester, 17, 31
New Bridge near Billingshurst 35
Newbuildings, near Southwater 14
Newhaven 113, 121, 129, 148; Jolly Sailor beer house 121

Newick 52; pump on village green *51*, 52
Newtimber 67, 138
Newtimber Hill 67, 134, 138
Nore Folly, Slindon 161
Norfolk, Dukes of 10, 20, 21, 22, 92, 146
Norman Conquest (1066) 28–9, 40, 96, 127–8, 164, 166
Normans 8, 20, 26, 28–33, 40, 41, 54, 68, 96, 98, 112, 122, 127–8, 130, 142, 154, 155, 166, 167, 173
Northchapel 115
North Common nature reserve 51
North Downs 67, 138
Northiam 121–2
North Marden 116
North Stoke 31, 101
Nutley post-mill 24, 171
Nyetimber 122
Nyetimber Barton 122
Nymans, Handcross 65

Ockenden Manor, Cuckfield 65
Old Ice House, The (near Pagham) *182*
Orwell, George 150
Otway, Thomas 143, 150
Ouse River/Valley 19, 23, 24, *33*, 109, 110, 121, 128–9, 134, 142, 148, 151, 155, 167; round-towered Norman churches of 33, 110, 128
Oxenbridge, Sir Goddard (the Brede Giant) 43

Pagham, Pagham Harbour 93, 122, 123, 149; nature reserve 122; The Old Ice House near *182*; Salt House 122
Parham Manor 9, 122, 136
Partridge Green 177
Patching 57, 58
Patmore, Coventry 152
Peacehaven 93, 123–4
Penn, William 59–60, 140, 166
Perching Hill *66*, 135
Perching Manor Farm 67
Percy Earls of Northumberland 10, 125
Pestalozzi children's village, Sedlescombe 148
Petworth 10, 17, 98, 124–7
Petworth House 10, 12, 124, *124–5*, 125, 150
Pevensey 28, 68, 127–8
Pevensey Bay 128
Pevensey Castle 19, 23, 29, 92, *126–7*, 127–8
Pevensey Levels 70, 128, 132; Martello Towers on 128
Piddinghoe 128–30; brick kiln 129; St John's church 33, *33*, 110, 128, 142
'Piltdown Man' 79
Pinter, Harold 183
Piper, John 54, 55, 77
Plaistow 114, 180
Playden 145, *145*
Plumpton 70, 134
Plumpton Plain 134
Plumpton Racecourse 70
Poling 23, 68
Pope, Alexander 151
Portslade-by-Sea 105
Portsmouth to Arundel Canal 114
Pound, Ezra 151
Powell, Alfred 17
Powys, John Cowper 151
Priestley, J. B. 183
Prince Regent *see* George IV
Pulborough 114, 117, 130–1, 161
Pulborough Hill 130
Pulborough Park 130

Pyecombe 134, 135, 138; tapsel gate 138, *139*, 165

Rackham Banks 136
Rackham Hill 136
Racton 170
Racton Tower 170
RAF Tangmere 153
Rebecca, J. B. 183
Richard, Saint, Bishop of Chichester 54
Richmond, Dukes of 74, 82, 83, 85
Ringmer 20, 138, 140, 152, *152*
Ripe 16, 150; Old Cottage 16, *16*
Robertsbridge 140–1
Robertsbridge Abbey 141
Rock Mill 176
Rodmell, 142, 151
Rogate 142
Rollo the Norseman 28
Romans 8, 19, 23, 38, 40, 49, 52–4, 70, 78, 81, 82, 85, 87, 92, 105, 112, 121, 127, 130, 133, 136, 137, 148, 155, 161, 175, 180
Romney Marsh 146
Rother, River/Valley 36, 86, 115, 117, 122, 125, 126, 130, 141, 142, 143, 150; medieval stone bridges across 142, 143
Rother Navigation 12
Rottingdean 48, 90
Rowdell Farm 174
Royal Military Canal 146
Royal Military Police Museum, Roussillon Barracks 56
Russell, Dr Richard 44, 46, 88
Rustington 114
Rye 9, 14, 36, 143–5, 146, 149, 150, 178; Church Square *144*; Lamb House 145, 151, 152; Mermaid Street 145

Saddlescombe 67–8, 134, 148
St Leonard's 7, 10, 90, 97; Royal Victoria Hotel 97, *97*
St Leonard's Forest 99, 146–7; the dragon of 146–7
St Michael's school, Burton Park 98, 127
Salisbury Cathedral 56
Saltdean Lido, near Peacehaven *122*
Saxons, Anglo-Saxons 8, 17, 19, 23, 26, 28, 29, 32, 33, 35, 40, 63, 64, 78, 86, 87, 96, 98, 107, 109, 116, 117, 127, 135, 142, 149, 164, 174; Billa's people 34; Haestingas 96
Seaford 88, 93, 121, 142, 148, 176
Seaford Head 148; nature reserve 148
Sedlescombe 148; Pestalozzi children's village 148; village green 148, *149*
Selham 127
Selingcourt, Hugh de 167
Selmeston 15–16
Selsey 30, 148–9
Selsey Bill 36, 76
Seven Sisters 81, 133, 148
Seven Sisters Country Park 148
Sheffield Park 79, 150, 154; Bluebell Railway *23*, 24, 79
Sheffield Park Garden 79
Shelley, Percy Bysshe 100, 150
Shelley family of Michelgrove 56–7, 59, 177
Shernfold Park house, Frant 81
Shimmings, River/Valley 125, 126
Shipley 12, 67, 153, 154, 164, 177, 178; King's Land and Windmill *152*, 154–5; St Mary the Virgin's church 32, 154, *154*
Shoreham by Sea 32–3, 100, 112, 122, 123, 154, 155, 158, 166, 170; Church of St Nicholas 32, 41, 155; The Marlipins 32, 155; New Shoreham 32, 41, 42, 93, 98, 113, 155, 164; Old Shoreham 32, 41, 155, 156; St Mary de Haura Church *32*, 33, 41, 93, 155, 166
Shoreham Beach 93, 156; 29 Old Fort Road 93, *93*; 43, Riverside Road *92*, 93
Shoreham Fort 156
Siddal, Elizabeth 151
Sidlesham 122
Sidlesham Ferry 122
Singleton 74, 83, 85, 135, *158*, 158–9; Weald and Downland Museum 43, 56, 159, *159*, *160–1*, 170
Slindon 137, 159–61, *162–3*
Slindon House 160–1
Slinfold 161
Snow Hill Creek 180
Society of Sussex Downsmen 87, 124, 175
Sompting 164; St Mary's church 8, 32, 164
Sompting Abbots 164
Sompting Peverel 164
South Common 52
Southdown sheep 81
South Downs 7, 12, 14, 15, 43, 46, 49, 52, 65–8, 70, 76, 78, 82, *86*, 87, 88, 93, 101, 123, 148, 155, 159
South Downs Way, The 15, 19, 43, 67, 86, 87, 107, 132–7, 138, 148, 161, 166, 170, 174, 175, 176; the Adur to the Arun 135–6; the Arun to Hampshire border 136–7; Eastbourne to the Ouse 132–4; the Ouse to the Adur 134–5
Southease 134, 142; barn at *136*; round-towered church 33, 110, 128, 136, 142, *143*
Southern Cathedrals Festival 56
South Harting 68, *86*, 87
South Lancing 164
South of England Show 19–20
Southover 29–30
South Stoke 31, 101
Springate, Sir William 20, 140
Standen, near East Grinstead 75
Stane Street 49, 50, 70, 85, 137, 161; 'Roman Gate' junction 161
Stanmer 48; University of Sussex 48, 110
Stansted Chapel 150
Stansted Park 170, *171*
Steyning 9, 20, 28, 29, 42, 57, 76, 98, 116, 136, 161, 166, 178; The Old Market House 166; *168*; St Andrew's church 32, 166
Steyning Round Hill 135
Stone Age sites 17, 81, 133, 159; New 76
Stone Hall, Balcombe 24
Stonehill House, near Chiddingly 56
Stopham Bridge *128–9*, 130
Storrington 122, 166–7, 169
Storrington Priory 150
Stoughton 169–70
Strettington 86
Sullington 167; tithe barn 15, 167, *167*
Sullington Warren 167
Sussex Archaeological Society 54, 68, 110, 155, 178, 184
Sussex Industrial Archaeology Society 126, 127
Sussex Wildlife Trust 98, 126
Sutherland, Graham 54, 55
Sutton 50
Swanborough Hill 134
Swanborough Manor, Rodmell 142

Talman, William 170, 172
Telegraph House, near Beacon Hill 137
Telscombe 142; Fore Hill and Fore Farm near *140–1*
Temple Grove 152
Tennyson, Alfred Lord 7, 115
Thakeham 169
Thomson, Francis 150
Three Bridges 61, 62, 64, 75
Ticehurst 170
Tillington 127
Tottington Barn youth hostel 67, 135
Tower Hill 137
Town and Country Planning Act (1947) 14
Treyford 10, 87, *87*
Treyford Hill 137
Trollope, Anthony 87
Trotton 142–3
Trotton Bridge 143
Truleigh Hill *66*, 67, 135
Trundle, The, Trundle Hill *13*, 82, *84*, 158, *158*
Turner, J. M. W. 12, 44, 125, 150

Uckfield 98, 171
Uckfield Preservation Society 171
University of Sussex, Stanmer 48, 110
Up Marden 116
Uppark 56, 87, 137, 170, 171–3
Uppark Tower 137
Upper Beeding 42, 43, 67; bridge 142
Upper Dicker 68
Upwaltham 137

Victoria, Queen 88, 89

Wadhurst 173–4; Bewl Lake Reservoir near *172*; old 'quarters' of 173–4
Wakehurst Place 19, 75; Royal Botanic Gardens 19
wall paintings 19, 23, 31–2, 68, 131, *131*, 138, 142, 143, 164, 169, 179–80
Walmisley, T. A. 76
Walpole, Horace 8, 140
Warenne, William and Gundrada de 26, 29–30, 64, 106, 109, 110
Warminghurst 59–60, 140; Church of the Holy Sepulchre 60, *60–1*
Warnham 115, 150
Warnham Court, near Horsham 100
Warnham nature reserve 100
Warr, Earls de la 23, 34
Washington 136, *173*, 174
Watersfield 50
Waverley Abbey (Surrey) 120
Weald, The 7, 8, 10, 14, 23, 35, 56, 63, 65, 67, 75, 86, 97, 99, 101, 114, 115, 116, 117, 128, 132, 133, 135, 154, 166, 173, 174, 176, 179; High 24, 64, 74, 81, 147
Weald and Downland Museum 43, 56, 159, *159*, *160–1*, 170
Webb, Sir Aston 64, 100
Webb, Philip 75
Weir Wood reservoir 75
Wells, H. G. 145, 150, 151, 172
West Burton 50
West Burton Hill 136
West Chiltington 167, 169
West Dean (East Sussex) 176
West Dean (West Sussex) 137, 176; arts and crafts college 176
West Dean House and Gardens *175*, 176
West Firle 78, 154; Piper's 'Tree of Life' window 77
West Grinstead 151, 154, 176–8; Catholic community 177–8; Priest's House 178; St George's church 177, *177*

Westham 128
Westhampnett 85; Old Schoolhouse *85*
West Harting 87
West Hoathly 24; Priest's House museum 24
West Marden 116
Westmeston 68
West Sussex 7, 10, 14, 33, 67, 74, 127, 132
West Tarring 183–4
West Wittering 56, 180
Wey and Arun Canal 12, 35, 114, 115, 130
Wey and Arun Junction Canal Company 115
Wey and Arun Navigations 114
West Sands Leisure Centre 149
White, Gilbert 87, 140, 151–2
Wilberforce, Samuel, Bishop of Winchester 86
Wilberforce, William 42
Wild Brooks, Amberley 17, 19, 50
Wilde, Oscar 183
Wildfowl Trust, Arundel 21
Wildham Wood 116, 170
Wilds, Amon 47, 104, 183
Wilfrid, St 40, 149
William I the Conqueror, King 8, 20, 26, 28–9, 40, 41, 49, 92, 109, 127–8, 130
William of Waynflete, Bishop of Winchester 42
Willingdon Hill 133
Wilmington, Long Man of 133, *134*, 178
Wilmington Priory 178
Wilton Park 176
Winchelsea 149, 178–9; New 178; Old 9, 178
Winchester Cathedral 56
Windover Hill 133, *133*
windmills 24, 75, 85, 134, 138, *138*, 149, *152*, 153, *153*, 154–5, 169, 171
Wisborough Green *179*, 179–80; St Peter ad Vincula church 179
Wiston 135, 136, 176
Withyham 23
Witterings, The 180
Wolstonbury Hill 67, 134, 138
Woodard, Canon Nathaniel 19, 98, 106, 164
Woods Mill: Sussex Wildlife Trust 98
Woolavington 86
Woolbeding 150
Woolf, Virginia and Leonard 142, 151
Wordsworth, William 151
Worth 63–4; Church of St Nicholas 64, *64*
Worth Abbey (Paddockhurst) 64
Worth Forest 14, 64
Worth Way 62, 64, 75
Worthing 7, 10, 66, 88, 91, 180, 183–5; Beach House 183; Museum 43, 183, 185
Wyatt, James 75, 79, 82, 176

Yeats, W. B. 151
youth hostels 17, 67, 135